COOKING WITH HERBS & SPICES

Merry Christmas!
Mom ~
All Our Love
Tony, Claudia, & Michael

COOKING WITH
HERBS & SPICES

NEW REVISED AND ENLARGED EDITION OF
AN HERB AND SPICE COOK BOOK

by CRAIG CLAIBORNE

DRAWINGS BY ALICE GOLDEN

GALAHAD BOOKS
NEW YORK

For Pierre Franey

COOKING WITH HERBS & SPICES:
New Revised and Enlarged Edition of An Herb and Spice Cookbook.

First Galahad Books edition published in 2000.

Galahad Books
A division of BBS Publishing Corporation
386 Park Avenue South
New York, NY 10016

Galahad Books is a registered trademark of BBS Publishing Corporation.

Published by arrangement with HarperCollins Publishers.

Library of Congress Control Number: 00-133032

ISBN: 1-57866-105-6

Printed in the United States of America.

Contents

Recipes by Categories

Consult index, page 339, for page numbers

APPETIZERS

Anchoiade
Anchovies with dill and pimento
Aniseed beef
Anticuchos
Baba ghanouj
Bagna caude
Beer garden cheese spread
Cabbage and fennel
Canapé parisien
Celery root rémoulade
Cheese straws
Chopped chicken livers
Chick peas ciboulette
Crab marinated with musta sauce
Curried stuffed eggs
Eggplant antipasto
Eggplant caponata
Fine liver pâté
Fresh mushroom salad
Hush puppies
Italian shrimp
Lamb in dill sauce
Meat and dill piroshki
Mussles marinara
Pan Bania
Peppers in oil
Peter Dohanos' swordfish seviche
Pickled shrimp
Pickled snap beans
Rocket canapés
Rumanian hamburgers
Sesame eggplant appetizers
Shrimp in beer
Shrimp Provençale
Switzerland cheese toast
Tapénade
Walnut and watercress sandwiches

SOUPS

Asparagus and tomato soup
Billi Bi
Chicken stock
Corn soup with spareribs
Fish stock
Gazpacho
Iced cucumber and mint soup
Kidney bean soup
Minestra di pasta
Navy bean soup
New England clam chowder
Onion soup
Oyster stew
Philadelphia pepper pot
Senegalese soup
Sorrel soup
Soupe de poissons au vermicelle
Vichyssoise à la Ritz

MEATS

Beef

Aniseed beef
Beef with ginger
Beef and mushrooms Florentine
Beef with rosemary
Bill Clifford's keema with peas
Boiled brisket of beef
Boiled tongue vinaigrette
Brisket of beef pot roast
Cecelia's sauerbraten
Chile con carne
Chopped steak viennoise
Curried pot roast
Ginger soy sauce beef
Hamburgers with ginger
Lombardy meat loaf
Marinated beef bordelaise
Meat and dill piroshki
Meat balls alla romana
Meat balls for spaghetti sauce
Mexican torte
Rumanian hamburgers
Tuscan meat loaf

Ham

Glazed Virginia ham
Ham omelet
Szekely goulash

Lamb

Blanquette of lamb
Herb Farm roast lamb
Keema with peas
Lamb country style
Lamb curry with melon and
  mangoes
Lamb in dill sauce
Lamb shanks with eggplant and
  thyme
Roast lamb
Roast lamb with herbs
Roast racks of lamb
Shish kebab with caraway seeds
Spit-roasted leg of lamb

Veal

Blanquette de veau
Herny Creel's veal and pepper loaf
Herbed veal loaf
Jellied veal
Ossi buchi milanese
Sausage-stuffed breast of veal
Tarragon veal croquettes
Veal birds with scallions
Veal pot roast with dill gravy
Veal maison with rosemary
Veal rondelles with egg-and-lemon
  sauce
Veal saumonée

Pork

Barbecued spareribs
Caraway sauerkraut with pork
  butt
Choucroute garnie
Corn soup with spareribs
Farm-style homemade sausage
Fennel-flavored spaghetti sauce
Indonesian pork saté
Pork chops with capers
Pork chops charcutière
Pork chops hongroise
Pork loin roast with thyme
Roast pork au vin blanc
Spareribs and sauerkraut
Szekely goulash
Tony Clarke's mandarin pork

Miscellaneous meats

Anticuchos (beef heart)
Boiled tongue vinaigrette
Chinese chrysanthemum pot
Farm-style homemade sausage
Italian sausage sauce
Kidneys à la moutarde
Kielbasa (Polish sausage)
Leek and sausage pie
Philadelphia pepper pot

EGGS, CHEESE, RICE, PASTA

VEGETABLES

Beans

Beans à la charente
Beans à la Grecque
Chick peas ciboulette
Chili con carne
Flageolets en casserole
Marinated lentils
Navy beans with savory
Pickled snap beans
Pinto beans with sage
Pinto beans vinaigrette

Beets

Beet preserves
Beets with caraway seeds
Beets with parsley butter
Beets with sour cream

Broccoli

Broccoli purée

Cabbage

Cabbage with capers
Cabbage and carrot relish
Cabbage and fennel
Cole slaw with caraway
    mayonnaise
Cole slaw vinaigrette with herbs
Creamed cabbage with savory
Herbed Creole cabbage
Mustard cabbage
White cabbage with caraway seeds

Cauliflower

Braised cauliflower
Cauliflower à la Grecque

Carrots

Carrot purée

Celery

Celery root rémoulade
Celery with dill
Puréed celery root and potatoes

Corn

Corn soup with spareribs
Fresh corn relish
Fresh corn and oyster casserole

Cucumbers

Cucumbers in cream
Cucumbers with sour cream
Cucumbers in yoghurt
Cucumber sauce
Cucumber slices with lemon
Cucumbers with dill
Iced cucumber and mint soup
Senfgurken

Eggplant

Eggplant and tomatoes, Riviera
    style
Eggplant antipasto
Eggplant caponata
Eggplant Parmigiana
Eggplant pizza
Eggplant with macaroni-sausage
    stuffing
Eggplant and sesame sauce
Eggplant, yoghurt and dill relish
Lamb shanks with eggplant and
    thyme
Ratatouille
Roasted eggplant in yoghurt
Sautéed sliced eggplant
Sesame eggplant appetizers
Stuffed eggplant with clams
Stuffed sliced eggplant
Tomato and eggplant casserole

Escarole

Escarole and eggs au gratin
Herbed escarole

Fennel

Cabbage and fennel
Fennel à la Grecque
Fennel and cucumber salad
Fennel Mornay
Fennel Parmigiana

Leeks

Leeks au gratin
Leek and sausage pie
Leeks vinaigrette
Polenta with leek gravy

Mushrooms

Beef and mushrooms Florentine
Fresh mushroom salad
Mushrooms à la Grecque
Mushrooms Chantilly
Mushrooms with fennel
Mushrooms Maryland
Mushrooms paprikash

Onions

Baked whole onions
Creamed onions
Chili-creamed onions and peppers
Onion soufflé
Onion soup
Onions with chicken-liver stuffing
Orange-and-onion salad
Pickled white onions
Sage-stuffed onions
Steamed onions in vinaigrette
    sauce

Peas

Bill Clifford's keema with peas
Chick peas ciboulette
Dal
Green peas with mint

Peppers

Chili-creamed onions and peppers
Parsley-stuffed peppers
Peppers in oil
Shrimp-stuffed peppers

Potatoes

Chive potato soufflé
Creamed potatoes with garlic
Creamed potatoes with scallions
Dauphin potatoes au gratin
New potatoes with caraway velouté
    sauce
Potatoes and anchovies vinaigrette
Potato dumplings
Potato salad with cucumbers
Puréed celery root and potatoes
Ragout of potatoes

Sauerkraut

Caraway sauerkraut with pork butt
Choucroute garnie
Spareribs and sauerkraut
Szekely goulash

Spinach

Beef and mushrooms Florentine
Spinach salad with mustard
    dressing

Squash

Squash with chicken stuffing
Zucchini purée
Zucchini-tomato casserole

Tomatoes

Asparagus and tomato soup
Cherry tomatoes à l'ail
Tomato-and-eggplant casserole
Tomatoes and eggplant, Riviera
    style
Tomato and scallion salad
Tomatoes à la provençale
Zucchini-tomato casserole

SALADS

Caesar salad
Cole slaw with caraway mayonnaise
Cole slaw vinaigrette with herbs
Fresh mushroom salad
Italian salad
Lobster salad with basil
Orange-and-onion salad
Pinto beans vinaigrette
Potato salad with cucumbers
Riviera salad

Shrimp salad with greens
Spinach salad with mustard
  dressing
Tabbouleh (parsley and mint
  salad
Tomato and scallion salad

Salad dressings

Alsatian salad dressing
Green Goddess salad dressing
Mustard salad dressing

SAUCES

Aïoli
Anchovy sauce
Avgolemono
Béarnaise
Béchamel
Brown chicken sauce
Brown sauce
Caper sauce
Chive hollandaise sauce
Chive mayonnaise
Cucumber sauce
Egg-and-lemon sauce
Fennel sauce for fish
Green sauce
Green mayonnaise

Hollandaise
Horseradish sauce
Mayonnaise
Parsley and sesame paste sauce
Poppy seed sauce
Poulette cream sauce
Rémoulade
Sauce chinoise for shrimp
Seafood cocktail sauce
Sour cream and dill sauce

Spanish omelet sauce
Tapénade
Tartar sauce
Taratour bi taheeni (sesame
  sauce)
Vinaigrette sauce

Sauces for pasta

Basil and tomato sauce
Fennel-flavored spaghetti sauce
Italian sausage sauce
Marinara sauce
Marisa Zorgniotti's base for Pesto

Butters

Basil butter
Blender butter
Clarified butter
Garlic butter
Herb butter
Maître d'hôtel butter
Parsley butter
Rosemary butter
Snail butter
Tarragon butter

BREADS

Bacon-and-onion bread
Blender crepes
Caraway seed loaf
Cheese-and-pepper bread
Croutons
Curry-cheese biscuits
Curried crepes

Entrée crepes
Fried toast triangles
Herb bread.
Hush puppies
Pan Bania
Rye bread
Sesame seed bread

RELISHES AND PRESERVES

Apple chutney
Beet preserves
Bread-and-butter pickles
Cabbage and carrot relish
Chowchow
Crystal tomatoes
Cucumber oil pickles
Cucumber relish
Curried vegetable relish
Eggplant, yoghurt and dill relish
Fresh corn relish
Fresh mint chutney
Fresh peach chutney

Fresh pineapple chutney
Mango chutney
Mustard pickles
Pickled scallions
Pickled snap beans
Pickled white onions
Rose hip jam
Rose petal jam
Seafood cocktail sauce
Senfgurken
Spiced lemon pickles
Tomato catchup
Uncooked cabbage relish

DESSERTS

Baked apples Cantonese
Black and white soufflé
Blueberry pudding
Bread pudding with raisins
Charlotte aux pommes
Charlotte russe with kirsch
Cinnamon-chocolate sponge roll
Cream rice mold
Crème brûlée
Curried fresh pears
Edward Lowman's raspberry
  ginger cream
Ginger cream mold
Gingered fresh blueberry compote
Glazed fresh pears

Honey-baked pears
Indian pudding
Lime-mint sherbet
Mace-pineapple charlotte
Maria von Trapp's Linzertorte
Melon delight
Minted cantaloupe and blueberries
Mont blanc aux marrons
Oranges in red wine
Pears Hélène
Pineapple-mint sherbet
Poppy seed strudel
Rice pudding
Sicilian cassata
Vanilla bread-and-butter custard
Zabaglione

Dessert sauces

Creamed fudge sauce
Custard sauce
Hot blueberry sauce
Vanilla sauce
Zabaglione

Pies

Cinnamon chocolate pie
Ginger cheese pie
Mace lemon soufflé pie
Pumpkin pie
Rum chocolate pie

Cakes

Almond-mace cake
Applesauce cake
Cinnamon-chocolate sponge roll
Duchess spice cake
Dutch apple cake
Ladyfingers
Nutmeg cake
Paula Peck's princess cake
Poppy seed cake
Saffron cake
Seed cake

Cakes

Spiced applesauce cake
Swedish apple cake with vanilla
  sauce
Vanilla crumb cake

Frostings

Almond-mace cream frosting
Cassata frosting
Chocolate butter cream
Cinnamon-chocolate frosting

Cookies and candies

Anise cookies
Benne wafers
Brandy snaps
Caraway seed cookies
Cardamom cookies
Cream taffy
David Dugan's spritz Christmas
  cookies
Sesame seed brittle
Swiss honey cookies
Vanilla divinity
White sugar cookies
White taffy

BEVERAGES

Blanche Knopf's eggnogg
Lüchow's May wine bowl
Mexican chocolate

Mint julep
Rose petal wine

Foreword

There is nothing arcane about cooking with herbs and spices. It is an art and an act as universal and almost as ancient as fire. It ranges from the cuisines of primitive lands where the singular spice might be ground capsicums to the more sophisticated delights of the French with the subtle *fines herbes,* the leeks and shallots. These are the things which a master chef ranks in spirit with butter and cream and the glorious bouquet of wine.

Aside from these culinary virtues, there is sheer poetry in the very names of herbs and spices that are commonly called on to contribute countless nuances in the world of food. Savory, sorrel, basil and clove, saffron, sage and more by the score to which this book is dedicated. Let it be said that this is a modest volume created for pleasure. It does not pretend to include the culinary uses of every herb and spice known from here to Zanzibar. It is rather a book for those who like to dine well and, on occasion, with a sense of adventure. It deals with well-known herbs and spices as well as some that are only "reasonably" known in the United States.

There has been an earnest attempt here to place each recipe with the herb or spice that is dominant in the recipe. It is clearly true that this has not been possible in every instance. Many recipes depend for their success not on one but on many herbs.

I am greatly indebted to Mrs. C. F. Leyel, author of *Herbal Delights* (Faber & Faber, 1937). I have used her volume as an authority for the herb and spice symbols noted throughout this book.

This book was first published in 1963 under the title *An Herb and Spice Cook Book*. It is now out of print in its original edition. For the present revised edition I have deleted some recipes and added new ones. The format has been redesigned and enlarged.

CRAIG CLAIBORNE

A Note About Herbs and Spices

In cooking with herbs and spices the eye and the nose are nearly as important as a knowing palate. It is virtually impossible to judge the relative age and quality of a dried herb or spice in the home kitchen except by sight and smell. The greener the herb, such as tarragon, or the redder the spice, such as paprika, the more likely that it has retained its best flavor traits.

Spices keep best in tightly sealed glass bottles and should be kept away from heat, preferably in a cool place. Spices freshly ground at the time they are used are invariably superior to their commercially ground counterparts. This is notably true of peppercorns and nutmeg.

Fresh herbs are much to be desired over their dried counterparts. But where they are not available, then use the dried by all means.

COOKING WITH HERBS & SPICES

Basic Sauces

CLARIFIED BUTTER

Place butter in the top of a double boiler over hot water. Place over low heat and let stand just until the butter melts. When the thin milky sediment has separated from the melted fat, pour off the clear fat (which is the clarified butter) and discard the thin sediment.

HERB BUTTERS

½ cup (one stick) butter, at room temperature
1 tablespoon lemon juice
3 tablespoons finely chopped fresh herb (parsley, tarragon, rosemary or other. Or use one to three teaspoons dried herb, depending on its strength; to make garlic butter use finely minced garlic to taste)
Salt and freshly ground pepper to taste

1. Cream the butter and beat in the lemon juice, a little at a time.
2. Beat in the herb and season with salt and pepper. Chill, if desired.

Yield: About three-quarters cup.

Basil Butter: Use two teaspoons lemon juice and two table-spoons fresh basil or one teaspoon dried. The basil butter may be served on top of poached eggs, as a spread for hot biscuits, on freshly cooked vegetables and on top of fish. Eggs also may be fried in basil butter.

Maître d'Hôtel Butter: Use parsley as the herb and beat in one teaspoon Worcestershire sauce with the lemon juice. Serve with grilled meats.

Snail Butter: Add one teaspoon each finely chopped garlic and shallots to the recipe for maître d'hôtel butter. Add, if desired, a little ground thyme and rosemary. Use for stuffing snails in the shell.

Parsley Butter: Use on broiled fish or meat.

Tarragon Butter: Use on broiled fish or meat.

Rosemary Butter: Use on broiled lamb, chicken or pork.

Garlic Butter: Use on steak or lamb.

BÉARNAISE SAUCE

1 teaspoon chopped shallots
1 small sprig tarragon, chopped
1 small sprig chervil, coarsely chopped
2 peppercorns
Pinch of salt
¼ cup tarragon vinegar
5 egg yolks
¾ cup butter, melted
Pinch of cayenne pepper
1 teaspoon mixed tarragon and chervil, minced

1. Simmer the shallots, tarragon, chervil, peppercorns and salt in the vinegar over low heat until the vinegar is almost evaporated. Cool to lukewarm.

2. Add the egg yolks and beat briskly with a wire whisk. Place over low heat and gradually add the butter. Whisk until the sauce thickens. Strain. Season with cayenne and stir in the minced tarragon and chervil.

Yield: One and one-half cups.

QUICK BÉARNAISE

2 tablespoons white wine
1 tablespoon tarragon vinegar
2 teaspoons chopped tarragon
2 teaspoons chopped shallots or onion

¼ teaspoon freshly ground black pepper
½ cup (one stick) butter
3 egg yolks
2 tablespoons lemon juice
¼ teaspoon salt
Pinch of cayenne pepper

1. Combine the wine, vinegar, tarragon, shallots and black pepper in a skillet. Bring to a boil and cook rapidly until almost all the liquid disappears.

2. In a small saucepan heat the butter to bubbling, but do not brown.

3. Place the egg yolks, lemon juice, salt and cayenne in the container of an electric blender. Cover the container and flick the motor on and off at high speed. Remove the cover, turn the motor on high and gradually add the hot butter.

4. Add the herb mixture, cover and blend on high speed four seconds.

Yield: Three-quarters to one cup sauce.

BÉCHAMEL (WHITE SAUCE)

2 tablespoons butter
2 tablespoons flour
1 cup milk

Salt and freshly ground pepper
Nutmeg (optional)

1. Melt the butter in a saucepan over moderate heat without letting it brown. Add the flour, accurately measured, and stir, preferably with a wire whisk, until it is well blended.

2. Meanwhile, bring the milk almost but not quite to the boiling point. While stirring the flour and butter mixture vigorously, add the hot milk all at once. When the mixture comes to a boil it will thicken automatically. Simmer, if time allows, for five minutes. Season to taste with salt and pepper and, if desired, a pinch of nutmeg.

Yield: One cup.

Note: Some quarters recommend that the butter-flour roux be stirred on and off the heat for five minutes before the milk is added, taking care that the mixture does not brown. Although this does away with the raw taste of the flour, it is not absolutely essential.

VARIATIONS

Thin White Sauce: Follow directions above, using one table-spoon butter and one tablespoon flour for each cup of milk.

Thick White Sauce: Use three tablespoons each of flour and butter for each cup of milk.

Sauce Mornay: Add one-half to one cup grated Cheddar or American cheese to the hot sauce and stir over low heat until melted. Season with mustard and Worcestershire sauce to taste.

Sauce Velouté: Substitute chicken, beef or fish broth for the milk and proceed as for white sauce.

Mustard Sauce: Combine one teaspoon dry mustard with the flour when making white or velouté sauce.

Fresh Herb Sauce: Add one teaspoon freshly chopped herbs, such as parsley or fresh dill.

Dried Herb Sauce: Add one-half teaspoon dried herbs, such as thyme or orégano.

BROWN SAUCE

5 pounds veal bones, cracked
1 onion, quartered
3 stalks celery, chopped
5 carrots, scraped and
   quartered
¾ teaspoon thyme
3 bay leaves
1 teaspoon coarsely cracked
   black peppercorns

3 cloves garlic, unpeeled
1 tablespoon salt
½ cup flour
3 quarts water
1 ten-and-one-half-ounce can
   tomato purée
3 sprigs parsley

1. Preheat the oven to 475 degrees.
2. Combine the veal bones, onion, celery, carrots, thyme, bay leaves, pepper, garlic and salt in a large baking pan. Bake forty-

five minutes. If the bones start to burn, reduce the heat slightly. When cooked, the bones should be quite brown.

3. Sprinkle the bones with the flour and stir the bones around with a fork to distribute the flour evenly. Return the pan to the oven and bake fifteen minutes longer.

4. Spoon the ingredients into a large, heavy kettle with at least a seven-quart capacity. Add three cups of water to the baking pan and place the pan over moderate heat. Stir with a wooden spoon to dissolve brown particles clinging to the bottom and sides of the pan.

5. Pour the liquid from the pan into the kettle and add the tomato purée. Add the remaining water and the parsley and bring to a boil. Simmer two hours, skimming occasionally to remove fat and foam as it rises to the surface. Strain the stock. It may be used immediately or it may be frozen and defrosted as desired.

Yield: About two quarts.

BROWN CHICKEN SAUCE

2½ pounds bony chicken
   parts (neck or wings)
2½ pounds veal bones
 5 carrots, chopped
 3 cloves garlic, unpeeled
 4 cups coarsely chopped
   onions
 3 large leeks, trimmed, cut
   into one-inch lengths and
   washed well
 4 stalks celery, coarsely
   chopped

½ pound fresh mushrooms,
   quartered (optional)
1½ tablespoons bruised peppercorns
 3 bay leaves
 2 teaspoons thyme
 9 quarts water
 6 sprigs parsley
 1 ten-and-one-half-ounce
   can tomato purée

1. Preheat the oven to 475 degrees.

2. Place the chicken and veal in a large baking pan and sprinkle with carrots, garlic, onions, leeks, celery, mushrooms, peppercorns, bay leaves and thyme. Bake forty-five minutes. If necessary, reduce the heat to prevent burning.

3. Transfer the chicken and veal mixture to a large kettle and add four cups of water to the baking pan. Place the pan over

moderate heat and stir with a wooden spoon to dissolve brown particles clinging to the bottom and sides of the pan.

4. Pour the liquid over the bones in the kettle and add the remaining water. Add the parsley and tomato purée. Cook, uncovered, over medium heat for five hours, stirring occasionally.

5. Strain the sauce through a sieve or colander lined with a double thickness of cheesecloth. Cool. Spoon into glass jars and seal tightly. The sauce may be frozen and defrosted as necessary.

Yield: About two quarts.

CAPER SAUCE

¼ cup butter   2 cups well seasoned beef broth
¼ cup flour   3 tablespoons capers

1. Melt the butter in a saucepan and add the flour. Stir with a wire whisk until blended and smooth.

2. Bring the broth to a boil and add it all at once to the butter-flour mixture, stirring vigorously with the whisk. The sauce may be served immediately but the flavor is more refined if the sauce is simmered fifteen minutes or longer, stirring frequently so that it does not stick to the bottom. Add the capers and serve hot.

Yield: About two cups of sauce.

EGG-AND-LEMON SAUCE

2 cups chicken broth   3 tablespoons lemon juice,
2 tablespoons cornstarch   or to taste
2 egg yolks

1. Bring one and one-half cups of the chicken broth to a boil. Combine the cornstarch with the remaining half cup of broth and stir well to blend. Add the hot chicken broth to the cornstarch mixture, stirring constantly. Return to the pan and heat until the mixture is thickened and smooth. Remove from the heat.

2. Combine the egg yolks and lemon juice and beat lightly. Add a little of the hot chicken broth to the yolks, then pour the egg-yolk mixture into the remaining hot broth, stirring rapidly. Place

over very low heat and cook, stirring, to thicken and reheat but do not allow to boil or the eggs will curdle. Serve hot.

Yield: Two cups of sauce.

HORSERADISH SAUCE

Substitute one tablespoon or more freshly grated or bottled horseradish for the capers in the above recipe. The horseradish should be added according to taste.

HOLLANDAISE SAUCE

3 egg yolks
1 tablespoon cold water
½ cup (one stick) soft butter

¼ teaspoon salt
1 tablespoon lemon juice, or to taste

1. Combine the egg yolks and water in the top of a double boiler and beat with a wire whisk over hot (not boiling) water until fluffy.
2. Add a few spoonfuls of butter to the mixture and beat continuously until the butter has melted and sauce starts to thicken. Care should be taken that the water in the bottom of the boiler never boils. Continue adding the butter, bit by bit, stirring constantly.
3. Remove from the heat, and add the salt and lemon juice. If a lighter texture is desired, beat in a tablespoon of hot water.

Yield: About one cup.

QUICK HOLLANDAISE SAUCE

½ cup (one stick) butter
3 egg yolks
1 tablespoon lemon juice, or to taste

¼ teaspoon salt
Pinch of cayenne

1. Heat the butter to bubbling in a small saucepan.
2. Place the egg yolks, lemon juice, salt and cayenne in the container of an electric blender. Cover and turn the motor on low

speed. Immediately remove the cover and pour in the hot butter in a steady stream. When all the butter is added, turn off the motor.

Yield: Four servings.

MARINARA SAUCE

1 clove garlic, finely minced
½ cup chopped onion
¼ cup olive oil
4 cups canned Italian tomatoes
½ teaspoon orégano

½ cup chopped parsley
4 whole basil leaves or one
teaspoon dried basil
Salt and freshly ground
black pepper to taste

1. Cook the garlic and onion in the oil until golden brown.
2. If desired, put the tomatoes through a food mill. Combine all the ingredients and simmer, uncovered, until thickened, about one hour and fifteen minutes.

Yield: About three cups.

Next to French dressing, mayonnaise is perhaps the most versatile of cold sauces. The name derives from the town of Mahón on the island of Minorca near Spain where it was first created—by hand, of course. Here are the traditional recipes and a quick version made in a blender.

MAYONNAISE

1 egg yolk
½ teaspoon salt
Dash of cayenne pepper
½ teaspoon dry mustard

1 to two tablespoons vinegar
or lemon juice
1 cup olive oil

1. Mix egg yolk, salt, cayenne and mustard. Stir in one tablespoon of vinegar.
2. Add oil drop by drop until mixture begins to thicken, beating vigorously with a rotary beater.

3. Add remaining oil in a fine stream while beating. If mixture becomes too thick, add remaining vinegar gradually, alternating with the oil.

Yield: About one cup.

BLENDER MAYONNAISE

1. Place one tablespoon wine vinegar or lemon juice, one-half teaspoon each of dry mustard and salt in the container of an electric blender.

2. Break a whole egg into the container and add one-quarter cup of olive oil. Cover and turn the motor on low speed.

3. Remove the cover (or center disk, if there is one) and add three-quarters cup olive oil. Blend until mayonnaise makes, about thirty seconds.

Yield: About one and one-half cups.

Allspice

ALLSPICE symbolizes compassion. It is the berry of the allspice tree, which is native to the West Indies. Allspice is pungent and sharply aromatic, and is available commercially both as a dried berry and powdered.

The principal uses of allspice are in marinades, curries and spice cakes and for pickling fruits and vegetables. A little whole allspice may be used in almost any marinade, particularly those for game.

FINE LIVER PÂTÉ

1 teaspoon rendered chicken or pork fat

2 pounds chicken or pork liver

3 eggs

⅓ cup cognac

1½ cups heavy cream

⅔ cup diced fresh unrendered chicken fat or fresh pork fat

1 onion, coarsely chopped

½ cup flour

5 teaspoons salt

½ teaspoon monosodium glutamate

2 teaspoons freshly ground white pepper

1 teaspoon ground allspice

1. Lightly grease a three-quart mold with the rendered fat.

2. In an electric blender, make a fine purée of the livers, eggs, cognac and cream. From time to time add a little diced fat, onion and flour. (It will not be possible to do the entire mixture at one time. Three or four separate blendings will be needed.)

3. Add all the seasonings to the liver purée and mix well. Pour into the prepared mold and cover the top with a double thickness of aluminum foil.

4. Place the mold in a pan of water and bake in a 325-degree oven one and one-half hours. Cool the pâté, then store it in the refrigerator. If desired, the top may be decorated with slices of truffle and a clear aspic poured over.

Yield: Three quarts pâté.

BRISKET OF BEEF POT ROAST

3 or four pounds fresh brisket of beef	1 bay leaf, crushed
1½ teaspoons salt	4 whole allspice
¼ teaspoon freshly ground black pepper	Flour
	1 tablespoon chopped parsley
3 large onions, thinly sliced	

1. Trim off part of the beef fat. Wipe the meat with a damp paper towel.

2. Place the beef in an enamel-lined, cast-iron casserole or a heavy saucepan over moderate heat. Let brown in its own fat on all sides, seasoning with salt and pepper as it browns. Remove the beef.

3. Pour off all the fat from the pan and add the sliced onions. Lay the beef over them. Add the bay leaf and allspice. Cover and simmer one hour. Turn the brisket over and simmer two hours longer, basting occasionally. Remove the meat to a platter.

4. Strain the liquid, measure it and return it to the pot. Blend the flour (one and one-third tablespoons for each cup of broth) with as little cold water as possible. Stir into the broth. Bring to a boil and add seasonings if needed. Lower the heat, replace the beef in the gravy and simmer one hour or until tender.

5. Cut the meat into thin slices. Arrange on a hot platter, slices overlapping. Cover partially with gravy and garnish with chopped parsley.

Yield: Six to eight servings.

TOMATO CATCHUP

8 pounds firm ripe toma- toes, coarsely chopped
4 large onions, sliced
1 clove garlic, finely minced
2 bay leaves
2 red peppers, fresh or dried
¾ cup firmly packed brown sugar

2 tablespoons whole all- spice
1 one-inch length of stick cinnamon
1 teaspoon ground cloves
1½ tablespoons salt, or to taste
1 teaspoon freshly ground black pepper
2 cups cider vinegar

1. Place the tomatoes in a large kettle with the onions, garlic, bay leaves and red pepper pods. Cook until soft and strain through a sieve or put through a food mill. This should yield about two quarts of tomato purée.

2. Return the purée to the kettle and add the brown sugar. Tie the allspice and cinnamon in a small cheesecloth bag and add it to the kettle along with the cloves, salt and pepper. Cook quickly, stirring frequently, until reduced to about half the original volume.

3. Season the mixture to taste with additional salt, if needed. Remove the spice bag and add the vinegar. Simmer ten minutes longer and pour at once into hot sterilized bottles. Seal the bottles with paraffin.

Yield: About eight pints.

Anise

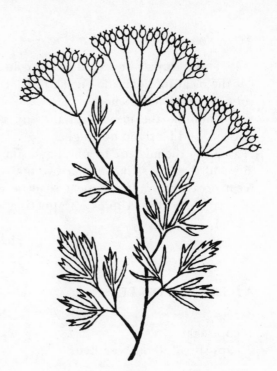

ANISE (ANN-iss) is one of the sweetest-smelling of herbs and it produces aniseed. The plant has feathery leaves and is a member of the carrot family. It is found principally in Egypt, Greece and Asia Minor but is a popular flavoring throughout Europe.

A principal use for anise is in the manufacture of liqueurs, but it also is important in the preparation of certain sauces and as a flavoring for cookies, cakes and breads. Some people steep aniseed in brandy (one teaspoon of seed for each pint of brandy) and it produces a most interesting drink.

ANISEED BEEF

2½ pounds cross-cut beef shank or shin
¾ cup imported Chinese or Japanese soy sauce
2 tablespoons brown sugar

3 tablespoons sherry
2 tablespoons aniseed, tied in cheesecloth
1 cup water

1. This dish may be served hot or cold. If it is to be served hot, cut the meat into one-and-one-half-inch cubes. If it is to be served cold, leave the meat whole.

2. Combine the meat with the soy sauce, sugar, sherry and aniseed, and let stand overnight.

3. Bring the mixture to a boil and simmer ten minutes. Gradually add the water and simmer two hours, turning or stirring the meat occasionally. If the meat is to be served cold, chill it and slice it wafer thin. Use as an appetizer or on an assorted meat platter.

Yield: Four to six servings.

ANISE COOKIES

3 eggs
1 cup sugar
2 cups sifted all-purpose flour

1 tablespoon ground aniseed
½ teaspoon baking powder

1. Beat the eggs until they are very light and pale yellow in color. Add the sugar and beat vigorously about three minutes.

2. Sift the flour together with the ground aniseed and baking powder; add to the egg mixture. Continue beating about five minutes.

3. Drop the batter by teaspoonfuls onto a well-greased cooky sheet. Leave one inch of space between each cooky. Do not cover. Let stand in a warm place overnight to dry.

4. Preheat the oven to 350 degrees. Bake the cookies eight minutes.

Yield: About three dozen cookies.

Basil

BASIL (BAZZ-il) symbolizes, in many books, hatred. In Italy it symbolizes love. Whatever the symbol, it is one of the most delicate and fragrant of herbs and has a particular affinity for tomatoes.

Basil makes a splendid pot plant, and its handsome green leaves, when chopped, make an excellent ingredient in almost all cold salads, such as those with tomatoes, potatoes, cucumbers or seafood.

LOBSTER SALAD WITH BASIL

3 one-and-one-half-pound lobsters
Water
Salt
½ cup mayonnaise, approximately (page 8)
1 tablespoon anchovy paste
Lemon juice to taste

2 tablespoons finely chopped onion
3 tablespoons finely chopped celery
2 tablespoons coarsely chopped basil
Chopped parsley, tomato wedges and hard-cooked egg halves for garnish

1. Place enough water in a large kettle to cover the lobsters when they are added later. Add one teaspoon of salt for each quart of water. Bring to a rolling boil and plunge the lobsters into the water, head first. Return to a boil, cover and simmer eight to ten minutes. Let the lobsters cool and remove the meat from the shells. Chill the lobster meat.

2. Mix the mayonnaise with the anchovy paste, lemon juice, onion, celery and basil. Combine with the lobster meat, adding more mayonnaise if necessary. Serve the lobster salad on lettuce leaves, sprinkled with chopped parsley. Garnish with tomato wedges and hard-cooked egg halves.

Yield: Six servings.

POTATO SALAD WITH CUCUMBERS

Salt and freshly ground
   black pepper
6 tablespoons olive oil
2 tablespoons vinegar
3 cups sliced boiled potatoes
½ cup finely sliced, peeled
   cucumbers
¾ cup mayonnaise

3 tablespoons heavy cream
3 tablespoons finely chopped
   onion
1 tablespoon chopped fresh
   basil or one-half teaspoon
   dried basil
1 teaspoon lemon juice

1. Place one-half teaspoon salt and a little black pepper in a small mixing bowl. Add the oil and, stirring with a fork, add the vinegar, little by little.

2. Add the sliced potatoes and cucumbers to the dressing in the bowl and let stand in the refrigerator one or two hours. Drain.

3. Add the remaining ingredients to the vegetables and mix well. Add salt and pepper to taste and chill until ready to serve. Serve garnished with fresh basil leaves.

Yield: Six servings.

PASTA RUSTICA

1 cup parsley
2 cloves garlic
1 large onion
½ pound bacon
1 large leek
2 radishes
2 medium carrots
3 teaspoons fresh basil
¼ cup olive oil
3 large tomatoes, chopped
1 cup bouillon
3 cups shredded cabbage
2 medium zucchini, chopped
Salt and freshly ground black pepper to taste
2 to three cups cooked cannellini (white kidney beans)
1 pound rigatoni, cooked according to package directions
¼ cup (one-half stick) butter
½ cup freshly grated Parmesan cheese

1. Mince together the parsley, garlic, onion, bacon, leek, radishes, carrots and basil.

2. Heat the oil in a large kettle and cook the minced ingredients in it until they are soft, stirring frequently.

3. Add the tomatoes, bouillon, cabbage, zucchini, salt and pepper. Cover and cook over low heat, stirring frequently, until the vegetables are tender, about ten minutes. Add the beans and cook five minutes longer.

4. Toss the rigatoni with the butter and grated cheese. Combine with the vegetables.

Yield: Six to eight servings.

RATATOUILLE

½ cup olive oil, approximately

1 onion, finely chopped

2 cloves garlic, finely minced

1 small eggplant, peeled and cubed

Flour for dredging

2 small zucchini, sliced

3 green peppers, seeded and cut into strips

Salt and freshly ground black pepper to taste

2 tablespoons chopped fresh basil or 1 teaspoon dried basil

6 ripe tomatoes, peeled, seeded and chopped

1. Heat about one-quarter of the oil (two tablespoons) in a skillet. Sauté the onion and garlic in the oil until golden.

2. Dredge the eggplant with flour. Heat the remaining oil in a separate skillet and brown the eggplant in it lightly, about ten minutes. Add more oil, if necessary.

3. Combine the eggplant, onion and garlic in a heat-proof casserole or large saucepan. Add the zucchini, green peppers, salt and pepper, basil and tomatoes. Simmer, uncovered, until the mixture is thick and well blended, thirty minutes or longer.

Yield: Six servings.

BASIL AND TOMATO SAUCE

3 tablespoons olive oil

2 medium-size onions, thinly sliced

1 clove garlic, finely minced

3 stalks celery, chopped

1 carrot, scraped and sliced

16 or more fresh basil leaves or one teaspoon dried basil

1 one-pound-three-ounce can of tomatoes, preferably the Italian kind

¾ cup tomato purée

1 cup water

Salt to taste

2 bay leaves

½ teaspoon orégano

1. Heat the olive oil in a saucepan and cook the onions and garlic until the onions are wilted and transparent.

2. Add the remaining ingredients and simmer, partially covered, three to four hours. Put the mixture through a sieve or a food mill and cook one or two hours longer. This sauce is best when it is cooked for a total of five hours.

Yield: Two to three cups of sauce.

MARISA ZORGNIOTTI'S BASE FOR PESTO

5 cups (about five bunches) basil leaves
½ cup olive oil

Salt to taste, preferably kosher salt

1. Rinse the basil well in cold water and remove the tough stems. Drain well.

2. Place the leaves in a blender until it is full but not overcrowded. Add the oil and salt and blend, pushing it down carefully with a rubber spatula, until thoroughly homogenized. Pour and scrape this into a freezer container. Freeze.

Yield: About one cup.

PASTA WITH PESTO GENOVESE

1 cup frozen pesto base (see recipe above)
1 clove garlic, finely chopped
2 tablespoons olive oil
2 tablespoons melted butter
½ teaspoon freshly chopped or dried marjoram

¾ to 1 cup grated Parmesan cheese
2 pounds spaghetti or linguine
¼ cup boiling water in which pasta cooked

1. Empty the frozen pesto base into a mixing bowl. When it is thoroughly defrosted, add the garlic, oil, butter and marjoram. Stir in just enough cheese until the pesto's color changes from dark green to pea green. Mix well with a fork.

2. Cook the spaghetti or linguine in a large kettle in boiling salted water. Just before it is done ladle the quarter-cup of boiling liquid into the pesto mixture; blend well. This must not be done too much in advance. When the spaghetti is done, drain it quickly, remove to a hot platter and add the pesto. Toss and serve immediately on hot plates.

Yield: Eight servings.

Bay Leaf

BAY LEAF stems from the bay tree, which symbolizes glory. The bay leaf itself is supposed to mean "I change but in death." The botanical name for the bay or laurel tree is Laurus nobilis. *It is found principally on the shores of the Mediterranean.*

Like wine, thyme and leeks, bay leaf or laurier is a foundation flavor of la cuisine française *and it is virtually impossible to conceive of French cuisine without it. From* le bon bouillon *through the entire repertoire of meat, fish and poultry cookery, there is almost always a touch of bay leaf in one form or another. It is used in soups and stews and marinades.*

NAVY BEAN SOUP

2 cups navy beans
2½ quarts water
1 ham hock
3 medium onions, chopped
2 carrots, diced
2 cups chopped celery with leaves

2 bay leaves
Salt and freshly ground black pepper to taste
1 cup finely chopped potato (optional)

1. Cover the beans with the water and let soak overnight. Or bring to a boil and simmer two minutes. Cover and let stand one hour.

2. Add the ham hock, onions, carrots, celery, bay leaves, salt and pepper to the beans in the kettle. Cook until the beans are tender, about two hours. Remove the bay leaves and ham hock. If desired, remove the meat from the bone and return the meat to the soup.

3. If a thicker soup is desired, add the potato and cook, stirring occasionally, until the potato is mushy. Adjust the seasonings.

Yield: About six servings.

Note: For additional flavor, add along with the vegetables listed one cup canned tomatoes, one clove garlic, minced, and one-quarter cup minced parsley.

PHEASANT BEAU SÉJOUR

2 three-pound pheasants, cut into serving pieces
2 teaspoons salt
Freshly ground pepper
⅓ cup butter, approximately
8 cloves garlic, split
6 bay leaves
2 teaspoons thyme
1 cup dry white wine
1½ cups brown sauce or canned beef gravy
¼ cup (one-half stick) cold butter
2 teaspoons chopped parsley

1. Season the pheasants with salt and pepper. In a Dutch oven or casserole, brown the birds slowly on all sides in one-third cup of butter.

2. Add the garlic, bay leaves, thyme and wine. Cover and simmer until the meat is tender, about fifteen to thirty minutes. (Older birds may require longer cooking.)

3. Transfer the pheasants to a hot platter and keep them warm.

4. Add the beef gravy to the casserole and cook, stirring with a wire whisk, until smooth. Remove from the heat and stir in the quarter cup of cold butter.

5. Pour the sauce over the pheasants and sprinkle with chopped parsley.

Yield: About six servings.

The following dish is a traditional French accompaniment to lamb. It is made with dried green beans, known as flageolets. These beans are available from many sources in New York including the Atlas Importing Company, 1109 Second Avenue, and Trinacria Importing Company, 415 Third Avenue.

FLAGEOLETS EN CASSEROLE

1 cup dried flageolets
1 onion, studded with one clove
1 bay leaf
1 sprig parsley
Salt and freshly ground black pepper to taste
1 onion, chopped

1 clove garlic, finely minced
2 tablespoons butter
3 tomatoes, peeled, seeded and coarsely chopped
2 tablespoons chopped parsley
3 tablespoons natural juices from roast leg of lamb

1. Cover the beans with water and let soak overnight. Or bring to a boil, simmer about two minutes, cover and let stand one to two hours.

2. Place on the heat and add the onion studded with the clove, the bay leaf, parsley and salt and pepper to taste. Bring to a boil and simmer until the beans are tender but not mushy, one and one-half to two hours.

3. In a large saucepan cook the chopped onion and garlic in the butter until the onion is transparent.

4. Add the tomatoes and simmer five minutes. Add the tomato mixture to the beans. Add the chopped parsley and lamb juices and simmer ten minutes longer.

Yield: Six servings.

Capers

CAPERS like cloves are unopened flower buds. The caper bush grows wild on mountain slopes, principally those that border the Mediterranean Sea. It is not surprising that the flavorful and tender delicacy figures prominently in Mediterranean cuisine, whether it be that of France, Spain, Italy or Southern Greece.

Capers are used primarily in sauces, both cold and hot, and have a particular affinity for tomatoes as well as for eggplant. In triumvirate, they are a triumph. Capers are sold commercially packed either in salt or in vinegar.

EGGPLANT CAPONATA

1 medium eggplant
6 tablespoons olive oil
1 clove garlic, minced
1 onion, thinly sliced
3 tablespoons tomato sauce
¾ cup chopped celery
2 tablespoons capers

12 stuffed green olives, cut into halves
2 tablespoons wine vinegar
1 tablespoon sugar
Salt and freshly ground black pepper to taste

1. Peel the eggplant and cut it into cubes. Sauté in five tablespoons of the olive oil.

2. Remove the eggplant from the skillet and add the remaining tablespoon of olive oil. Cook the garlic and onion in it until the onion is brown.

3. Add the tomato sauce and celery and simmer until the celery is tender. If necessary, add a little water to the skillet.

4. Return the eggplant to the skillet and add the capers and olives. Heat the vinegar with the sugar and pour it over the eggplant. Add salt and pepper to taste and simmer the mixture ten to fifteen minutes longer, stirring frequently.

5. Serve hot or cold with lemon wedges and buttered toast fingers. Cold caponata may be served on lettuce leaves.

Yield: Six to eight servings.

Traditionally, in Provence this sauce is made by pounding the ingredients in a large mortar with a pestle. Today an electric blender is more effective and the results are similar, although the handmade version is coarser.

TAPÉNADE

(A MEDITERRANEAN APPETIZER)

¼ cup capers
3 two-ounce cans flat anchovy fillets
1 seven-ounce can tuna fish
1 clove garlic, or more to taste

18 black olives (preferably Greek or Italian), pitted
Juice of two lemons
½ cup olive oil
3 tablespoons cognac
Freshly ground black pepper to taste

1. Place the capers, anchovies and tuna, with the oil in which they were packed, and the garlic, olives and lemon juice in the container of an electric blender.

2. Blend on medium speed two to five minutes, stopping the motor to stir down occasionally with a rubber spatula. (It may be

stirred with the motor running, but care must be taken not to touch the blades.)

3. Gradually add the olive oil. When all the oil is blended, the sauce should be like medium-thick mayonnaise.

4. Blend in the cognac and pepper. Serve at room temperature over hard-cooked eggs, cold poached fish or cold boiled beef.

Yield: About two and one-half cups of sauce.

PORK CHOPS WITH CAPERS

6 pork chops, three-quarters inch thick
Flour for dredging
Salt and freshly ground black pepper to taste
2 tablespoons oil
¼ cup finely chopped onion
1 green pepper, finely chopped
1 cup hot beef stock or bouillon
¼ cup dry white wine
2 tablespoons capers
Parsley for garnish

1. Dredge the pork chops with flour which has been seasoned with salt and pepper.

2. Heat the oil in a skillet and brown the chops on both sides. Remove the chops and add the onion and green pepper. Cook, stirring, until the onion is wilted. Return the chops to the skillet and add the stock and wine. Cover and cook slowly over moderate heat forty minutes.

3. Add the capers and cook, uncovered, until thoroughly done, about fifteen minutes longer. Serve garnished with fresh parsley.

Yield: Six servings.

CHICKEN WITH CAPER SAUCE

2 two-pound frying chickens
2 stalks celery, leaves removed
2 sprigs parsley
2 carrots, scraped and quartered
½ bay leaf
¼ teaspoon thyme
10 peppercorns
Salt to taste
Chicken stock or water
¼ cup (one-half stick) butter
¼ cup flour
3 tablespoons capers

1. Truss the chickens and place them in a kettle with the celery, parsley, carrots, seasonings and chicken stock or water to cover. Bring to a boil and simmer, partially covered, until the chicken is tender, thirty to forty-five minutes.

2. Melt the butter in a saucepan and stir in the flour. Add two cups of the strained stock in which the chicken cooked and stir vigorously with a wire whisk over very low heat. When the sauce is thickened and smooth, add the capers. Transfer the chickens to a hot serving platter and cut into serving pieces. Pour a little of the sauce over the chickens and serve the remainder in a sauceboat.

Yield: Four to six servings.

EGGPLANT AND TOMATOES, RIVIERA STYLE

1 medium eggplant	1 cup canned tomatoes
¼ cup olive oil	¼ cup chopped parsley
1 cup chopped onion	1 tablespoon chopped basil
1 clove garlic, finely minced	2 tablespoons capers
½ cup chopped celery	Salt and freshly ground black
1 large green pepper, seeded and cut into strips	pepper to taste
	Lemon wedges

1. Preheat the oven to 350 degrees.

2. Wrap the eggplant in aluminum foil and bake one hour. Meanwhile, heat the oil in a casserole and cook the onion, garlic and celery until the onion is transparent. Add the green pepper and cook until the pepper is slightly wilted.

3. Add the tomatoes, parsley, basil and capers to the casserole and simmer until the mixture is slightly thickened, about thirty-five minutes. Add salt and pepper to taste.

4. Remove the eggplant from the oven and open the aluminum foil. Carefully split the eggplant open, scoop out the flesh and add it to the casserole. Correct the seasonings and serve the stew hot or cold with lemon wedges.

Yield: Six servings.

CABBAGE WITH CAPERS

½ cup chopped onion
1 clove garlic
1 whole clove
2 tablespoons bacon drippings
1 cup chopped cooked ham
2 tablespoons capers
1 tablespoon cider vinegar

1 cup diced fresh tomatoes
6 cups shredded cabbage
¼ teaspoon freshly ground black pepper
¾ teaspoon salt
¼ cup stock or water
½ cup soft bread crumbs

1. Sauté the onion, garlic and clove in hot bacon drippings until the onion is limp and transparent.

2. Add the ham, capers, vinegar, tomatoes, cabbage, pepper, salt and stock or water. Mix well. Sprinkle with the bread crumbs. Cover and cook until the cabbage is tender, about ten minutes.

Yield: Six servings.

ANCHOVY SAUCE

4 anchovies
1 tablespoon capers
1 tablespoon wine vinegar
½ cup chopped onion
1 clove garlic, finely minced
¼ cup finely chopped parsley
¼ cup lemon juice

1 teaspoon chopped basil or half the amount dried
Tabasco to taste
½ cup peanut oil
Salt and freshly ground pepper to taste

Combine all the ingredients except salt and pepper in the container of an electric blender. Blend thoroughly. Taste the sauce and add salt and pepper to taste. Serve with cold poached fish.

Yield: About one and one-half cups.

GREEN SAUCE

¼ cup finely chopped parsley

¼ cup finely chopped spinach

¼ cup finely chopped watercress
1½ tablespoons drained capers (if the Italian salty
ones are used, they should
be rinsed and dried)
½ clove garlic
1 tablespoon chopped sour

cucumber pickle
1 slice bread, crusts re-
moved, crumbled
Salt and freshly ground black
pepper
¼ cup olive oil
¼ cup wine vinegar

1. Mash together, preferably in a wooden bowl, the parsley, spinach, watercress, capers, garlic, pickle, bread and salt and pepper to taste.

2. Gradually stir in the oil and vinegar. Serve with boiled meats.

Yield: About one cup.

Caraway

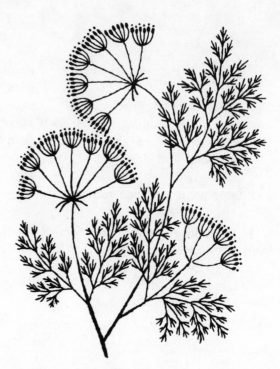

CARAWAY is a principal ingredient in much of the rye bread produced in America. Many people have believed mistakenly that the caraway seeds found in rye bread are in reality rye seeds.

The magical properties ascribed to caraway are lengthy and range from the belief that they prevent theft and infidelity in love to a cure for hysteria. In the kitchen they are a delight, both in savory dishes and desserts, and go particularly well with beets, potatoes and cabbage, especially the last mentioned. One of the best-known cakes ever made is the seed cake made with caraway seeds.

BEER GARDEN CHEESE SPREAD

1 cup cottage cheese
2 teaspoons anchovy paste
2 teaspoons dry mustard
1 tablespoon caraway seeds
1 tablespoon capers
1 teaspoon minced onion
½ cup (one stick) softened butter

Put the cottage cheese through a sieve. Blend in the anchovy paste and seasonings. Add the butter and mix well. Serve garnished with additional capers.

Yield: About one and three-quarters cups.

SHISH KEBAB WITH CARAWAY SEEDS

2 pounds lean lamb, cut into one-inch cubes
1 teaspoon orégano
1 teaspoon caraway seeds

Salt and freshly ground black pepper to taste
¾ cup olive oil
2 tablespoons onion juice
1 clove garlic, finely minced

1. Combine all ingredients in a mixing bowl and gently stir until all pieces of lamb are well coated. Let stand one to two hours. Turn the meat in the marinade occasionally.

2. String the meat on skewers and broil over charcoal or under the broiler. Cook to the desired degree of doneness, basting occasionally with the marinade. Turn the meat once as it broils.

Yield: Four servings.

CARAWAY SAUERKRAUT WITH PORK BUTT

2 pounds lean pork butt
1 bay leaf
¼ teaspoon black peppercorns

2 pounds fresh sauerkraut
2 tablespoons caraway seeds
½ cup brown sugar
2 cups diced green apples

1. Place the pork in a saucepan containing two inches of boiling water, the bay leaf and peppercorns. Cover and cook until tender, about forty-five minutes. Remove the pork and keep it warm.

2. Stir the remaining ingredients into the cooking water, cover and cook fifteen minutes or to the desired degree of doneness. Serve hot with sliced pork butt.

Yield: Six to eight servings.

SPARERIBS AND SAUERKRAUT

3 pounds spareribs
2 pounds sauerkraut
2 cloves garlic, freshly chopped
1 onion stuck with four cloves
1 teaspoon caraway seeds
10 peppercorns and six juniper berries (optional) tied in a cheesecloth bag
Dry white wine

1. Cut the spareribs into serving portions and brown them in a skillet.

2. Drain the sauerkraut and press it to remove some of the liquid. Put the sauerkraut in a kettle and add the garlic, onion, caraway seeds, peppercorns and juniper berries. Add enough dry white wine to barely cover the sauerkraut. Add the browned spareribs. Cover and simmer one to two hours, piling the sauerkraut on top of the ribs as they cook.

Yield: Three to four servings.

BEETS WITH CARAWAY SEEDS

2 cups cooked or canned sliced beets, drained
2 tablespoons butter
1 tablespoon lemon juice
½ teaspoon salt
Dash of freshly ground black pepper
¾ teaspoon caraway seeds
¼ cup sour cream (optional)

Place all the ingredients in a saucepan and heat, but do not boil. Serve immediately.

Yield: Four servings.

WHITE CABBAGE WITH CARAWAY SEEDS

1 medium head white cabbage
Boiling salted water
2 teaspoons caraway seeds
Few drops of lemon juice
¼ cup (one-half stick) butter, melted

1. Remove the tough outer leaves and cut the cabbage into quarters.

2. Drop the cabbage into boiling salted water and, when the water returns to the boil, reduce the heat and simmer for ten to fifteen minutes, until tender but still crisp.

3. Drain the cabbage carefully and place it in a serving dish. Add the caraway seeds and lemon juice to the butter and pour over the cabbage.

Yield: Four servings.

COLE SLAW WITH CARAWAY MAYONNAISE

4 cups shredded cabbage
½ cup mayonnaise
2 tablespoons vinegar or lemon juice
1 tablespoon grated onion

1 teaspoon caraway seeds
1 teaspoon sugar
½ teaspoon salt
⅛ teaspoon freshly ground black pepper

1. Crisp the shredded cabbage in ice water, if necessary.

2. Combine the mayonnaise, vinegar or lemon juice, onion, caraway seeds, sugar, salt and pepper.

3. Drain the cabbage thoroughly and mix with the dressing. Serve in lettuce cups, garnished with a dash of paprika, a ring of green pepper or a strip of pimento.

Yield: Six to eight servings.

COLE SLAW VINAIGRETTE WITH HERBS

3 cups finely shredded cabbage
½ cup green pepper, chopped
2 teaspoons caraway seeds
1 teaspoon finely chopped parsley
1 tablespoon finely chopped onion
1 teaspoon salt

Freshly ground black pepper to taste
½ teaspoon dry mustard (or one teaspoon prepared Dijon mustard)
2 tablespoons sugar
¼ cup olive oil
2 tablespoons red wine vinegar

1. Place the cabbage in a large salad bowl and sprinkle with green pepper, caraway seeds, parsley and onion.

2. Combine the remaining ingredients and beat well with a fork. Add more oil or vinegar according to taste. Pour the oil over the cabbage and toss it lightly. Chill until ready to serve.

Yield: Four to six servings.

NEW POTATOES WITH CARAWAY VELOUTÉ SAUCE

2 tablespoons butter
1 tablespoon caraway seeds
2 tablespoons flour
1 cup beef stock
1/2 teaspoon salt

1/8 teaspoon white pepper
1/4 cup heavy cream
2 pounds new potatoes, cooked

1. Melt the butter in a saucepan. Add the caraway seeds and blend in the flour. Stir in the stock and cook, stirring, over moderate heat until thickened.

2. Add the seasonings and cream and heat, stirring, one-half minute. Serve over hot cooked potatoes.

Yield: Six servings.

ALSATIAN SALAD DRESSING

1 tablespoon caraway seeds
2 tablespoons water
1 cup olive or salad oil
1/3 cup vinegar
1 teaspoon salt

1/8 teaspoon freshly ground black pepper
1 clove garlic, minced
1 teaspoon grated onion

1. Cook the caraway seeds in the water until all the water is absorbed, about five minutes. Remove from the heat.

2. Combine the remaining ingredients and stir in the caraway seeds. Serve on crisp greens.

Yield: One and one-third cups of dressing.

CARAWAY SEED LOAF

1 long loaf French bread   ¼ cup (one-half stick) soft-
2 teaspoons caraway seeds   ened butter

1. Preheat the oven to 425 degrees.
2. Slicing to within one-quarter inch of the bottom crust, make ten cuts in the bread one inch apart.
3. Mix the seeds with the butter and spread between slices. Wrap the loaf in aluminum foil and heat twenty to twenty-five minutes. Serve hot.

Yield: Five servings.

RYE BREAD

3 packages yeast   2 tablespoons shortening
1 cup warm water   3½ cups sifted all-purpose
1 tablespoon salt   flour
2 tablespoons caraway seeds   2¾ cups sifted rye flour
½ cup light molasses   Cornmeal
½ cup hot water

1. Dissolve the yeast in the warm water.
2. Combine the salt, caraway seeds, molasses, hot water and shortening. Cool to lukewarm. Add the dissolved yeast.
3. Mix the flours. Gradually stir them into the yeast mixture. Rub a little flour into the pastry board. Turn the dough out and knead until smooth and satiny. Form into a ball and place in a greased bowl. Coat all sides with fat, cover and let rise in a warm place (80 to 85 degrees) until doubled in size, about one and one-half to two hours.
4. Punch the dough down. Form it into a ball, cover and let rest ten minutes.
5. Shape the dough into two loaves and place them in greased 9 x 5 x 3-inch pans sprinkled with cornmeal. Cover and let rise in a warm place until doubled in size, about one hour.
6. Brush lightly with cold water and bake ten minutes in a preheated 450-degree oven. Reduce the heat to 350 degrees and

bake twenty-five to thirty minutes longer. Cover with brown paper after baking twenty-five minutes to prevent the crust from burning.

Yield: Two loaves.

SEED CAKE

2 cups (one pound) sweet butter
2 cups sugar
9 eggs
1 teaspoon vanilla

½ teaspoon mace
4 cups sifted cake flour
½ teaspoon cream of tartar
½ teaspoon salt
⅓ cup caraway seeds

1. Preheat the oven to 350 degrees. Line two 9 x 5 x 3-inch loaf pans with a double thickness of wax paper, allowing the paper to project an inch above the long sides for easy removal.
2. Cream the butter thoroughly. Add the sugar slowly, beating thoroughly. Continue beating for several minutes after all the sugar is added.
3. Add the eggs, one at a time, beating well after each. Add the vanilla and mace.
4. Sift the cake flour together with the cream of tartar and salt. Add the flour mixture gradually to the batter, folding gently until thoroughly blended. Fold in the caraway seeds.
5. Pour the batter into the prepared pans and bake until golden, about one and one-half hours. Cool in the pans ten minutes; finish cooling on racks.

Yield: Two loaves.

CARAWAY SEED COOKIES

1¾ cups sifted flour
¼ teaspoon salt
1 teaspoon baking powder
2 tablespoons caraway seeds
⅔ cup butter

1 cup light-brown sugar
½ teaspoon finely grated lemon rind
1 egg
2 tablespoons milk

1. Preheat the oven to 375 degrees. Lightly grease several cooky sheets.

2. Sift the flour with the salt and baking powder. Stir in the caraway seeds.

3. Cream the butter with the sugar and lemon rind. Beat in the egg. Add the milk and gradually stir in the flour, beating until smooth.

4. Drop the mixture from a teaspoon onto the prepared cooky sheets.

5. Bake the cookies on the lower shelf of the oven until browned, twelve to fifteen minutes.

Yield: About four dozen cookies.

Cardamom

CARDAMOM (CAR-da-mum) also is spelled cardamum *and* cardamon. *Only the dried, ripe seeds of the cardamom plant are used and they are decidedly aromatic. Scandinavians have a particular fondness for the spice and use it liberally in pastries. It is a usual ingredient in curry powders and there are those who admire the flavor of a bruised cardamom seed in after-dinner coffee. Orientals (and a few New Yorkers) chew it to sweeten the breath.*

CURRIED SHRIMP

1½ pounds shrimp
2 teaspoons turmeric
¼ cup vegetable oil
2 medium onions, sliced
1 medium green pepper chopped
1 clove garlic, diced

1½ teaspoons salt
1 teaspoon powdered cardamom
2 teaspoons fresh ginger, diced, or one-half teaspoon powdered ginger
12 cloves

38

1. Wash the shrimp and sprinkle them with turmeric. Place in a skillet, cover and steam without additional water until the shrimp turn pink, two or three minutes. Shell and devein the shrimp.

2. Brown the shrimp in the oil. Add the remaining ingredients and cook over low heat, stirring frequently, until most of the liquid in the skillet evaporates.

Yield: Six servings.

CURRY OF CHICKEN

2 frying chickens, cut into serving pieces
1 cup (one-half pint) yoghurt
4 teaspoons turmeric
2 teaspoons tamarind juice (optional, see note below)
3 tablespoons butter
6 medium onions, thinly sliced
4 cloves garlic, finely minced

1½ inches green ginger, grated, or one-half teaspoon powdered ginger
2 sticks cinnamon
8 cardamom seeds, peeled
2 bay leaves
1½ tablespoons powdered coriander
Water
4 ripe tomatoes, peeled, or two cups canned Italian plum tomatoes, drained
Crushed red pepper and salt to taste

1. Marinate the chicken for one hour in a mixture of the yoghurt, one teaspoon of the turmeric and the tamarind juice.

2. Heat the butter in a large casserole or Dutch oven. Add the onions, garlic, ginger, cinnamon, cardamom seeds and bay leaves. Cook, stirring occasionally, until the onions are well browned.

3. Add the coriander and the remaining turmeric and cook three minutes longer.

4. Add the chicken pieces and remaining marinade and cook until the moisture evaporates. Add water to barely cover the chicken and cook ten minutes longer.

5. Add tomatoes, crushed red pepper and salt. Cover and sim-

mer until the chicken is tender, thirty to forty-five minutes. Serve with chutney and rice. Serve hot tea as a beverage.

Yield: Eight to ten servings.

Note: Tamarind may be purchased in Puerto Rican grocery stores, at Trinacria Importing Company, 415 Third Avenue, and at M. Kehayan, 380 Third Avenue. To make tamarind juice, soak the tamarind in a little water, then squeeze it and rub part of the pulp through a sieve.

CARDAMOM COOKIES

1 cup (two sticks) butter	2 cups light-brown sugar, firmly packed
2 teaspoons baking soda	
1 teaspoon ground cardamom	2 eggs
½ teaspoon salt	4½ cups sifted all-purpose flour
	2 teaspoons cream of tartar

1. Cream the butter and add the soda, cardamom and salt; mix well. Gradually blend in the sugar. Beat in the eggs.
2. Sift together the flour and cream of tartar. Gradually stir into the butter mixture. Chill the dough until stiff enough to handle, three to four hours.
3. Preheat the oven to 350 degrees.
4. Shape the chilled dough into half-inch balls. Place on ungreased cooky sheets. Dip a fork into flour and press into each cooky in criss-cross style. Bake ten minutes.
5. Cool and store in tightly closed tin box or cooky jar.

Yield: About eight dozen cookies.

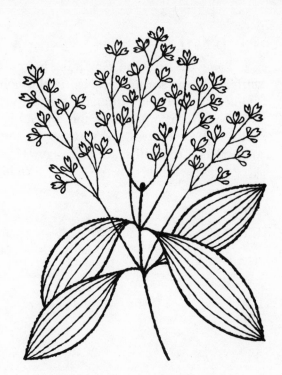

Cassia

CASSIA (KASH-ya or KASS-ya) once referred to cassia bark, otherwise known as Chinese cinnamon. Today it generally applies to any of the coarser varieties of cinnamon bark. Genuine cassia bark is stronger than genuine cinnamon and the scent is not so delicate, but the uses are practically interchangeable.

SHRIMP IN BEER

2 pounds shrimp
2 twelve-ounce cans or bottles of beer
1 clove garlic, peeled
1 onion, studded with cloves
½ teaspoon broken cassia pieces
2 teaspoons salt
½ teaspoon thyme
2 bay leaves
1 teaspoon celery seed
2 parsley sprigs
½ teaspoon crushed red pepper
Juice of half a lemon

1. Wash the shrimp and split them down the back with kitchen scissors. Rinse well to remove intestinal tract but do not remove the shells.

41

2. Bring the beer and remaining ingredients to a boil in a deep kettle. Add the shrimp. Return to the boil and reduce the heat. Simmer two to five minutes, depending on the size of the shrimp.

3. Remove from the heat and drain. Leave the shrimp in their shells and serve them hot with lemon butter or chill and serve with seafood cocktail sauce (see page 143).

Yield: Four to six servings.

Cayenne

CAYENNE (kye-EN) is a powder ground from the seeds and pods of various peppers grown in the Cayenne district of Africa. The uses for cayenne are legion. For centuries it has added zest and piquancy to soups and sauces, eggs and meats and, used sparingly, it seems to accent the natural flavors of most savory foods.

The following recipe is for a dramatic and utterly delicious dish. It is somewhat tedious to prepare but well worth the effort.

SOUFFLÉ WITH LOBSTER BORDELAISE

Generously butter a three-quart soufflé dish. Pour lobster bordelaise (see recipe below) into the dish. Top lobster with uncooked cheese soufflé mixture (page 188) and bake in a preheated 375-degree oven until well puffed and browned, thirty to forty minutes. Serve immediately.

Yield: Six servings.

The following is a classic of French cuisine and, of course, the basis for the above soufflé. It may seem incredible but professional chefs consider the touch of cayenne pepper one of the most important of its ingredients.

LOBSTER BORDELAISE

3 one-and-one-half-pound live lobsters
2 tablespoons olive oil
Salt and freshly ground black pepper
1 clove garlic, minced
2 tablespoons finely chopped shallot (optional)
½ cup finely chopped onion
½ cup finely minced celery
½ cup finely minced carrot
Pinch of thyme
1 bay leaf

3 tablespoons cognac, or more to taste
1½ cups dry white wine
2 cups peeled, chopped fresh tomatoes
1 one-pound can tomato purée
¼ cup brown sauce or canned beef gravy
2 sprigs fresh tarragon or one teaspoon dried
6 sprigs fresh parsley
Cayenne pepper to taste
3 tablespoons butter, at room temperature
3 tablespoons flour

1. Kill each lobster by plunging a knife into the thorax. Break off the tail and cut it crosswise into thirds with the shell on. Cut the body in half and remove the coral and liver. Refrigerate them for later use. Discard the remaining body. Break off the claws and crack them.

2. Heat the oil and cook the tails and claws in it over high heat about five minutes, stirring occasionally. When the meat and shell are red, sprinkle lightly with salt and liberally with black pepper.

3. Add the garlic, shallot, onion, celery and carrot. Continue to cook, stirring, and add the thyme and bay leaf. Sprinkle lobster with the cognac and add wine. Cover and simmer five minutes.

4. Add the tomatoes, tomato purée and gravy. Add the tarragon and parsley, tied in a cheesecloth bag, and the cayenne. Cover and cook fifteen minutes longer.

5. Remove the claws and tails. Discard the shells and reserve the meat. Discard the tarragon and parsley and cook the sauce remaining in the pan over high heat, stirring occasionally, about thirty minutes, or until the sauce is reduced by half and slightly thickened. Remove and discard all bits of shell from the sauce.

6. Combine the coral and liver with the butter and flour. Blend to make a smooth paste. Turn off the heat under the sauce and stir in the paste, a little at a time, with a wire whisk, to thicken the sauce. Add a little more cognac, if desired, and salt and pepper to taste. Combine the reserved meat with half the sauce and heat thoroughly but do not boil. The remaining sauce may be used on another occasion with cooked shrimp or fish.

Yield: Three or four servings.

CHEESE STRAWS

1 cup grated sharp cheese	½ teaspoon cayenne
3 tablespoons butter	1½ cups fine soft bread
4½ tablespoons milk	crumbs
½ teaspoon salt	¾ cup flour

1. Preheat the oven to 400 degrees. Grease baking sheets.

2. Mix the cheese and butter. Add the remaining ingredients, mix and knead until smooth.

3. Roll on a lightly floured pastry cloth to about three-eighth-inch thickness and cut with a pastry wheel or knife into strips that are six inches long and one-half inch wide. Place on prepared baking sheets. If desired, one-quarter of the strips may be shaped into rings with the overlapping ends brushed with egg before pressing them together. After baking, three straws may be run through each ring for serving.

4. Bake until lightly browned, about twelve minutes.

Yield: Thirty-six straws.

Celery Seed

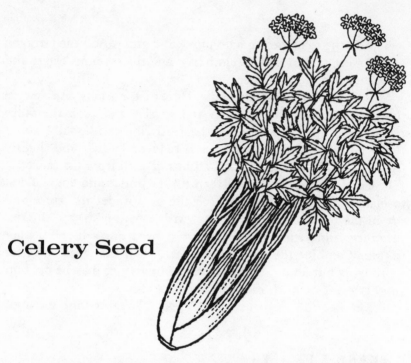

CELERY produces a seed that gives an on ne sait quoi *to thousands of salads, roasts, sauces and stews. By and large, it can be used in almost any dish calling for fresh celery. It goes with cheese and cocktail juices, pastries and sandwich spreads.*

CABBAGE AND FENNEL

½ head green cabbage	Salt and pepper to taste
4 stalks fennel	3 shallots, chopped
¾ cup olive oil	1 teaspoon celery seed
¼ cup wine vinegar	

Cut the vegetables into julienne strips and blend with remaining ingredients. Chill. Serve as an appetizer or first course.

Yield: Four to six servings.

OYSTER STEW

1 pint oysters
¼ cup (one-half stick) butter
1 quart milk, scalded (one-half cup heavy cream may be substituted for one-half cup of the milk)

½ teaspoon salt
Pepper to taste
Celery seed to taste
½ teaspoon Worcestershire sauce (optional)

1. Pick over the oysters and heat them with their liquid until the edges begin to curl.

2. Add the butter, scalded milk and seasonings. Serve at once, sprinkled, if desired, with paprika.

Yield: Four servings.

CHOPPED STEAK VIENNOISE

¾ pound ground round steak
¾ pound ground veal
2 teaspoons salt
Freshly ground black pepper to taste
½ teaspoon paprika
1 teaspoon celery seed

Nutmeg to taste
1 teaspoon onion juice
2 teaspoons lemon juice
1 egg, well beaten
2 tablespoons butter
¾ cup sour cream

1. Combine the meats, salt, pepper, paprika, celery seed, nutmeg, onion and lemon juices. Add the egg and mix lightly with the fingers. Shape into twelve patties, each one-half inch thick.

2. Heat the butter in a large skillet. Brown the patties on both sides and cook to the desired degree of doneness. (They should not be overcooked or they will tend to be dry.)

3. Remove the patties to a heated serving platter and add the sour cream to the skillet. Heat through without boiling. Pour the hot sauce over the patties and serve immediately.

Yield: Four servings.

FRESH CORN AND OYSTER CASSEROLE

3 cups (about six medium ears) fresh cut corn
1¼ cups soft bread crumbs
1 cup drained oysters
1 egg, beaten

1¼ teaspoons salt
½ teaspoon celery seed
⅛ teaspoon freshly ground black pepper
4 tablespoons butter

1. Preheat the oven to 350 degrees.

2. Combine the cut corn, one-quarter cup of the bread crumbs, the oysters, egg, salt, celery seed and pepper. Break two tablespoons of the butter into small pieces and add. Turn into a greased one-quart casserole.

3. Melt the remaining butter, mix with the remaining cup of crumbs and sprinkle over the top of the casserole. Bake until the crumbs are brown, about forty minutes.

Yield: Six servings.

SAUTÉED SLICED EGGPLANT

1 medium eggplant
⅔ cup fine dry bread crumbs
⅓ cup freshly grated Parmesan cheese
2 teaspoons salt
½ teaspoon celery seed

¼ teaspoon freshly ground black pepper
2 eggs
2 tablespoons milk
Flour for dredging
Oil or melted shortening

1. Peel and cut the eggplant into slices one-half inch thick. Set aside.

2. Combine the bread crumbs, cheese, salt, celery seed and pepper. Set aside.

3. Beat together the eggs and milk. Set aside.

4. Dip the eggplant slices in the flour, then in the egg and milk, then in the seasoned bread crumbs.

5. Sauté in a ten-inch skillet in hot oil or shortening until golden, turning to brown both sides. Drain on paper toweling.

Yield: Six to eight servings.

CABBAGE AND CARROT RELISH

3 cups scraped and chopped carrots
5 cups chopped sweet red or green peppers or a mixture of both
4 cups chopped cabbage
2 cups chopped onions

3½ cups white or cider vinegar
1¼ cups sugar
3 tablespoons salt
2 tablespoons celery seed
1 tablespoon mustard seed

1. Mix all the vegetables together well.
2. Boil the vinegar, sugar, salt, celery and mustard seeds together for two or three minutes. Add the vegetables and bring to a boil. Cook for exactly one minute and pack into hot sterilized jars. Seal at once.

Yield: About three quarts.

Note: If the relish is to be consumed within a few weeks after it is made, it is not necessary to cook the vegetables with the vinegar mixture. Simply spoon the vegetables into jars and pour the hot vinegar over them. Seal at once and refrigerate.

FRESH CORN RELISH

9 cups fresh cut corn
2 cups finely ground cabbage
1½ cups finely ground onion
2 cups finely ground green peppers, seeded
2 teaspoons crushed red pepper

2 teaspoons celery seed
1 teaspoon mustard seed
2 teaspoons turmeric
2½ tablespoons salt
1 cup sugar
2 cups cider vinegar
½ cup chopped pimento

1. Bring to a boil the vegetables, spices, salt, sugar and vinegar. Cook uncovered twenty minutes, or until relish has thickened. Stir in pimento.
2. Ladle into hot sterilized jars at once. Seal immediately. Let stand six weeks before using.

Yield: Five pints.

Chervil

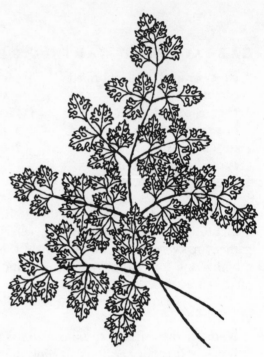

CHERVIL (CHUR-vil) has delicate and feathery leaves
and belongs to the carrot family. The resemblance ends
with the leaves, however. Chervil is used widely in
Europe and is scarcely known in America. It is one of
the four traditional fines herbes, the others being tarragon, parsley and chives. It is excellent with cream
cheese or cottage cheese, in omelets and soups.

If it is possible to be prodigal with chervil (if it is
grown in the home garden, that is), it makes a handsome
garnish for meat platters and the like. Chervil symbolizes
sincerity.

COLD ASPARAGUS WITH PARISIAN SAUCE

1 six-ounce package cream
cheese
1 teaspoon salt
1½ teaspoons paprika
Dash of white pepper
1 tablespoon lemon juice

6 tablespoons olive or other
salad oil
1 teaspoon chopped fresh
chervil
2 pounds cold cooked
asparagus

Blend the softened cream cheese with the salt, paprika and pepper. Beat in the lemon juice, oil and chervil. Continue beating until fluffy. Serve over cold asparagus.

Yield: About one cup sauce.

CAULIFLOWER À LA GRECQUE

1 medium head cauliflower, cut into flowerets
2 cups water
1 cup olive oil
Juice of three lemons
1 stalk celery, sliced
1 clove garlic, minced
1 branch whole fresh fennel or one-half teaspoon dried fennel

1 teaspoon freshly chopped chervil or one-half teaspoon dried chervil
½ teaspoon thyme
½ bay leaf
¾ teaspoon freshly ground coriander
8 peppercorns
¾ teaspoon salt

1. Bring all ingredients to a boil. Reduce the heat and simmer five minutes, stirring occasionally.

2. Turn into a bowl, cool and then marinate overnight in the refrigerator.

Yield: Six servings.

Mushrooms à la grecque: Follow recipe for cauliflower à la grecque but substitute one and one-half pounds whole small mushrooms or medium-sized mushrooms, quartered, for the cauliflower.

Chili Powder

CHILI is also spelled chile *and* chilli. *The chili is purely and simply a pepper, and there are many kinds. All the world (most of it, anyway) knows about chili through chili con carne.*

Chili powder is made not only with the ground pods of several varieties of Mexican peppers but with such other powdered herbs and spices as cumin, garlic and orégano.

CHILI CON CARNE

1 pound ground boneless chuck
1 large onion, minced
1 clove garlic, minced
3 tablespoons butter or oil
1 eight-ounce can tomato sauce
1 six-ounce can tomato paste
½ teaspoon celery salt
½ teaspoon caraway seeds
¼ teaspoon crushed red pepper
1 bay leaf, crumbled
1 tablespoon chili powder
¼ cup chopped fresh basil or one tablespoon dried basil
1½ teaspoons salt
1 pint cooked chili beans (or one can)

1. Sauté the beef, onion and garlic slowly in the hot butter or oil.

2. Add the tomato sauce, tomato paste and seasonings. Continue simmering over low heat about ten minutes. Add the beans, cover and let simmer one hour or longer. If additional liquid is needed, add beef bouillon so that the mixture has the consistency of soup.

Yield: Four servings.

Note: This dish may be frozen in ice cube trays. When frozen, the cubes may be wrapped in clear plastic or aluminum foil and kept frozen until ready for use.

CHILI-CREAMED ONIONS AND PEPPERS

1 cup thinly sliced green pepper rings
2 tablespoons butter
2 tablespoons flour
1 cup milk
¾ teaspoon freshly ground black pepper
1 teaspoon chili powder or to taste
18 small whole white onions, cooked

1. Sauté the pepper rings in the butter. Blend in the flour and stir in the milk. Cook, stirring constantly, until mixture is of medium thickness.

2. Remove from the heat and stir in the seasonings and onions. Return to the heat and heat slowly. Serve hot.

Yield: Six servings.

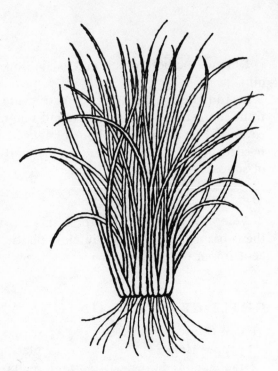

Chives

CHIVES are the most delicate member of the onion family and, according to most sources, have added a happy touch to the world's cuisine for at least the past five thousand years. Chives may be used in almost any recipe calling for a touch of raw onion as a flavoring ingredient. Chopped chives are another of the four fines herbes and they make a very pretty garnish. They are excellent when linked with cream cheese or cottage cheese or used discreetly in an omelet.

CANAPÉ PARISIEN

6 slices white bread
3 hard-cooked eggs
¼ cup (one-half stick) butter, at room temperature
3 tablespoons chopped chives
Salt and freshly ground black pepper to taste
6 tablespoons mashed foie gras, ham or sardine spread

6 ripe tomato slices, peeled
½ cup mayonnaise, preferably homemade (page 8)
½ cup sour cream
1 tablespoon lemon juice
3 tablespoons capers, drained and chopped
1 tablespoon tomato paste or catchup
½ cup finely chopped fresh parsley or watercress

1. Toast the bread and, using a large biscuit cutter, cut out the center of each slice. Butter the toast rounds and reserve trimmings for another use.

2. Cut the eggs in half and mash the yolks well. Mix with butter and chives and season to taste with salt and pepper. Fill the cavities of the hard-cooked whites with the yolk mixture.

3. Spread the toast rounds with the mashed foie gras or ham spread and top with a slice of tomato. Place one stuffed egg half, stuffed side down, in the center of each tomato slice.

4. Combine the remaining ingredients and mix well. Spoon the mixture over the canapés and serve garnished with a sprig of parsley or watercress.

Yield: Six servings.

CHICK PEAS CIBOULETTE

2 cups cooked or canned chick peas, drained
1½ cups mayonnaise (page 8)

2 tablespoons mustard
1 tablespoon chopped chives
Salt and pepper to taste

Combine all ingredients and chill. Serve as an appetizer.

Yield: Six to eight servings.

CHICKEN LEGS GRILLED IN FOIL

Wrap each leg securely in foil with a pat of butter, a teaspoon of chopped chives and salt and pepper to taste. Grill the packages over hot coals, turning once. Total cooking time will be about forty minutes.

CHIVE POTATO SOUFFLÉ

¾ cup shredded sharp Cheddar cheese
2 cups hot mashed potatoes
½ cup sour cream

1½ teaspoons salt
3 tablespoons chopped chives
3 eggs, separated

1. Preheat the oven to 350 degrees.
2. Combine the shredded cheese with the mashed potatoes, sour cream and seasonings.
3. Beat the egg whites until stiff but still moist; set aside. Beat the egg yolks until smooth and add them to the potato mixture. Whip until light. Fold in the beaten egg whites and pour into a buttered one-and-one-half-quart casserole.
4. Bake forty-five minutes and serve immediately. Garnish with additional chopped chives, if desired.

Yield: Four to six servings.

CHIVE MAYONNAISE

1 clove garlic, split
1 cup mayonnaise
3 tablespoons finely chopped chives
1 tablespoon finely chopped green pepper

1 tablespoon chopped fresh parsley
1 tablespoon chopped pimento
¼ teaspoon salt
⅛ teaspoon freshly ground black pepper

Rub the bowl in which the dressing is to be mixed with the cut side of the garlic. Discard the garlic. Combine the remaining ingredients in the bowl and mix well. Serve with chilled shrimp.

Yield: One and one-quarter cups.

CHIVE HOLLANDAISE SAUCE

Follow the recipe for hollandaise sauce (page 7). Along with the salt and lemon juice add a dash of cayenne pepper and one and one-half teaspoons finely chopped chives. Serve over hot asparagus or broccoli.

Yield: One cup sauce.

GREEN GODDESS SALAD DRESSING

1 two-ounce can flat anchovies, chopped
3 tablespoons chopped fresh chives
1 tablespoon lemon juice
3 tablespoons tarragon vinegar

1 cup sour cream
1 cup mayonnaise
½ cup chopped parsley
Freshly ground black pepper to taste
½ teaspoon salt

Combine all ingredients in the container of an electric blender and blend two seconds, or beat thoroughly with a rotary beater. Chill and use on salad greens, chilled seafood or hard-cooked eggs.

Yield: About two and one-quarter cups.

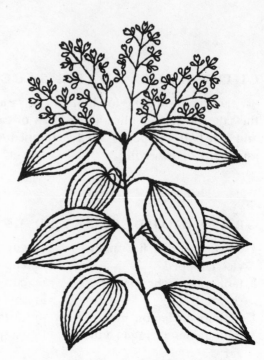

Cinnamon

CINNAMON is the bark of the cinnamon tree, and its value can scarcely be estimated. It is one of the oldest spices known to man and is one of the predominant scents used in the incense burned for ritual purposes. The uses of cinnamon in cooking are without number and it is used equally in savory dishes and desserts. It it important for pickling and it is difficult to imagine rice pudding without it.

STUFFED SLICED EGGPLANT

1 large eggplant (two and one-half pounds)
½ cup olive or salad oil
½ cup finely chopped onion
1 clove garlic, minced
½ pound ground beef
2 tablespoons chopped fresh parsley
2 cups soft bread crumbs
1 teaspoon ground cinnamon
3 teaspoons salt
¼ teaspoon freshly ground black pepper
2 eggs, beaten

1. Preheat the oven to 350 degrees.
2. Wash, peel and cut the eggplant into lengthwise slices one-

half-inch thick. Heat the oil in a skillet. Sauté the eggplant in the oil until almost cooked, but still firm. If necessary, add more oil. Remove the eggplant from the skillet and reserve the oil in which it cooked.

3. Sauté the onion and garlic until limp in one tablespoon of the oil. Add the beef and cook until it loses its red color. Blend in the parsley, bread crumbs, cinnamon, salt, pepper and eggs.

4. Spread the filling sandwich-fashion between each two slices of eggplant. Hold together with food picks or skewers. Place in a baking pan and pour the reserved oil over all. Bake thirty to forty-five minutes.

Yield: Six servings.

FRESH PINEAPPLE CHUTNEY

1 large fresh pineapple (six to seven pounds)	1¾ cups seedless raisins
1 tablespoon salt	1¼ cups light-brown sugar
½ large clove of garlic, mashed	1 cup cider vinegar
	2 two-inch cinnamon sticks
	¼ teaspoon ground cloves

1. Peel, slice and finely chop the pineapple. Sprinkle with salt and let stand one and one-half hours. Drain.

2. Put the garlic and raisins through a food chopper using the medium blade. Add to the pineapple.

3. Combine the sugar, vinegar and spices in a saucepan and bring to the boiling point. Add the fruit mixture and cook over medium heat until thickened, about forty-five minutes. Ladle into hot, sterilized half-pint jars and seal at once.

Yield: Four jars.

CRYSTAL TOMATOES

5 pounds green or under-ripe tomatoes	3½ cups sugar
3 tablespoons slaked lime (calcium hydroxide, available at a drugstore)	3 two-inch cinnamon sticks
	1 teaspoon nutmeg
	1 tablespoon pieces of whole dried ginger
2 quarts plus one cup water	1 teaspoon salt
	4 cups vinegar

1. Cut the tomatoes into one-quarter-inch slices.

2. Dissolve the lime in two quarts of the water and add the tomatoes. Stir gently to separate the pieces. Let stand six hours or overnight.

3. Drain and rinse the tomatoes in several changes of cold water; drain.

4. Place the sugar, the spices tied loosely in cheesecloth, the salt, vinegar and one cup of water in a six-quart kettle. Boil for five minutes.

5. Add the tomatoes and boil until the syrup is thick and the tomatoes are clear. Pack at once into hot sterilized jars, sealing immediately.

Yield: About ten cups.

CINNAMON CHOCOLATE PIE

1 cup sugar	2 cups scalded milk
¼ teaspoon salt	3 tablespoons butter
½ teaspoon ground cin-	3 egg yolks
namon	1 teaspoon vanilla
¼ cup cornstarch	1 nine-inch baked pastry
⅓ cup cocoa	shell
¼ cup cold milk	Meringue (recipe follows)

1. Preheat the oven to 300 degrees.

2. Combine one-half cup of the sugar with the salt, cinnamon, cornstarch and cocoa in the top of a double boiler. Blend in the cold milk. Stir in the hot milk and cook over hot water until thick, about three to five minutes, stirring constantly. Cover and continue cooking until very thick, about eight minutes, stirring occasionally. Add the butter.

3. Beat the egg yolks lightly and blend them with the remaining one-half cup sugar. Add a little of the hot mixture, then stir

into the remaining hot mixture. Cook, uncovered, over hot (not boiling) water until very thick, about ten minutes. Add the vanilla. Cool.

4. Turn the mixture into the baked pie shell. Top with meringue and bake twenty minutes.

Yield: Six to eight servings.

Meringue: Combine three egg whites with one-eighth teaspoon salt and beat until the whites stand in soft peaks. Beat in four tablespoons sugar, one tablespoon at a time, until stiff.

DUTCH APPLE CAKE

1½ cups sifted all-purpose
　　flour
⅓ cup sugar
2 teaspoons baking powder
¾ teaspoon salt
⅓ cup shortening
1 egg, beaten

½ cup milk
3 medium apples, peeled,
　　cored and sliced
½ teaspoon ground cinna-
　　mon
2 tablespoons butter
2 tablespoons maple syrup

1. Preheat the oven to 375 degrees.
2. Sift together the flour, three tablespoons of the sugar, the baking powder and the salt. Cut in the shortening with two knives or a pastry blender.
3. Combine the egg and milk and add to the dry ingredients. Mix to a soft dough. Spread the dough in a greased, shallow, eight-inch-square pan.
4. Place the apples on the dough in rows of overlapping slices. Mix the remaining sugar and cinnamon and sprinkle over the apples. Dot with butter.
5. Bake for forty to forty-five minutes. Remove from oven and pour the maple syrup over the apple topping.

Yield: Nine servings.

MARIA VON TRAPP'S LINZERTORTE

1 cup (two sticks) butter
1 cup sugar
1 tablespoon grated orange
  or lemon peel
2 egg yolks
1½ cups sifted all-purpose
  flour
1 teaspoon baking powder
2 teaspoons cinnamon
½ teaspoon cloves
¼ teaspoon salt
1 cup ground nuts (filberts,
  almonds or walnuts)
1 cup currant or plum
  preserves
Whipped cream

1. Cream the butter and add the sugar slowly while continuing to cream. Add the grated peel. Add the egg yolks, one at a time, beating well after each.

2. Sift together the flour, baking powder, spices and salt. Add slowly to the creamed mixture, stirring in. Stir in the nuts. Mix with the hands until all the ingredients are thoroughly combined. Chill.

3. Preheat the oven to 350 degrees.

4. Pat two-thirds of the dough into the bottom of a nine-inch layer-cake pan (preferably one with a removable bottom). Spread the preserves over the dough in the pan. Roll out the remaining dough and cut it into eight strips, each three-quarters of an inch wide. Place lattice fashion on top of the preserves.

5. Bake until the edges of the strips recede from the sides of the pan, fifty to sixty minutes. Cool. Garnish with whipped cream and cut into small wedges to serve.

Yield: Ten to twelve servings.

DUCHESS SPICE CAKE

1¾ cups sifted flour
¼ teaspoon salt
1 teaspoon baking soda
1 teaspoon cinnamon
½ teaspoon nutmeg
½ teaspoon cloves
½ cup (one stick) butter
1½ cups brown sugar, firmly
  packed
2 eggs, well beaten
1 cup sour cream
1 cup seeded raisins, simmered, drained and
  cooled (optional)
½ cup broken nut meats
  (optional)

1. Preheat the oven to 350 degrees. Lightly grease a 9 x 5 x 3-inch loaf pan.

2. Sift together the flour, salt, soda and spices; set aside.

3. Cream the butter, adding the sugar gradually; blend well. Add the eggs. Stir in the sifted dry ingredients alternately with the sour cream. Add the raisins and nuts.

4. Pour the batter into the prepared pan and bake forty-five to fifty minutes.

Yield: One loaf.

SPICED APPLESAUCE CAKE

½ cup shortening
1¼ cups sugar
2 eggs, beaten
1 cup light or dark raisins, chopped
½ cup chopped walnuts
1 cup thick unsweetened applesauce

2¼ cups sifted all-purpose flour
1 teaspoon salt
1 teaspoon cinnamon
½ teaspoon nutmeg
½ teaspoon ground cloves
½ teaspoon soda
1 teaspoon baking powder
Sweetened whipped cream

1. Preheat the oven to 375 degrees.

2. Cream the shortening and sugar together thoroughly. Add the eggs, raisins, walnuts and applesauce. Beat well.

3. Sift together the flour, salt, spices, soda and baking powder. Blend into the applesauce mixture thoroughly.

4. Spoon into two greased, nine-inch layer-cake pans and bake about thirty minutes. When cool, fill and frost with sweetened whipped cream.

Yield: One nine-inch layer cake.

CINNAMON-CHOCOLATE SPONGE ROLL

4 eggs
¾ teaspoon baking powder
¼ teaspoon salt
¾ cup sugar
½ teaspoon ground cinnamon

1 teaspoon vanilla
¾ cup sifted cake flour
Confectioners' sugar
Cinnamon-chocolate frosting (recipe follows)

1. Preheat the oven to 400 degrees. Line a greased 15 x 10 x 1-inch jelly-roll pan with wax paper and grease the paper.

2. Beat the eggs until foamy with the baking powder and salt in a bowl set over, not in, hot water.

3. Mix the sugar with the cinnamon and gradually beat into the eggs. Continue beating until the mixture is very thick. Remove the bowl from over the hot water and beat in the vanilla. Fold in the cake flour.

4. Pour the batter into the prepared pan and spread it evenly. Bake until the cake springs back when touched gently with the finger, about twelve or thirteen minutes.

5. Turn out upside down on a cloth dusted with confectioners' sugar. Quickly remove the wax paper and trim off the edges of the cake. Roll up in the cloth jelly-roll fashion. Cool.

6. Unroll the cake and spread it with cinnamon-chocolate frosting. Roll again. Frost the outside of the cake with the same frosting or dust with confectioners' sugar.

Yield: Twelve servings.

CINNAMON-CHOCOLATE FROSTING:

1 twelve-ounce package semi-sweet chocolate pieces
¼ cup (one-half stick) butter
⅔ cup sifted confectioners' sugar
¾ teaspoon ground cinnamon
¼ cup evaporated milk
1 teaspoon vanilla
⅛ teaspoon salt

Melt the chocolate and butter in the top of a double boiler over hot water. Remove from the heat and stir in the sugar, cinnamon, milk, vanilla and salt. Beat until smooth and of spreading consistency.

Yield: Enough frosting for inside of roll.

The following recipe has an interesting history. It was sent to me by Mrs. Mary Jane Kaniuka of State College, Pennsylvania.

"Our family feels very strongly about Indian pudding

and my parents never fail to order it when it appears on a menu. They always agree that Mother's is infinitely superior. This is her recipe, which she clipped from the Boston Globe, *probably twenty-five years ago. Printed with the recipe was the following note:*

" 'This recipe was taken from a seared and yellow scrapbook in Widener Library of Harvard University, and without a doubt can't be beat.' "

It is excellent.

INDIAN PUDDING

4 cups milk	¾ teaspoon salt
1 cup yellow cornmeal	½ teaspoon cinnamon
2 eggs, lightly beaten	¼ teaspoon ground cloves
⅓ cup finely minced suet	¼ teaspoon ground ginger
½ cup sugar	⅛ teaspoon allspice
⅔ cup light molasses	⅛ teaspoon nutmeg

1. Preheat the oven to 325 degrees.
2. Bring the milk to a boil and add the cornmeal gradually, beating vigorously with a wire whisk. When mixture starts to thicken set it aside to cool.
3. When the mixture is nearly cool stir in the remaining ingredients and mix well.
4. Pour the mixture into a buttered baking dish and bake two hours. Serve piping hot with vanilla ice cream on top.

Yield: Ten to twelve servings.

BLUEBERRY PUDDING

1 quart fresh blueberries	4 slices firm white bread
½ teaspoon cinnamon	¼ pound butter
2 tablespoons sugar	⅔ cup sugar
1 cup heavy cream	

1. Wash the blueberries and drain them well. Mix cinnamon and sugar together.

2. Whip cream until stiff but still moist. Fold in cinnamon-sugar mixture. Put cream in a serving dish and refrigerate until well chilled.

3. Remove the crusts from the bread slices and discard. Dice the bread into pieces that are about one-third inch square. Melt the butter in a skillet and sauté the bread cubes until they are crisp and golden. Add the sugar and stir so that the croutons are coated thoroughly.

4. Just before the dessert is to be served, reheat the croutons, add the berries and warm them well. Serve with the well-chilled whipped cream.

Yield: Six servings.

SWISS HONEY COOKIES

¾ cup honey
1¼ cups sugar
Grated rind and juice of one-quarter lemon
½ cup ground candied orange peel
¼ cup ground candied lemon peel
1½ cups unblanched almonds, ground

3 tablespoons kirsch or cognac
4 cups sifted flour
Dash of salt
1 teaspoon baking soda
1 teaspoon cinnamon
⅛ teaspoon ground cloves
⅛ teaspoon nutmeg
1 cup sifted confectioners' sugar
3 tablespoons water

1. Heat the honey and sugar to the boiling point but do not boil. Add the grated lemon rind and juice. Set aside to cool slightly.

2. Stir in the ground candied fruits, the ground almonds and the kirsch.

3. Sift together the flour, salt, baking soda and spices onto a board. Make a well in the center of the flour mixture and pour in the honey mixture. Knead with the hands until the dough holds together. This is a very stiff dough and requires energetic kneading.

4. Preheat the oven to 350 degrees.

5. Divide the dough into quarters and roll, one at a time, to a thickness of one-quarter inch. Cut into 2 x 1½-inch rectangles.

6. Place on greased baking sheets and bake until golden, about ten to fifteen minutes. Cool on racks.

7. While the cookies are still warm, brush the tops with a glaze of the confectioners' sugar mixed with the water.

8. Store the cookies in an airtight container.

Yield: Seven to eight dozen cookies.

ORANGES IN RED WINE

1 cup dry red wine	2 or three slices of tangerine
1 cup water	(optional)
¾ cup sugar	2 slices of lemon
1 cinnamon stick	6 large oranges
2 cloves	

1. Combine the wine, water, sugar, cinnamon, cloves, tangerine and lemon. Bring to a boil and simmer three minutes. Strain and keep hot.

2. Meanwhile, peel the oranges and reserve the skins. Section the oranges, keeping the segments as whole as possible. Discard the fibrous membranes. Drop the orange sections into the hot syrup.

3. Pare away the white part of the orange skins and cut the skins into very fine julienne strips. Sprinkle the strips over the oranges in red wine; chill.

Yield: Six servings.

HONEY-BAKED PEARS

8 pear halves	¾ teaspoon cinnamon
3 tablespoons lemon juice	2 tablespoons butter
½ cup honey	

1. Preheat the oven to 350 degrees.

2. Place the pear halves in a buttered baking dish. Combine

the lemon juice with the honey and pour this mixture over the pears. Sprinkle with cinnamon and dot with butter.

3. Bake until the fruit is tender, about thirty-five to forty minutes, basting occasionally.

Yield: Eight servings.

GLAZED FRESH PEARS

8 firm, ripe pears	¾ cup currant or apple jelly
24 whole cloves	3 cups water, approximately
½ cup sugar	2 two-inch cinnamon sticks

1. Peel the pears, leaving them whole and with the stems attached. Stud each with three cloves.

2. Mix the sugar, jelly and water. Add the cinnamon, mix well and bring to the boiling point.

3. Place four of the pears in the hot syrup. (The syrup should cover three-quarters of the pears. If not, add more water.) Cover and simmer until the pears are tender, about twenty minutes. Remove the pears from the syrup.

4. Repeat the process, using the remaining four pears. Cool all the pears in the syrup. Carefully lift the pears from the syrup and place in serving dishes. Chill.

Yield: Eight servings.

HOT BLUEBERRY SAUCE

1½ cups fresh blueberries	¼ teaspoon nutmeg
¼ cup sugar	½ teaspoon grated lemon
¾ teaspoon cinnamon	rind

1. Wash the blueberries and drain well. Mix with the remaining ingredients.

2. Bring to a boil and simmer slowly for five minutes, stirring occasionally. Serve hot over ice cream, waffles, pancakes, puddings or cake.

Yield: One cup.

MEXICAN CHOCOLATE

4 ounces unsweetened chocolate
½ cup boiling water
4 cups milk, scalded
2 cups cream
6 tablespoons sugar

¼ teaspoon salt
Pinch each of nutmeg and allspice
2 teaspoons cinnamon
2 eggs
2 teaspoons vanilla

1. Grate the chocolate into the top of a double boiler over boiling water. Add the half cup of boiling water and, when the chocolate is melted, beat with a wooden spoon until smooth.

2. Stir in the hot milk, cream, sugar, salt and spices. Cook one hour, beating vigorously at intervals of ten minutes.

3. When ready to serve, beat the eggs with the vanilla. Add a little of the hot chocolate to the eggs, then stir into the remainder of the chocolate. Beat vigorously three minutes. Serve at once.

Yield: Six to eight servings.

Note: The chocolate should be served in preheated cups or mugs, preferably earthenware. Although it is not authentically Mexican, the chocolate may be served topped with whipped cream and sprinkled with cinnamon.

Cloves

The CLOVE, one of the most fragrant of all aromatic spices, looks like a little brown nail. The clove tree flourishes in the Philippines and is said to be exquisitely scented, exhaling a perfume both rare and delicious. Cloves serve a double purpose in both savory and sweet dishes. The clove symbolizes dignity.

ASPARAGUS AND TOMATO SOUP

1½ cups cooked asparagus
5 cups chicken stock or water
1 medium onion, chopped
1 carrot, sliced
⅛ teaspoon freshly ground black pepper
1 teaspoon chopped parsley
½ teaspoon thyme

1 teaspoon salt
1 bay leaf
3 whole cloves
½ teaspoon sugar
2 cups cooked tomatoes
2 tablespoons melted butter
2 tablespoons flour

1. Combine all ingredients except butter and flour. Cover and cook slowly about forty-five minutes. Press through a sieve.

2. Blend the butter and flour; add to the soup and cook slowly twenty minutes longer. Serve hot.

Yield: Six servings.

CECELIA'S SAUERBRATEN

1 cup red wine vinegar	¼ teaspoon nutmeg
½ bottle red wine	3 stalks celery, chopped
10 peppercorns	2 carrots, chopped
1 teaspoon salt	3 sprigs parsley
1 bay leaf	1 six-pound rolled top round
6 cloves	of beef
2 cloves garlic	2 cups beef stock
2 strips lemon rind	3 tablespoons cornstarch or
1 onion, halved	arrowroot

1. Combine the vinegar, wine, peppercorns, salt, bay leaf, cloves, garlic, lemon rind, onion, nutmeg, celery, carrots and parsley. Add the beef, cover and refrigerate three days, turning occasionally.

2. Remove the meat and reserve the marinade. Dry the meat well with paper towels. Bring the marinade to a boil and simmer it over low heat while the meat is cooking. It will be used to baste the meat.

3. Heat a Dutch oven or heavy kettle. Add the meat, fat side down, and brown it well on all sides for one hour. After browning, pour off excess fat from the kettle.

4. Add one cup of the beef stock to the meat. Cover with a close-fitting lid and cook over low heat for three and one-half hours. Baste occasionally with the remaining cup of stock and the hot marinade until all the marinade has been added.

5. Remove the meat to a hot platter. Strain the gravy, pressing the vegetables through a sieve. Remove the fat from the surface. Thicken the gravy with the cornstarch mixed with a little water. The sauce should be served separately from the meat. Serve with potato dumplings (see page 225).

Yield: Eight to ten servings.

BLANQUETTE DE VEAU

2 pounds breast or shoulder of veal
4 cups water
12 small white onions
1 medium carrot, cut into half-inch pieces
1 medium onion, studded with two cloves
1 bay leaf
Pinch of thyme

½ teaspoon salt
¼ teaspoon white pepper
1 tablespoon butter
1 tablespoon flour
½ cup sliced mushrooms
⅛ cup heavy cream
2 egg yolks
1 teaspoon lemon juice
1 tablespoon chopped parsley

1. Cut the veal into twelve pieces and place in a large, heavy saucepan. Add the water, bring to a boil and skim. Add the small onions, carrot, onion studded with cloves, bay leaf, thyme, salt and pepper. Cover and simmer until the meat is tender, about one and one-half hours. Remove the meat, small onions and carrot to a heated serving dish and keep warm. Discard the bay leaf and the onion studded with cloves.

2. In another saucepan melt the butter. Stir in the flour and cook, stirring, until smooth. Add the liquid in which the veal cooked and the mushrooms. Cook over low heat fifteen minutes, stirring occasionally.

3. In a bowl, combine the cream and egg yolks. Stir in five tablespoons of sauce from the pan, one at a time. Then stir the egg mixture into the sauce in the pan. Add the lemon juice. Cook over low heat five minutes, stirring constantly, but do not allow to boil. Pour the sauce over the meat and sprinkle with chopped parsley. Serve hot.

Yield: Four to six servings.

SPICED LEMON PICKLES

9 large lemons
2¼ cups sugar
⅛ teaspoon salt
¼ cup water
1 cup cider vinegar

1 cinnamon stick
½ teaspoon whole allspice
1 small ginger root
4 or five whole cloves

1. Wash and thoroughly dry the lemons. Cut them, without peeling, into crosswise slices one-quarter inch thick.

2. Combine the sugar, salt, water and vinegar in a saucepan. Tie the spices in a cheesecloth bag and add to the syrup. Boil five minutes.

3. Drop the lemon slices into the boiling syrup and boil one minute.

4. Discard the spice bag and pack the lemons into hot sterilized half-pint jars. Cover with the boiling syrup and seal at once.

Yield: Six jars.

Coriander

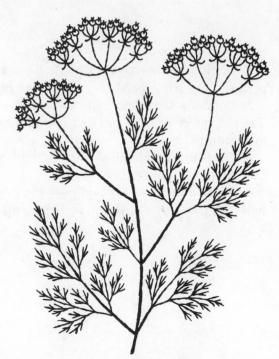

CORIANDER (cori-ANDER) symbolizes hidden worth and that is a sermon in itself. The use of coriander seeds ranges from the humble frankfurter to some of the most exotic dishes of North Africa. It is welcome in soups and stews and gives a fresh, spicy flavor to chili dishes and curries. It is interesting, too, with some of the more delicate cheeses, such as cream or cottage. The leaf of coriander is widely used in international cuisines.

INDONESIAN PORK SATÉ

2 pounds lean pork
1 cup salted peanuts
2 tablespoons coriander seeds, finely ground
2 cloves garlic, minced
1 teaspoon crushed red pepper, or to taste
1½ cups chopped onions

3 tablespoons lemon juice
2 tablespoons brown sugar
5 tablespoons soy sauce
½ teaspoon black pepper
½ cup melted butter
½ cup chicken stock or water

1. Trim all fat, bone and sinews from the pork and cut it into one-inch cubes.

2. Combine the peanuts, coriander, garlic, red pepper, onions, lemon juice, sugar, soy sauce and black pepper in the container of an electric blender, or put them through a food mill. Blend or grind to a fine purée.

3. Pour the purée into a saucepan and bring to a boil. Add the butter and chicken stock. Let cool and pour over the pork. Let stand one or two hours.

4. Thread the meat on skewers and grill over charcoal, basting occasionally with the sauce. If any sauce remains, reheat it and serve it with the meat.

Yield: Six servings.

TANDOORI CHICKEN

1 five- to six-pound roasting chicken or capon	½ teaspoon dry mustard
2 cups yoghurt	½ teaspoon cardamom
1 clove garlic, minced	½ teaspoon ginger
2 teaspoons coriander	½ teaspoon cumin
½ teaspoon crushed red pepper	⅓ cup cider vinegar
½ teaspoon freshly ground black pepper	2 tablespoons fresh lime or lemon juice
	4 teaspoons salt
	Salad oil

1. Wash the chicken and place it in a close-fitting bowl. Combine the yoghurt, garlic, spices, vinegar, lime juice and salt. Mix well and pour over the chicken. Turn to coat well with the marinade. Place in the refrigerator and marinate at least twelve hours, or overnight.

2. Preheat the oven to 325 degrees.

3. Remove the chicken from the mixture and place it on a rack in a shallow baking pan or roaster. Bake until tender, about three and one-half hours. Baste with the marinade for just one and one-half hours of the cooking time. Baste with salad oil as often as the chicken looks dry, about three times, during the remaining

cooking time. If necessary, cover the chicken with aluminum foil during the last forty-five minutes of baking. If a gravy is desired, add one-half cup hot water to the roasting pan. Cook only until hot, scraping the bottom of the pan well.

Yield: About six servings.

STEAMED ARTICHOKES

8 large artichokes   8 coriander seeds
Boiling salted water   Juice of two lemons

1. Trim the tough outer leaves and stalks from the artichokes and drop the vegetables into boiling salted water to cover. Add the coriander seeds and lemon juice.

2. Simmer, covered, until the outer leaves pull off easily, about forty minutes. Serve hot with melted butter, hollandaise (page 7) or mousseline sauce, or cold with French dressing or sauce vinaigrette (page 228).

Yield: Eight servings.

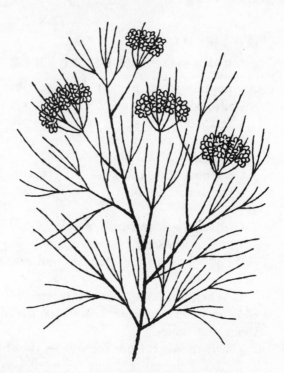

Cumin

CUMIN (KUMM-in) was a symbol of greed to the ancient Greeks. On the Roman side, it is said that Marcus Aurelius was nicknamed Cumin because of a pronounced cupidity.

Those who dote on Mexican food generally have a strong liking for cumin, or comino as it is known south of the border, and it figures prominently as a flavor in many of that country's characteristic dishes. Mexican cooks aver that the best way to get the full effect from cumin seeds is to rub them briskly between the palms of the hand, letting the bruised seeds fall naturally into the stew as it cooks. Cumin figures prominently in many international cuisines, including that of India.

CORN SOUP WITH SPARERIBS

2½ pounds spareribs, cut
    into serving pieces
3 teaspoons salt
1 teaspoon cumin seed
¼ teaspoon black pepper
½ teaspoon orégano
1 bay leaf, crumbled

½ clove garlic, chopped
1 small onion, chopped
1½ tablespoons cider vinegar
4 cups cold water
3 medium ears fresh corn
1½ cups shredded potatoes
½ cup milk

1. Place the spareribs in a bowl. Combine one teaspoon of the salt, the cumin seed, pepper, orégano, bay leaf, garlic, onion and vinegar. Mix with the spareribs and marinate eight to ten hours or overnight.

2. When ready to cook, transfer the mixture to a saucepan, add the water, cover and simmer until the meat is well cooked, about one hour.

3. Cut the corn from the cob by running the point of a sharp knife down the center of each row of kernels lengthwise, cutting them in half; shave a thin layer off the entire cob. Repeat, removing another layer. Scrape the cob well, using the bowl of a tablespoon.

4. Add the corn to the meat and broth, along with the potatoes, milk and remaining two teaspoons of salt. Simmer until the vegetables are tender, about ten minutes. Serve in bowls with a piece of sparerib in each.

Yield: Six to eight servings.

KIDNEY BEAN SOUP

½ cup dried kidney beans
Water
2 ounces salt pork
1 medium onion, chopped
1 carrot, diced
3 stalks celery with leaves,
    diced
½ bay leaf

3 peppercorns
1 teaspoon ground cumin
    seed
Salt and freshly ground black
    pepper to taste
Avocado slices
Lemon juice

1. Cover the beans with water and soak them overnight. Or boil two minutes, cover and let stand for one hour. Drain, discarding the water.

2. Cut the salt pork into cubes and cook it slowly in a heavy kettle to render the fat.

3. Add the onion, carrot and celery to the fat in the kettle. Sauté five minutes.

4. Add the drained beans, four cups of boiling water, the bay leaf, peppercorns and cumin to the kettle. Cover and simmer two and one-half to three hours.

5. Put the soup through a sieve or purée it in an electric blender. Reheat the soup and correct the seasonings with salt and pepper, if needed.

6. Serve the soup topped with avocado slices which have been dipped into the lemon juice.

Yield: Six servings.

MEXICAN TORTE

¾ cup coarsely chopped onion

1 or two cloves garlic, finely minced

3 tablespoons olive oil

1 pound ground round steak

2 cups canned Italian plum tomatoes

1 cup water or beef stock

3 tablespoons chili powder, or to taste

1 teaspoon ground cumin

Salt and freshly ground black pepper to taste

9 tortillas (approximately), fresh or canned

1 cup grated cheese, preferably Monterey Jack although Cheddar may be used

½ cup finely chopped onion

½ cup sour cream, approximately

6 black olives, pitted and halved

1. Cook the onion and garlic in the olive oil five minutes, but do not brown. Add the meat and cook, stirring, until it loses its red color.

2. Add the tomatoes, water, chili powder, cumin, salt and pepper. Simmer forty-five minutes.

3. Preheat the oven to 350 degrees.

4. Spoon a little of the sauce over the bottom of a buttered casserole and cover it with three tortillas, overlapping them if necessary.

5. Sprinkle with one-third of the cheese, one-third of the finely chopped onion and add a tablespoon of sour cream. Continue adding layers, including sauce, until all the ingredients are used, ending with a top layer of sauce. Spoon the remaining sour cream into the center of the torte and garnish around it with the black olives.

6. Bake the casserole until it bubbles, about twenty minutes. Serve piping hot.

Yield: Four to six servings.

CHICKEN À LA MEXICAINE

2 two-and-one-half-pound chickens, cut into serving pieces
Salt and freshly ground black pepper
3 tablespoons chicken fat or olive oil
¾ cup finely chopped onion
2 cloves garlic, finely chopped
8 pimentos
½ teaspoon ground cumin
3 cups hot chicken stock or water
3 tablespoons butter
3 tablespoons flour

1. Sprinkle the chicken with salt and pepper and brown it on all sides in chicken fat in a casserole with a tight-fitting lid. Add the onion and garlic to the casserole and cook briefly, stirring.

2. Put the pimentos through a food mill or purée in an electric blender. Pour them over the chicken and sprinkle with cumin. Pour the hot chicken stock over the chicken, cover the casserole and simmer until the chicken is tender, about forty-five minutes.

3. Transfer the chicken to a serving dish. Prepare a beurre manié by kneading the butter and flour together. Add it, bit by bit, to the liquid in the casserole, stirring after each addition.

When the sauce is thickened and smooth, simmer one minute and pour it over the chicken.

Yield: Six servings.

CUCUMBERS IN YOGHURT

3 pints plain yoghurt, lightly whipped
1 small onion, finely chopped
2 cucumbers, finely grated
½ teaspoon freshly ground black pepper
1 teaspoon cumin seed, preheated in a dry skillet
¼ teaspoon crushed red pepper
1 teaspoon finely chopped Chinese parsley (optional)
Salt to taste

1. Combine all ingredients and chill at least one hour.
2. Garnish with paprika and, if available, sprigs of Chinese parsley. Serve as an accompaniment to curries and other highly condimented dishes.

Yield: About ten servings.

Curry Powder

The name curry derives from a Hindustani word, turcarri, colloquially shortened in India to turri. This was corrupted slightly to be pronounced curry *in English.*

CURRY POWDER is a blend of, generally, ten or more spices. In India, where the curry originated, the word means sauce, and several curries, each of them with different flavors, may be served during the course of one meal. There may be meat curries, fish curries and vegetable curries. Indian women frequently grind and blend their own spices although preblended spices for curries are available at various bazaars. Typical spices in a commercially packaged curry powder might include turmeric, cardamom, coriander, mustard, saffron and allspice. The color of most curry powders is derived from the goldenrod yellow of turmeric.

SENEGALESE SOUP

¼ cup butter
2 medium onions, coarsely
  chopped
3 ribs celery, chopped
2 tablespoons flour
1 tablespoon curry powder

2 apples, peeled and
  chopped
1 cup diced cooked chicken
2 quarts chicken broth
1 bay leaf
1 cup light cream, chilled

1. Melt the butter in a skillet, add the onions and celery and cook until the vegetables are limp. Add the flour and curry powder and cook, stirring, several minutes.

2. Transfer the mixture to an electric blender. Add the apples, chicken and about one cup chicken broth. Blend until smooth.

3. In a saucepan combine the puréed mixture with the remaining broth, add the bay leaf and bring to a boil. Remove the bay leaf and chill. Before serving, stir in the chilled cream.

Yield: Ten servings.

LAMB CURRY WITH MELON AND MANGOES

3 pounds lean lamb
  shoulder or leg
⅓ cup butter
¾ cup finely chopped onion
3 tablespoons freshly grated
  or chopped preserved
  ginger
¼ teaspoon freshly ground
  black pepper
2 teaspoons salt
2 to three tablespoons curry
  powder

1 teaspoon chopped fresh
  mint leaves
½ cup lamb stock (recipe
  below)
½ cup coconut milk (recipe
  below)
1 cup melon balls—cantaloupe, honeydew or
  Persian
1 cup mango balls or pieces
½ cup lime juice
½ cup heavy cream

1. Wipe the meat and cut into two-inch cubes.

2. Melt the butter and sauté the onion in it until tender but not browned. Add the lamb and heat until it changes color, but do not brown.

3. Add the ginger, pepper, salt, curry powder, mint, stock and coconut milk. Cover and simmer twenty-five to thirty-five minutes until the lamb is tender.

4. Add the melon and mango balls and cook five minutes. Stir in the lime juice. Add the cream, stirring rapidly. Reheat but do not boil.

Yield: Six to eight servings.

Lamb stock: Simmer lamb bones with one cup water one to two hours.

Coconut milk: Blend one cup grated fresh coconut meat with one cup liquid drained from the coconut. Strain through several layers of muslin.

TURKEY MADRAS

½ cup white raisins
Boiling water
3 tablespoons butter or
  poultry fat
¾ cup chopped celery
¾ cup chopped onion
1 clove garlic, crushed
4 mushrooms, finely chopped

1 to three tablespoons curry
  powder, according to taste
¼ cup flour
1 tablespoon tomato paste
2 cups turkey broth
1 cup heavy cream
Salt and freshly ground black
  pepper to taste
3 cups cubed cooked turkey

1. Place the raisins in a bowl and cover with boiling water. Let stand three minutes. Drain.

2. Heat the butter in a Dutch oven or kettle and cook the celery, onion, garlic and mushrooms until the vegetables are tender. Stir occasionally. With a wooden spoon, stir in the curry powder, flour and tomato paste until well blended.

3. Meanwhile, bring the broth to a boil and add it all at once to the kettle, stirring with a wire whisk. Cook the mixture forty-five minutes and pass through a food mill or sieve. Stir in the heavy cream. Season to taste with salt and pepper.

4. Add the turkey and raisins and bring to a boil. Serve with rice, chutney and, if desired, chopped hard-cooked egg whites, chopped hard-cooked egg yolks, chopped peanuts or toasted almonds, shredded coconut, chopped cucumber and chopped onion or scallion.

Yield: Six servings.

CECILY BROWNSTONE'S BROILED CHICKEN

1 two-and-one-half-pound chicken
¼ cup (one-half stick) butter
1 teaspoon salt
1 teaspoon dry mustard
1 teaspoon paprika
½ teaspoon curry powder
1 clove garlic, peeled and crushed

1. Preheat the broiler.
2. Cut the chicken into eight pieces. Wash it and dry it.
3. Cream the butter with the remaining ingredients and spread the underside of the chicken with half the mixture.
4. Broil the chicken, seasoned side up, until brown. Turn and spread the other side with the remaining butter mixture. Continue broiling until brown and cooked through, about forty-five minutes, basting occasionally with the drippings.

Yield: Four servings.

FIRE ISLAND CURRY

¼ cup (one-half stick) butter
2 cups thinly sliced onions
2 cloves garlic, finely chopped
1 three-pound chicken, cut into serving pieces
1 teaspoon freshly grated ginger or one-half teaspoon ground ginger
1 teaspoon poppy seeds
1 teaspoon cumin
1 teaspoon coriander seeds
1 teaspoon salt
1 teaspoon hot chili pepper
1 cinnamon stick, broken
2 bay leaves
1 teaspoon cardamom, peeled and crushed
5 whole cloves
2 cups water
1 cup coconut cream (see below)

1. Melt the butter in a large skillet and cook the onions and garlic in it until golden brown. Add the chicken pieces and brown on all sides. Then, sprinkle the chicken with the ginger, poppy seeds, cumin, coriander seeds and salt. Cook the chicken ten minutes longer, turning once and stirring around.

2. Add the chili pepper, cinnamon stick, bay leaves, cardamom and cloves to the skillet. Add the water, cover the skillet loosely and simmer thirty minutes, or until chicken is done.

3. Remove the bay leaves and cloves and add the coconut cream. Bring to a boil and simmer three minutes. Serve hot with rice and chutney.

Yield: Two to four servings.

Coconut Cream: Coconut cream as it exists in tropical countries is taken from green coconuts, generally unavailable here.

To prepare coconut cream from ripe coconut, which is available here, pare the brown skin from the coconut meat. Chop the meat, discarding the liquid, and blend with one cup fresh scalded milk in an electric blender. Let stand twenty minutes, then strain the mixture through cheesecloth.

In lieu of freshly grated coconut meat, about one cup of packaged shredded coconut may be used.

CURRIED CREPES AUX FRUITS DE MER

1 large onion, finely chopped
5 tablespoons butter
2 green apples, peeled, cored and chopped
2 ribs celery, chopped
3 sprigs parsley, chopped
2 medium leeks, chopped
3 tablespoons curry powder, or to taste
6 tablespoons flour
1 bay leaf
¼ teaspoon thyme
½ teaspoon salt
2½ cups chicken stock or clam juice
3 cups cooked seafood (crab, shrimp or lobster)
1 cup heavy cream
12 to fourteen entrée crepes (recipe follows)
1 bottle Escoffier Sauce
2 or three drops Worcestershire sauce

1. Sauté the onion in the butter in a saucepan until tender and golden. Add the apples. celery, parsley and leeks. Cook two minutes. Sprinkle with the curry powder and cook two minutes longer.

2. Sprinkle the flour over the vegetables. Add the bay leaf, thyme and salt. Gradually stir in the stock. Bring the mixture to a boil, cover and simmer gently two to three hours.

3. Put the sauce through a food mill or purée in an electric blender.

4. Return the puréed sauce to the pan and stir in the seafood and one-half cup of the heavy cream. Reheat the mixture and stuff the crepes with it. Spoon the remaining sauce over one-half of each crepe.

5. Combine the Escoffier Sauce with the remaining cream and the Worcestershire sauce. Heat and spoon over the other half of each crepe.

Yield: Six to eight servings.

ENTRÉE CREPES

2 cups flour
½ teaspoon salt
4 eggs, lightly beaten
1 cup milk

1 cup water
¼ cup melted butter
Vegetable oil

1. Sift the flour and salt into a mixing bowl. Gradually beat in the eggs with a wire whisk. Add liquids a little at a time, beating after each addition. When batter is smooth, stir in the butter. Let batter stand in the refrigerator two to three hours.

2. Heat a crepe pan or a small iron skillet and brush lightly with the oil. When the skillet is hot and the film of oil almost smoking, pour in three or four tablespoons of batter, tipping the skillet in all directions so that batter forms a single layer. If there is too much batter, it may be poured back into the bowl. The important thing in making crepes is the timing. The batter must be poured and tilted in seconds.

3. Let the crepe cook about forty-five seconds, shaking the pan so that it does not stick. When crepe is golden brown, turn it

over. Cook the other side about thirty seconds, so it is barely brown, if at all. Slip the crepe onto a plate and keep it warm. The crepes should be about one-sixteenth of an inch thick. If they are too thick, the batter may be thinned with additional milk or water.

4. Brush the skillet with more oil and repeat process until all batter is used.

Yield: Twelve to fourteen six-inch crepes.

Blender Crepes: Combine the eggs, water, milk and salt in the container of an electric blender. Blend briefly. Add the flour and melted butter. Cover and blend sixty seconds. With the motor off, use a spatula to dislodge bits of flour from the sides of the jar. Blend again briefly and let stand in the refrigerator at least two hours. Proceed as in Step 2 above.

Note: The crepes may be made several hours ahead and kept covered until serving time, or they may be frozen in a stack with a small sheet of aluminum foil between each. Wrap the whole stack in foil and freeze. The crepes may then be reheated in a slow oven or in the sauce with which they are to be served.

SHRIMP-STUFFED GREEN PEPPERS

6 green peppers
2 quarts plus one cup boiling water
1½ cups cooked rice
1½ cups chopped cooked shrimp
1 teaspoon grated onion
1 cup chopped fresh tomatoes
1 teaspoon salt
¼ teaspoon freshly ground black pepper
½ clove garlic, minced
2 teaspoons curry powder
⅓ cup tomato paste
¼ cup melted butter
1 cup fresh bread crumbs

1. Preheat the oven to 350 degrees.
2. Cut a one-quarter-inch slice from the stem end of each pepper and remove the seeds. Place the peppers in a saucepan, add two quarts of the boiling water, cover and steam five minutes. Remove the peppers from the pan and drain them.

3. Mix the cooked rice with the shrimp, onion, tomatoes, salt, pepper, garlic, curry powder, remaining cup of water and the tomato paste. Mix thoroughly and fill the peppers with this mixture. Mix the melted butter with the bread crumbs and use to top the stuffed peppers.

4. Place the stuffed peppers in a baking dish and cook twenty minutes.

Yield: Six servings.

CURRIED STUFFED EGGS

6 hard-cooked eggs
3 tablespoons mayonnaise
1 teaspoon grated onion
1 cup chopped cooked
  shrimp or lobster
Salt and pepper
3 tablespoons butter

3 tablespoons flour
2 teaspoons curry powder,
  or more to taste
2 cups milk
½ cup buttered fine fresh
  bread crumbs

1. Preheat the oven to 375 degrees.

2. Cut the eggs in half lengthwise, remove the yolks and mash them. Add mayonnaise, onion, seafood, salt and pepper to the yolks. Mix well and pack into the egg whites.

3. Melt the butter and add the flour and curry powder. Blend well. Add the milk and cook, stirring, until the mixture boils. Add salt and pepper to taste and more curry powder if desired.

4. Stand the eggs in a shallow baking dish and pour the sauce over them. Sprinkle with the crumbs.

5. Bake until heated through and lightly browned.

Yield: Six servings.

CURRY-CHEESE BISCUITS

2 cups sifted flour
½ teaspoon salt
½ teaspoon dry mustard
1½ teaspoons curry powder
Dash of cayenne pepper

⅔ cup butter
1 cup grated sharp Cheddar
  cheese
1 egg, beaten
2 tablespoons milk

1. Preheat the oven to 400 degrees.

2. Combine the flour, salt, dry mustard, curry powder and cayenne pepper in a mixing bowl. Cut in the butter to the consistency of fine crumbs. Blend in the cheese. Stir in the beaten egg and the milk.

3. While still in the crumbly stage, turn out onto a pastry board. Form it into a mound. Cut through the center of the mound with a spatula. Stack one half of the mound on the other half and again shape it into a mound. Repeat this process until the dough holds together, about ten or twelve times.

4. Roll the dough to a thickness of one-eighth inch. Cut with a two-inch biscuit cutter. Bake on a cooky sheet ten minutes.

Yield: About twenty-four biscuits.

CURRIED VEGETABLE RELISH

12 large cucumbers, peeled	12 large ripe tomatoes, peeled
6 large onions, peeled	
1 large sweet red pepper	1½ cups cider vinegar
1 large sweet green pepper	⅓ cup brown sugar
¼ cup plus one teaspoon coarse salt	2 teaspoons celery seed
	¼ cup curry powder

1. Grind separately the cucumbers, onions and peppers, using medium blade. Measure out eleven cups cucumbers, seven and one-half cups onions and one and one-quarter cups mixed peppers. Combine vegetables and add one-quarter cup salt. Let stand one hour. Drain.

2. Cut up tomatoes and stew until soft. Add vegetables, vinegar, sugar, spices and remaining salt. Cook uncovered twenty-five minutes, or until sauce thickens.

3. Ladle into hot sterilized jars. Seal at once. Let stand six weeks before using.

Yield: Five and one-half pints.

CURRIED POT ROAST

4 pounds top round or other meat for a pot roast
Salt and freshly ground black pepper
1 teaspoon curry powder
1 teaspoon turmeric
1 teaspoon ground ginger
2 tablespoons peanut oil
2 cups chopped onions
2 garlic cloves, finely minced
1 cup peeled and chopped fresh tomatoes or canned Italian plum tomatoes
1 bay leaf
3 fresh thyme sprigs or ½ teaspoon dried
1 cup water or beef broth

1. Rub meat with salt and pepper to taste, curry powder, turmeric and ginger.
2. Heat oil in a deep casserole or kettle and brown meat well on all sides. This should take about fifteen minutes. Pour off fat from kettle. Add remaining ingredients and bring to a boil. Cover and simmer until fork tender, three hours or longer.

Yield: Six servings.

CURRIED FRESH PEARS

3 fresh winter pears
3 tablespoons butter
3 tablespoons brown sugar
1 tablespoon curry powder
¼ teaspoon salt

1. Preheat the oven to 350 degrees.
2. Cut the pears in half and remove the cores. Arrange them in a greased baking dish. Combine the remaining ingredients and pile this mixture in the cavity of each pear half. Bake until tender, about forty minutes. Serve with ham.

Yield: Six servings.

Dill

DILL *produces a leaf and a seed, both of which are valuable in cookery. Dill leaves are feathery and fernlike and, when chopped, have a rare affinity for sour cream and cucumbers. Chopped dill is enormously complementary to eggs, light cream cheeses, poached salmon and other fish. Sprigs of dill are a frequent garnish for open-faced sandwiches of the sort served in Norway, Sweden and Denmark.*

Dill seeds are best known as an ingredient for dill pickles, but there are few dishes from sauerkraut to apple pie to which the seed would not add interest.

ANCHOVIES WITH DILL AND PIMENTO

2 two-ounce cans flat fillets
of anchovy
Juice of one lemon
1 teaspoon finely chopped
shallot or onion
¼ teaspoon finely minced
garlic
Coarsely ground black pepper

2 tablespoons chopped fresh
dill or one teaspoon dried
dill weed
1 tablespoon finely chopped
parsley
1 teaspoon chopped chives
(optional)
2 four-ounce cans whole
pimento

1. Drain the oil from the anchovies into a small bowl and add the lemon juice, shallot, garlic and pepper. Beat with a fork and add the dill, parsley and chives. If necessary, add a little olive oil.

2. Reserve one whole pimento and slice the rest into long, thin strips. Place the whole pimento in the center of a round dish. Arrange alternating strips of anchovy and pimento, like the spokes of a wheel, around the whole pimento.

3. Spoon the herb sauce over the strips of anchovy and pimento and let stand at room temperature one hour. Serve with buttered toast triangles.

Yield: Four to six servings.

*The following is a favored recipe of Nika Hazelton,
a cook book author of considerable merit. Mrs. Hazelton
received this recipe from the chef of the Kronprinssen
Restaurant in Malmö, Sweden.*

GRAVAD LAX (PICKLED SALMON)

7 to eight pounds fresh salmon, in one piece, with
bones in
⅔ cup salt
½ cup sugar
1 tablespoon whole white
pepper, coarsely crushed

1 teaspoon whole allspice,
coarsely crushed
6 tablespoons cognac
(optional)
2 large bunches fresh dill

1. Choose middle cut from salmon. Clean fish, leaving skin on, and carefully remove bone so that two big fillets remain. Rinse under cold water and dry carefully with kitchen towel, being careful that the fish does not break.

2. Mix together salt, sugar, pepper and allspice. Rub seasonings carefully into all surfaces of the fish. Sprinkle with cognac.

3. Wash dill and place one-third of it in bottom of deep pan or bowl. Use an enameled, china, stone or stainless steel bowl, but not an aluminum one. Place one piece of salmon, skin side down, on dill. Place another third of the dill on the salmon. Put the other piece of salmon, skin side up, on dill. Cover with remaining dill.

4. Set heavy plate or board on fish and keep in refrigerator from twenty-four to thirty-six hours, preferably the latter.

5. Drain fish, scrape off dill and spices and slice on the slant, away from the skin. Serve as a first course with lemon wedges and freshly ground black pepper. Boiled potatoes with dill are also a traditional accompaniment.

Yield: Fifteen to twenty small servings.

Note: The Gravad Lax keeps approximately eight days, but it must be refrigerated.

CRAB MARINATED IN MUSTARD SAUCE

1 tablespoon dry mustard
3 tablespoons dry white wine
1 clove garlic, finely minced
½ cup olive or other salad oil
¼ teaspoon salt
⅛ teaspoon freshly ground black pepper
1 tablespoon lemon juice
1 tablespoon finely snipped fresh dill
2 cups fresh or frozen crabmeat, picked over well

1. Mix the mustard with the wine, add the garlic and allow to stand at room temperature ten minutes.

2. Add the oil very slowly to the mustard mixture while beating vigorously by hand or electric mixer.

3. Beat in the salt, pepper and lemon juice and then the dill.

4. Add the crabmeat and marinate in the refrigerator one hour.

5. Serve the crabmeat in shells as an appetizer.

Yield: Eight servings.

MEAT AND DILL PIROSHKI

1 cup (two sticks) butter
8 ounces cream cheese
¼ cup heavy cream
2½ cups flour
1 teaspoon salt

Piroshki filling (recipe
   follows)
1 egg
1 teaspoon water

1. Cream butter and cheese and beat in cream. Blend in flour and salt. Chill well.

2. Preheat the oven to 400 degrees.

3. Roll out dough between wax paper to one-eighth-inch thickness. Cut into two-inch to three-inch rounds or squares.

4. Place one teaspoon filling on one side of each round. Combine egg and water. Moisten edges of dough with mixture.

5. Fold dough over filling, forming crescents or triangles. Seal and decorate edges. Put on a baking sheet. Brush with remaining egg mixture. Slash a small hole in the middle of each to allow steam to escape. Bake until golden, fifteen to twenty minutes. Serve hot or cold.

Yield: Thirty-six to forty piroshki.

PIROSHKI FILLING

2 onions, chopped
¼ cup butter
¾ pound ground beef
2 tablespoons sour cream
½ teaspoon Worcestershire
   sauce
½ cup cooked rice

2 tablespoons snipped fresh
   dill
½ teaspoon salt
¼ teaspoon freshly ground
   black pepper
2 hard-cooked eggs, chopped

1. Sauté the onion in the butter in a heavy skillet. Add beef and cook, stirring, until meat loses its color.

2. Remove from heat and add the sour cream, Worcestershire, rice, dill, salt and pepper. Add the eggs and mix well.

Yield: Filling for thirty-six to forty turnovers.

VEAL POT ROAST WITH DILL GRAVY

3 pounds boneless rolled shoulder of veal
1½ tablespoons cooking oil or butter
½ cup finely chopped onion
¾ cup hot water
1 bay leaf
6 medium potatoes
6 medium carrots
1 tablespoon salt
½ teaspoon freshly ground black pepper
3 tablespoons flour
3 tablespoons cold water
¼ to one-half teaspoon dill seed
½ cup sour cream
Paprika for garnish

1. Brown the veal on all sides in the oil or butter. Place on a rack in a Dutch oven. Sauté the onion briefly in the fat remaining in the pan. Transfer to the Dutch oven and add the water and bay leaf. Cover and cook slowly two hours.

2. Peel the potatoes and carrots, cut into halves and add to the Dutch oven. Sprinkle with salt and pepper. Cover and continue cooking until the meat and vegetables are tender, about thirty minutes.

3. Remove the meat and vegetables to a hot platter. Mix the flour and water to a smooth paste and stir into the liquid left in the Dutch oven. Blend in the dill seed. Cook until thickened. Stir in the sour cream and heat, but do not boil. Serve the gravy in a sauceboat. Sprinkle the top with paprika.

Yield: Six to eight servings.

GRILLED HERBED CHICKEN BREASTS

4 large chicken breasts.
Salt and freshly ground black
   pepper to taste
6 tablespoons (three-quarters
   stick) butter, at room
   temperature
¼ cup chopped parsley

2 tablespoons chopped fresh
   dill
2 tablespoons minced onion
1 tablespoon lemon juice
1 cup fine soft bread crumbs
Melted butter

1. Halve the breasts and remove the bone. Cut through the thickest part of each half breast to form a pocket. Season lightly with salt and pepper.

2. Cream the butter. Add the parsley, dill, onion and lemon juice. Mix well and stir in the bread crumbs.

3. Fill the pockets with the mixture and skewer to close.

4. Brush with melted butter and grill over hot coals or broil, turning to brown all sides. Total cooking time will be about twenty minutes.

Yield: Eight servings.

FINNAN HADDIE WITH DILL

1 pound fresh finnan
   haddie
2¼ cups milk, or more if
   needed
4 tablespoons (one-half
   stick) butter

4 tablespoons flour
2 tablespoons chopped fresh
   dill or one tablespoon
   dried dill
Sprigs of dill or parsley

1. Place the finnan haddie in a saucepan and cover with milk. Bring to a boil and simmer, covered, twenty to twenty-five minutes. Drain and reserve two cups of the milk. Tear the fish into bite-size pieces and reserve.

2. Heat the butter and blend in the flour, stirring with a wire

whisk. When the mixture is well blended, add the reserved milk, stirring vigorously with the whisk. When the sauce is thickened and smooth, add the finnan haddie. Stir in the chopped dill and serve garnished with sprigs of dill or parsley.

Yield: Four servings.

SALMON SOUFFLÉ

3 tablespoons butter
3 tablespoons flour
1 cup milk
5 egg yolks
½ teaspoon salt
¼ teaspoon dry mustard
¼ teaspoon Worcestershire sauce

1 cup fresh cooked salmon or one seven-ounce can salmon, drained, with skin and bones removed
1 teaspoon snipped fresh dill
6 egg whites

1. Preheat the oven to 375 degrees.
2. Melt the butter in a saucepan and blend in the flour. Add the milk slowly, stirring; bring to a boil, stirring, and simmer one minute. Cool the mixture.
3. Beat in the egg yolks, one at a time. Season with salt, mustard and Worcestershire sauce.
4. Flake the salmon and blend well into the sauce mixture. Add the dill.
5. Beat the egg whites until they stand in peaks; do not overbeat.
6. Fold the beaten whites gently into the salmon mixture with a rubber spatula. Do not overblend.
7. Pour the mixture into a two-quart soufflé dish, which may be greased or ungreased.
8. Bake until the soufflé is puffed and brown, thirty to forty minutes. Serve immediately.

Yield: Three or four servings.

SHAD ROE BAKED IN FOIL

1 pair shad roe
Salt and freshly ground black
  pepper
4 tablespoons (one-half stick)
  butter, at room temperature
2 tablespoons chopped fresh
  dill

2 tablespoons chopped
  parsley
2 tablespoons dry white wine
  (optional)
Lemon wedges

1. Preheat the oven to 350 degrees.
2. Sprinkle the shad roe on all sides with salt and pepper.
3. Cut a rectangle of aluminum foil large enough to enclose the roe envelope-fashion. Spread three tablespoons of the butter on the center of the foil and sprinkle with the dill and parsley. Cover the bed of herbs with the roe and dot the roe with the remaining tablespoon of butter. Bring up the edges of the foil. If desired, two tablespoons of wine may be poured over the fish. Seal the foil closely.
4. Bake twenty to twenty-five minutes, depending on size. Serve with lemon wedges.

Yield: Two servings.

QUICK SHRIMP WITH DILL

36 large shrimp
¼ cup (one-half stick) butter
Tabasco to taste
½ teaspoon Worcestershire
  sauce

1 teaspoon chopped fresh
  dill or one-half teaspoon
  dried dill weed
Juice of half a lemon

1. Shell and devein the shrimp and rinse them under cold running water.
2. Melt the butter in a skillet large enough to hold the shrimp and, when it is heated, add them.
3. Cook over moderate heat, turning the shrimp once, until they are pink, about three to five minutes.
4. Sprinkle the shrimp with Tabasco, Worcestershire, dill and

lemon juice. Stir well and serve hot as a luncheon dish with toast points or over rice.

Yield: Four to six servings.

CELERY WITH DILL

3 cups chopped celery	1 tablespoon butter
½ teaspoon salt	Freshly ground black pepper
½ teaspoon dill seed	to taste

1. Put the celery in a one-quart pan. Rinse, drain, cover and place over medium-high heat. When the cover is hot to the touch, reduce the heat to low and cook ten minutes.

2. Combine with the remaining ingredients and serve.

Yield: Four servings.

CUCUMBERS IN SOUR CREAM

2 teaspoons salt	1 tablespoon chopped chives
¼ teaspoon Tabasco	1 cup sour cream
1 tablespoon lemon juice	3 cucumbers, chilled
2 teaspoons chopped fresh dill	

1. Combine the salt, Tabasco, lemon juice, dill and chives with the sour cream.

2. Pare and slice the cucumbers; add them to the sour cream mixture. Chill and serve garnished with additional dill.

Yield: Six servings.

CUCUMBER SLICES WITH LEMON

2 cucumbers	2 tablespoons snipped fresh dill
Olive oil (optional)	Salt and freshly ground black
¼ cup lemon juice	pepper to taste

1. Peel the cucumbers and slice them thin. Brush the slices lightly with the oil, if desired.

2. Mix the lemon juice, dill, salt and pepper together. Pour the dressing over the cucumber slices and toss lightly to mix. Chill the mixture well before serving.

Yield: About six servings.

CUCUMBERS WITH DILL

2 large cucumbers
Salt
½ cup vinegar

2 tablespoons water
2 tablespoons sugar
Freshly ground black pepper
1 tablespoon fresh snipped dill

1. Peel cucumbers or score lengthwise with fork tines. Cut into very thin slices. Sprinkle lightly with salt and let stand two hours.

2. Wash off salt. Drain.

3. Combine remaining ingredients and pour over cucumber slices. Marinate at least one hour in refrigerator before serving.

Yield: Four to six servings.

MUSHROOMS CHANTILLY

¼ cup (one-half stick) butter
½ pound medium mush-
  rooms, sliced or quartered
Salt and freshly ground black
  pepper to taste

1 teaspoon chopped fresh
  dill or one-half teaspoon
  dried dill
½ cup heavy cream

1. Heat the butter in a skillet with a cover and, when it is melted, add the mushrooms. Cover and cook over medium heat, stirring or shaking the pan, about one minute.

2. Add the salt, pepper and dill. Cover and cook five minutes. Add the cream and simmer, uncovered, until the sauce is thickened and reduced somewhat. Taste and correct the seasonings with more salt, pepper or dill if desired.

Yield: Four servings.

PICKLED SNAP BEANS

3 pounds tender snap beans
1½ cups water
1½ cups white or cider vinegar
½ cup sugar
2 teaspoons salt
3 hot red peppers
1½ teaspoons dried dill seed
5 cloves garlic, coarsely chopped or sliced

1. Wash the beans thoroughly and snap off the ends. Cook them in the water until just crisp tender.

2. Meanwhile, simmer covered in a two-quart saucepan the vinegar, sugar, salt, red peppers and dill seed.

3. Add the beans with the water in which they were cooked and simmer, covered, fifteen minutes.

4. Continue simmering while packing one sterilized jar after another with the beans. Divide the raw garlic among the jars and pour the vinegar mixture over the beans. Fill the jars to one-eighth inch from the top. Seal at once and store in a cool, dry place.

Yield: Four or five pints.

SOUR CREAM AND DILL SAUCE

1 cup sour cream
1 small bunch dill with stems, broken into small pieces

Put the sour cream into the container of an electric blender. Add the dill, cover and blend on high speed twenty seconds. Pour into a bowl and refrigerate. The sauce will set in a few minutes. Serve with poached fish.

Yield: One cup sauce.

LAMB IN DILL SAUCE

4 pounds shoulder of lamb, cut into one-inch cubes, plus two or three lamb bones from the butcher

5 cups water

2 carrots, scraped and quartered

1 rib celery, quartered

1 leek, split, rinsed well and coarsely chopped

6 sprigs parsley

1 bay leaf

5 peppercorns

Salt to taste

1 parsnip, trimmed (optional)

3 tablespoons butter

1 cup finely chopped onions

3 tablespoons flour

1 teaspoon sugar (optional)

2 tablespoons lemon juice

3 tablespoons chopped fresh dill

1 cup sour cream

Dill sprigs for garnish

1. Place the lamb and bones in a large saucepan and add the water, carrots, celery, leek, parsley, bay leaf, peppercorns, salt and parsnip. Partly cover and bring to a boil. Simmer until the lamb is tender, about one hour, skimming the surface as necessary.

2. Remove the lamb pieces to a warm serving dish and strain the stock. Boil the stock uncovered until it is reduced to about two cups.

3. Melt the butter in a saucepan and add the onions. Cook until wilted and sprinkle with flour. Add the stock, stirring rapidly with a wire whisk. When smooth and thickened, add the sugar, lemon juice and chopped dill. Simmer 10 minutes, stirring frequently. Remove from the heat and stir in the sour cream. Add the lamb and heat thoroughly, but do not boil or the sauce may curdle. Serve garnished with dill sprigs.

Yield: Six servings.

EGGPLANT, YOGHURT AND DILL RELISH

1 large eggplant, unpeeled
¼ cup (approximately) olive oil
½ cup finely chopped onion
1 or 2 cloves garlic, finely minced
¼ cup finely chopped dill
Salt and freshly ground pepper to taste

½ cup sour cream
1 cup yoghurt
Juice of one lemon, approximately
Tabasco to taste
Chopped parsley for garnish

1. Cut off and discard the stem end of the eggplant. Cut unpeeled eggplant into one-inch cubes.

2. Heat the oil in a large skillet and add the eggplant and onion. Cook, stirring frequently, until the eggplant is soft and starts to brown. Add more oil if necessary.

3. Scoop the eggplant mixture into a mixing bowl and add the garlic, dill, salt and pepper. Blend in the sour cream and half the yoghurt. Chill thoroughly and stir in the remaining yoghurt. Season to taste with lemon juice, Tabasco and, if necessary, more salt and pepper. Serve sprinkled with parsley.

Yield: Six servings.

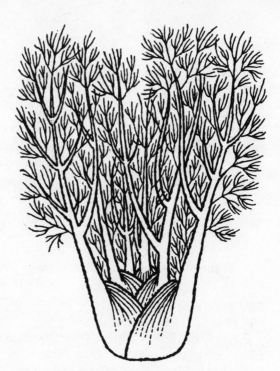

Fennel

FENNEL is a symbol of flattery and an emblem of heroism. It has long been admired in Italy (where it is known as finocchio*) and in France (where it is known as* fenouil*). It is, fortunately, becoming better known and appreciated in America. Almost all of the fennel plant is edible, including the seeds, bulb, stalks and lacy leaves. The bulb is delicious sliced and served cold and raw like celery. The bulb also may be quartered and cooked in any form appropriate to celery, onions or asparagus. Chopped fennel leaves add character to soups, fish and salads. Fennel seeds are widely used in European liqueurs and they are the soul of certain fresh hot or sweet Italian sausages.*

TUSCAN MEAT LOAF

1 pound ground round
  steak
½ cup fresh bread crumbs
½ cup milk
1 egg, lightly beaten
1 teaspoon salt
¼ cup finely chopped
  parsley
¼ teaspoon fennel seeds

½ teaspoon freshly ground
  black pepper
½ teaspoon paprika
½ teaspoon orégano
½ teaspoon basil
½ cup chopped onion
1 clove garlic, minced
3 tablespoons butter

1. Preheat the oven to 350 degrees.
2. With the hands work the meat with the bread crumbs, milk, egg, salt, parsley, fennel seeds, black pepper, paprika, orégano and basil.
3. Cook the onion and garlic in the butter until golden brown. Blend with the meat mixture. Shape into a loaf and bake one hour. Serve with tomato sauce (page 18).

Yield: Four servings.

ITALIAN SAUSAGE SAUCE

1 pound hot or sweet fennel-
  flavored Italian sausages
2 tablespoons water
1 large onion, chopped
½ cup finely chopped celery
1 tablespoon chopped parsley

1 seventeen-ounce can
  Italian plum tomatoes
2 eight-ounce cans tomato
  purée
2 bay leaves

1. Cook the sausages in the water until they begin to fry. Add the onion, celery and parsley and continue cooking until the sausages are brown, turning often.
2. Add the tomatoes, tomato purée and bay leaves. Simmer,

covered, one hour, stirring occasionally. Uncover and cook, stirring often, to desired thickness.

Yield: Enough sauce for one pound of spaghetti.

FENNEL-FLAVORED SPAGHETTI SAUCE

2 two-pound-three-ounce cans Italian plum tomatoes with basil

1 tablespoon chopped fresh basil or one teaspoon dried basil

Salt and freshly ground black pepper

3 tablespoons lard or olive oil

1 large onion, sliced

1 two-pound lean loin of pork

1 two-pound lean loin of lamb

8 sweet fennel-flavored Italian sausages

8 hot fennel-flavored Italian sausages

16 to twenty meat balls (recipe follows)

½ teaspoon dried thyme

½ teaspoon fennel seed

2 pounds vermicelli or spaghettini

Freshly grated Parmesan cheese

1. Put the tomatoes through a food mill or rub them through a fine sieve. Discard the seeds and pour the puréed tomatoes into a large kettle. Add the basil and season to taste with salt and pepper. Bring to a boil and simmer slowly. Simmer one hour before adding the remaining ingredients.

2. Heat the lard or oil in a large skillet and cook the sliced onion five minutes, stirring. Remove and discard the onion but retain the fat in the pan. Sprinkle the pork and lamb with salt and pepper and brown the meat on all sides in the fat. Add the meats to the simmering sauce. Stir frequently to insure that the sauce does not scorch as it cooks.

3. In the same skillet, brown the sausages and add to the sauce. Brown the meat balls in the same skillet and, thirty minutes before the end of the cooking time, add them to the sauce with the thyme and fennel seed.

4. Add a cup or so of the hot tomato sauce to the skillet and swirl it around. Scrape the contents of the skillet into the kettle.

The total cooking time for the sauce is two and one-half hours.

5. Cook the vermicelli or spaghettini according to package directions. Mix the drained pasta with a little of the tomato sauce and pile it into the center of a hot platter. Surround it with the meat balls, sausage and sliced pork and lamb, or serve the meats and sauce separately. Serve freshly grated Parmesan cheese separately.

Yield: Eight to ten generous servings.

Note: If a garlic flavor is desired, proceed as follows: Just before serving the sauce, heat four tablespoons butter in a skillet. It will bubble at first and then start to turn hazelnut brown. Watch carefully and, just as it starts to turn brown, remove from the heat. Add one or two cloves freshly chopped garlic and stir briefly. Stir the garlic butter into the sauce and serve immediately.

MEAT BALLS

1 pound ground round steak	2 eggs, lightly beaten
2 slices dry white bread, crusts removed	¼ cup finely grated Romano cheese
3 tablespoons milk or cream	¼ cup finely chopped parsley
Salt and freshly ground black pepper to taste	½ teaspoon grated nutmeg (optional)
1 or two cloves garlic, finely chopped	

1. Place the meat in a mixing bowl.

2. Prepare fine bread crumbs in an electric blender or by grating the bread. Moisten the crumbs with the cream. Let stand briefly and add the crumbs and cream to the meat.

3. Add the remaining ingredients and mix with the hands. Shape the mixture into sixteen to twenty one-inch balls and brown them in hot fat (see preceding recipe).

Yield: Sixteen to twenty meat balls.

CHICKEN WITH FENNEL

1 three-pound chicken, cut into serving pieces
¼ cup (one-half stick) butter
2 tablespoons flour
1½ cups sour cream
½ teaspoon salt
⅛ teaspoon freshly ground black pepper
¼ pound fresh mushrooms, sliced
1 tablespoon fennel seeds
1 tablespoon chopped chives
1 tablespoon lemon juice
1 teaspoon grated lemon rind
1 tablespoon chopped parsley

1. Preheat the oven to 325 degrees.

2. Brown the chicken pieces in a skillet on all sides in the butter. Transfer chicken to a casserole.

3. Stir the flour into the drippings remaining in the skillet. Add the sour cream and simmer five minutes. Add the salt, pepper, mushrooms, fennel seeds and chives. Pour the sauce over the chicken.

4. Cover and bake 25 to 30 minutes, or until chicken is tender. Stir in the lemon juice and rind, and sprinkle with the parsley.

Yield: Four servings.

COUNTRY-STYLE POLENTA

½ pound hot, fennel-flavored Italian sausages
2 tablespoons water
1 small onion, chopped
1 clove garlic, minced
¼ pound mushrooms, sliced
1 cup tomato purée
1 cup canned tomatoes with the liquid
Salt to taste
4 cups hot polenta
3 tablespoons grated Romano cheese

1. Prick the sausages, add water and cook until brown in a two-quart saucepan.

2. Add the onion and garlic and brown lightly. Add the mush-

rooms, tomato purée and tomatoes and simmer, covered, until the sausages are tender, about one hour. Add salt.

3. Turn the hot polenta onto a platter, cover with the sauce, sprinkle with cheese and garnish with sausages.

Yield: Four servings.

FENNEL À LA GRECQUE

2 cups water
6 tablespoons olive oil
⅓ cup lemon juice
Salt to taste
10 whole peppercorns
10 whole coriander seeds
2 tablespoons minced
  shallot or onion
5 sprigs parsley
1 small rib of celery
¼ teaspoon thyme
¼ teaspoon fennel seeds
  (optional)
4 small heads of fennel

1. Combine the water, oil, lemon juice, salt, peppercorns, coriander seeds and shallot in a large saucepan. Tie the parsley, celery, thyme and fennel seeds in cheesecloth and add them to the liquid. Cover, bring to a boil and simmer ten minutes.

2. Trim off the top leaves and tough outer stalks of the fennel. Cut the vegetable into quarters and add to the saucepan. Cover and simmer until the fennel is tender, thirty to forty minutes.

Yield: Four to six servings.

FENNEL MORNAY

6 heads of fennel
1 cup chicken broth
6 tablespoons (three-quarters
  stick) butter
6 tablespoons flour
2 cups milk
½ cup heavy cream
3 ounces Gruyère cheese, cut
  into small pieces
3 ounces freshly grated
  Parmesan cheese
Salt and freshly ground white
  pepper
Butter

1. Cut off the tops of the fennel and remove any outer stalks that may be discolored. Wash well and cut each head into wedges. Poach them in the chicken broth in a large pan with a tight-fitting lid for twenty minutes. When tender, lift out the fennel with a slotted spoon and place the wedges in a large, shallow baking dish. Reserve the broth.

2. Preheat the oven to 350 degrees.

3. To prepare the sauce, melt 6 tablespoons butter, blend in the flour and stir with a wooden spoon until smooth. When the mixture acquires a delicate, off-white color, slowly blend in the milk, cream and one-half cup of the broth in which the fennel was cooked. Bring the sauce to the boiling point, stirring constantly.

4. Add the cheeses and continue stirring until thoroughly melted. Add salt and pepper to taste. Pour the sauce over the fennel, dot with butter and bake just long enough for the butter to melt and the vegetable to heat through.

Yield: Eight servings.

FENNEL PARMIGIANA

4 heads of fennel
Salt and freshly ground black
 pepper

½ cup (one stick) butter,
 melted
⅔ cup freshly grated
 Parmesan cheese

1. Preheat the oven to 425 degrees.

2. Trim off the top leaves and tough outer stalks of the fennel. Trim the base. Slice the fennel from top to bottom into quarter-inch slices. Drop the slices into boiling salted water and simmer until tender, five minutes or longer. Do not overcook. Drain.

3. Season the fennel with salt and pepper and line a baking dish with half of it. Sprinkle half the butter and half the cheese over it. Add the remaining fennel, butter and cheese. Bake ten minutes, or until the cheese is golden brown.

Yield: Four to six servings.

FENNEL AND CUCUMBER SALAD

1 cucumber
2 heads of fennel
6 radishes
2 tablespoons lemon juice
⅓ cup olive oil
½ teaspoon fresh or dried
  chopped mint

1 clove garlic, finely minced
Salt and freshly ground black
  pepper to taste
2 or three hard-cooked eggs,
  quartered

1. Peel the cucumber and cut it into quarters. Slice it thin. Trim off the top leaves and tough outer stalks of the fennel. Cut the fennel into thin slices, then cut the slices into matchlike strips. Trim the radishes and cut them into thin slices. Combine and chill the vegetables until ready to use.

2. Combine the lemon juice, oil, mint, garlic, salt and pepper. Blend well and toss the dressing with the vegetables. Arrange the salad on a platter and garnish with wedges of hard-cooked eggs.

Yield: Four to six servings.

PICKLED SHRIMP

2 pounds raw shrimp in the
  shell
2 tablespoons mixed
  pickling spices
1 rib celery with leaves
Salt to taste
12 peppercorns
1 cup vegetable oil
½ cup white vinegar

1 lemon, thinly sliced
Freshly ground pepper
¼ cup finely chopped parsley
1 teaspoon crushed fennel
  or anise seeds
1 clove garlic, cut in half
Tabasco to taste
1 onion, thinly sliced

1. Place the shrimp in a saucepan and add pickling spices and water to cover. Break celery into quarters and add it. Add salt and peppercorns. Bring to a boil and simmer three minutes. Let the shrimp cool in the cooking liquid.

2. Drain the shrimp and shell them. Remove the black vein down the back.

3. Place the shrimp in a mixing bowl and add the remaining ingredients. Add salt to taste and, if necessary, a little more vinegar. Cover and refrigerate overnight. Serve on lettuce.

Yield: Six servings.

MUSHROOMS WITH FENNEL

5 tablespoons butter
1 small onion, finely chopped
½ cup diced fennel bulb
1½ pounds mushrooms, sliced
2 tablespoons chopped parsley

2 tablespoons all-purpose flour
1 cup milk
2 tablespoons fennel leaves
Salt and freshly ground black pepper
1 egg yolk
2 tablespoons sour cream

1. Melt four tablespoons of the butter. Sauté the onion and diced fennel in the butter until wilted and tender but not browned. Add the mushrooms and parsley. Cook until mushrooms are tender and most of the liquid has evaporated, about five minutes.

2. Melt the remaining butter in a small pan and blend in the flour. Gradually stir in the milk, bring to a boil and simmer, stirring constantly, one minute. Add the fennel leaves and pour over the mushrooms.

3. Bring the combined mixture to a boil and season with salt and pepper to taste. Blend together the egg yolk and the sour cream and stir into the mushroom mixture. Reheat, but do not allow to boil.

Yield: Six servings.

FENNEL SAUCE FOR FISH

½ cup (one stick) butter
¼ cup finely chopped fennel
leaves

1 tablespoon lemon juice
Salt and freshly ground black
pepper

1. Melt the butter but do not let it brown. Remove from the heat and let it cool slightly.
2. Add the remaining ingredients and serve immediately on poached or broiled fish.

Yield: About one-half cup sauce.

Garlic

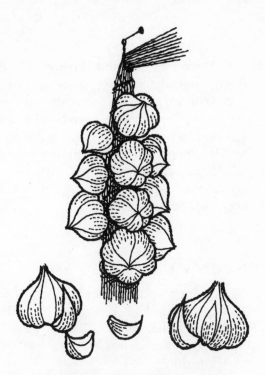

Horace, the Roman poet and satirist, considered the odor of GARLIC to be the essence of vulgarity.

Since antiquity garlic has been the one seasoning about which there is almost no middle ground of opinion. The old-time Romans are said to have attributed magical powers to it; early-day Greeks reputedly detested it.

Garlic, in short, is prized and disdained in just about equal measure. This volume holds it in highest esteem. Without garlic, what would the admirable cuisine of South Italy be? Or that of sun-swept Provence? The name garlic is of Anglo-Saxon origin, deriving from gar (a spear) and leac (leek).

ANCHOIADE

2 two-ounce cans flat anchovy fillets
3 cloves garlic, chopped
2 tablespoons bread crumbs
Water to moisten crumbs

Freshly ground black pepper to taste
1 tablespoon olive oil
½ teaspoon wine vinegar
6 slices French bread

1. Using a mortar and pestle or a food mill or a blender at low speed, mash the anchovy fillets with the garlic.

2. Dampen the bread crumbs with a little water and squeeze them dry. Combine the crumbs with the anchovy-garlic mixture, a little black pepper and one teaspoon of the olive oil. Using a wooden spoon, work the mixture to a paste with the vinegar.

3. Brush the bread slices with the remaining olive oil and spread them with the anchovy paste. Bake under the broiler until very hot. Serve piping hot.

Yield: Six servings.

BAGNA CAUDA

½ cup (one stick) butter
¼ cup olive oil
6 cloves garlic, or according to taste, peeled and sliced tissue-thin

1 two-ounce can flat anchovy fillets
Fresh vegetables

1. Combine the butter and oil in a saucepan and add the garlic. Cook over the lowest possible heat for about fifteen minutes without letting the mixture boil.

2. Chop the anchovies and add to the garlic-oil mixture. Stir until the anchovies are smooth. Do not let the sauce boil or brown. Keep it hot over a candle or a spirit lamp.

3. Prepare an assortment of raw vegetables, such as cucumber, cauliflowerettes, strips of green pepper, celery, carrots and leaves of endive. Serve the vegetables separately to dip into the hot sauce.

Yield: About ten servings.

MUSSELS MARINARA

5 pounds mussels
2 cloves garlic
6 to eight peppercorns
¼ cup water
2 tablespoons wine vinegar
¾ cup olive oil

¼ cup tomato paste
3 whole cloves, crushed in a mortar
Salt and coarsely ground black pepper to taste

1. Scrub and debeard the mussels. Place them in a pan with the garlic, peppercorns and water. Cover and steam until the shells open, about ten minutes. Discard all unopened shells.

2. Blend together the vinegar, oil, tomato paste, cloves, salt and pepper.

3. Remove the mussels from the shells and combine with the vinegar-oil mixture. Marinate in the refrigerator until serving time. Serve as an appetizer.

Yield: Six to eight generous servings.

PEPPERS IN OIL

3 large sweet red peppers
¾ cup pitted black Italian olives

2 cloves garlic, crushed
Salt to taste
Italian olive oil

1. Roast the peppers over charcoal or in a hot skillet, turning frequently with the fingers so as not to pierce the skins. Or bake, turning occasionally, in a 400-degree oven until the skin is black, about fifteen to twenty minutes.

2. Remove the skins from the peppers. Cut out and discard the core and seeds. Cut the peppers into strips and combine with olives, garlic and salt. Marinate in a little olive oil, turning occasionally. Discard the garlic, if desired, and serve as antipasto.

Yield: Six servings.

RUMANIAN HAMBURGERS

2 pounds ground beef chuck or round
1½ cloves garlic, or more to taste
3 or four fresh or canned green chili peppers (see

note) or chili powder to taste
Salt and freshly ground black pepper to taste
6 to 8 tablespoons butter

1. Put meat in mixing bowl.

2. Grate the garlic on a fine grater or mince it fine with a

knife. Chop the chili peppers, if available, and add them or the chili powder to the meat. Add the salt and pepper. Mix well with the hands.

3. Shape the meat into six or eight patties. Grill or broil them to the desired degree of doneness, top each with a tablespoon of butter and serve with hot, buttered, toasted buns.

4. This meat mixture is also delicious when made into cocktail balls. To make them, roll small portions of the meat mixture into balls about three-quarters inch thick and place on skewers. Broil or grill until done.

Yield: Six to eight hamburgers or about twenty-four cocktail balls.

Note: Canned chilies may be purchased at Casa Moneo, 218 West Fourteenth Street, and at other stores that carry Spanish specialties.

OSSI BUCHI MILANESE

3 veal shanks, each sawed into three pieces two inches thick
⅓ cup flour
2 teaspoons salt
½ teaspoon freshly ground black pepper
3 tablespoons olive oil
3 tablespoons butter
½ teaspoon ground sage
1 teaspoon rosemary
1 medium onion, finely chopped
3 cloves garlic
2 small carrots, diced
1 rib celery, diced
1½ cups dry white wine
1¼ cups chicken stock
2 tablespoons tomato paste
1½ tablespoons chopped parsley
1 tablespoon grated lemon peel

1. Dredge the meat with the flour, which has been seasoned with one teaspoon of the salt and the pepper.

2. Heat the oil and butter together in a large skillet. Using medium heat, cook the meat on all sides until golden brown. If necessary, add a little more oil or butter.

3. Arrange the meat in a Dutch oven, standing each piece on

its side so the marrow found in the bone does not fall out as the meat cooks. Sprinkle the veal with the sage and rosemary. Add the onion, one clove garlic, minced, the carrots and celery. Sprinkle the vegetables with the remaining teaspoon of salt. Cover the Dutch oven closely and braise ten minutes.

4. Remove the cover and add the wine, stock and tomato paste. Cover and simmer the dish on top of the stove for two hours.

5. Mince the remaining two cloves of garlic and combine with the parsley and lemon peel. Sprinkle the mixture, called *gremolata*, over the veal and serve immediately.

Yield: Six to eight servings.

BRANDADE DE MORUE

(BRANDADE OF SALT COD)

1½ pounds salt cod Water ¾ pound potatoes, freshly baked 1 cup heavy cream, at room temperature	¼ cup warm olive oil ½ teaspoon cayenne pepper, or to taste 3 large cloves garlic, finely chopped 1 truffle, sliced (optional)

1. Soak the salt cod in cold water for several hours, changing the water three times. Drain and cut it into three-inch squares. Place the fish in a skillet and add cold water to cover. Bring to a boil and simmer not more than eight minutes. Drain the cod and carefully remove the skin and bones.

2. Slice the hot baked potatoes in half and scoop the flesh into the bowl of an electric mixer. Discard the potato skins. Start the mixer on low speed and add the cod. Continue beating while adding the cream and olive oil, a little at a time. (The oil must be warm or it will not homogenize properly.)

3. Add the cayenne pepper and garlic and finish whipping briefly on high speed. The mixture should have the creamy consistency of mashed potatoes. The brandade should be served lukewarm, garnished with slices of truffle if desired. Serve with fried toast triangles (see directions that follow). Traditionally,

the brandade is molded into the shape of a dome before it is served.

Yield: Six to eight servings.

Fried toast triangles: Neatly trim the crusts from four slices of white bread to make four large squares. Cut the slices diagonally, both from the left and right, to make four triangles of each slice. Heat three tablespoons butter in a large skillet and cook the triangles on both sides until golden brown. Add more butter to the skillet if necessary. Drain on absorbent toweling.

SCALLOPS PROVENÇALE

1½ pounds scallops
Flour for dredging
  2 tablespoons olive oil
  6 tablespoons butter
  1 clove garlic or more to taste, finely chopped

Salt and freshly ground black pepper
½ cup chopped parsley
Lemon wedges

1. Wash and dry the scallops and roll them in flour.

2. Heat the oil and butter together, add the scallops and cook them very quickly, tossing them lightly in the hot fats so they brown delicately on all sides. While they are cooking, add the chopped garlic and mix it in well.

3. Add salt and pepper to taste and, just before removing the pan from the heat, add the parsley and toss until the scallops are covered with the parsley. Serve with lemon wedges.

Yield: Four servings.

SHRIMP CINTA

1 cup lemon juice
1 cup olive oil
6 cloves garlic, crushed
2 teaspoons parsley

1 teaspoon ground red pepper (optional)
24 large shrimp, shelled and deveined

1. Combine all the ingredients except the shrimp. Pour over the shrimp and marinate overnight in the refrigerator.

2. Remove the shrimp from the marinade and broil until brown, about five minutes on each side.

Yield: Four servings.

SWISS FONDUE

1 clove garlic, split
2 cups dry white wine
1 pound natural Switzerland cheese (Gruyère, Emmentaler or Appenzell), shredded or finely cut
1 teaspoon cornstarch
3 tablespoons kirsch

Nutmeg, pepper or paprika to taste
2 loaves Italian or French bread with hard crust, cut into bite-size pieces, each of which must have at least one side of crust

1. Rub the cooking utensil (which should be a heavy pan) with the cut sides of the garlic. Pour in the wine and set over low heat. When the wine is heated to the point that air bubbles rise to the surface, add the cheese by handfuls, stirring constantly with a wooden fork or spoon. Keep stirring until the cheese is melted.

2. Dissolve the cornstarch in the kirsch and add to the cheese mixture. Cook, stirring constantly, two or three minutes longer, adding the desired spice to taste.

3. To serve, transfer the fondue to a chafing dish or a casserole set over a small flame. Keep hot but below the simmering point. If the mixture becomes too thick, thin with a little white wine. Serve with the pieces of crusty bread, which may be speared on long-handled, two-pronged forks and dipped by each guest into the hot fondue.

Yield: Four servings.

SWITZERLAND CHEESE TOAST

2 tablespoons butter
1½ tablespoons flour
½ cup milk
½ cup natural Gruyère cheese, grated
3 tablespoons dry white Swiss wine

1 clove garlic, minced
1 egg, beaten
Salt and freshly ground black pepper
Grated nutmeg
1 long loaf French bread

1. Melt the butter and blend in the flour with a wire whisk. Meanwhile, bring the milk to a boil and add it all at once to the butter-flour mixture, stirring vigorously with the whisk. Continue stirring until the sauce is thickened and smooth. Cool to room temperature.

2. Add the cheese, wine, garlic and egg and the salt, pepper and nutmeg to taste. Mix well.

3. Cut ten to twelve slices of French bread diagonally, each half an inch thick, and toast each slightly on one side only.

4. Spread each untoasted side with about three tablespoons of the cheese mixture. It should be about one-half inch thick on the toast.

5. Broil under medium heat until the mixture is lightly browned and heated through. Serve with glasses of well-chilled white wine.

Yield: Five or six servings.

Here is a pilaff that also has a touch of garlic and the result is triumphant. It is the recipe of Mr. Cyrus Melikian, an industrialist and member of the Philadelphia Wine and Food Society.

PILAFF

¼ cup (one-half stick) butter
½ cup finely chopped onion
½ teaspoon finely chopped garlic
½ cup (approximately) very thin egg noodles

1 cup raw rice
2 cups chicken broth
¼ teaspoon monosodium glutamate

1. Heat the butter in a heavy three-quart saucepan. Add the onion and garlic; cook briefly, stirring, then add the noodles. Continue stirring over very low heat about three minutes. Add the rice and cook five minutes, still stirring.

2. Meanwhile, bring the chicken broth to a full rolling boil

and add it all at once to the rice. Add monosodium glutamate. If the chicken broth is not salty enough, add salt to taste.

3. Put on a tight-fitting lid and simmer, without removing the cover, exactly thirty-five minutes. Turn off the heat but do not remove the cover. Let the rice stand ten to thirty minutes before serving.

Yield: Four servings.

ROASTED EGGPLANT IN YOGHURT

2 small eggplants	Salt and freshly ground black
1 clove garlic, minced	pepper to taste
1 cup yoghurt	

1. Place the eggplants on a charcoal grill and turn them frequently until they are tender, about fifteen minutes (the outsides of the eggplants may become somewhat charred).

2. Cool the eggplants briefly, then, using the fingers, peel off skins and discard them.

3. Place the eggplant pulp on a hot platter and chop it into small pieces with a knife and fork. Add the remaining ingredients and mix thoroughly. Serve as a side dish with shish kebab (page 31).

Yield: Six servings.

ESCAROLE AND EGGS AU GRATIN

1 pound escarole	½ cup freshly grated
Water	Parmesan cheese
Salt	Freshly ground black
2 tablespoons olive oil	pepper
2 cloves garlic, minced	3 or four poached eggs
2½ tablespoons flour	3 or four teaspoons butter
1¼ cups milk (a portion of this may be sweet cream, if desired)	

1. Wash the escarole thoroughly, especially the outer leaves. Shred it coarsely and cook it, covered, in about one-quarter cup salted water until tender, about fifteen minutes. Drain it in a sieve and press out excess water.

2. Heat the olive oil in a saucepan and sauté the garlic in it until the garlic is beginning to turn golden.

3. Blend in the flour. Add the milk all at once and cook, stirring vigorously with a wire whisk, until the mixture is thickened and smooth. Add about one-third of the grated cheese and season the sauce to taste with salt and pepper.

4. Add about one-third of the sauce to the escarole. Blend well and spread the mixture in three or four individual shallow baking dishes.

5. Place a poached egg on each, cover the eggs with the remaining sauce and sprinkle with the remaining grated cheese. Dot each with a teaspoon of butter.

6. Brown lightly under the broiler or bake on the upper rack of a 400-degree oven until the tops are browned.

Yield: Three or four servings.

Note: If more substantial servings are desired, place two poached eggs in each baking dish.

CREAMED POTATOES WITH GARLIC

2 buds of garlic (about thirty to forty cloves)
½ cup (one stick) butter
2 tablespoons flour
1 cup light cream or milk
2½ pounds potatoes, peeled and quartered
Heavy cream
Salt and freshly ground pepper to taste
Chopped fresh parsley or dill for garnish

1. Place the garlic cloves in a small saucepan and add boiling water to cover. Simmer one minute and drain.

2. Peel the garlic cloves and return them to the saucepan. Add half the butter and cover. Cook over low heat until thoroughly tender but not brown, about twenty minutes.

3. Add the flour to the saucepan and stir with a wire whisk over moderate heat until well blended. Gradually add the light cream, stirring constantly with the whisk. Put the garlic sauce through a food mill or purée it in an electric blender. Return to the heat and cook briefly.

4. Meanwhile, cook the potatoes in boiling salted water to cover until they are tender. Drain them and put them through a food mill or potato ricer.

5. Combine the potatoes and garlic sauce; beat with a wooden spoon. Beat in the remaining butter and add heavy cream, a little at a time, until the potatoes have reached the desired consistency.

6. Season to taste with salt and pepper. Heap onto a hot serving dish and sprinkle with chopped parsley or dill.

Yield: Six servings.

CHERRY TOMATOES À L'AIL

36 ripe cherry tomatoes
  Boiling water
1 teaspoon salt
3 tablespoons butter

1 clove garlic, finely minced
¼ teaspoon freshly ground
  black pepper
1 tablespoon chopped chives

1. Place the tomatoes in a wire sieve and dip them into rapidly boiling water for about ten seconds, or until skins loosen. Remove from the water and remove the skins. Sprinkle with the salt and let stand fifteen minutes.

2. Preheat the oven to 350 degrees.

3. Melt the butter in a shallow, ovenproof dish. Add the garlic and pepper. Drain and add the tomatoes, shaking to coat them all over with the mixture. Place the dish in the oven just long enough to heat the tomatoes through, about one to two minutes. Do not overcook or the tomatoes will lose their shape. Sprinkle with the chives and serve immediately.

Yield: Six servings.

TOMATOES À LA PROVENÇALE

6 large ripe tomatoes
Salt and freshly ground black
  pepper
¼ cup chopped fresh basil
2 cloves garlic, finely minced

2 tablespoons finely chopped
  shallot or scallion
¼ teaspoon thyme
¾ cup fresh bread crumbs
Olive oil

1. Preheat the oven to 400 degrees.
2. Wash the tomatoes and dry them. Cut them in half horizontally and scoop out the seeds and juice with a small spoon or the fingers. Sprinkle each half with salt and pepper and invert on a cake rack to drain.
3. Combine the basil, garlic, shallot, thyme, bread crumbs and five tablespoons olive oil. Mix well and season to taste with salt and pepper. Use this mixture to stuff the tomato halves and sprinkle with a little additional oil.
4. Arrange the tomato halves in a large baking dish and bake until thoroughly heated and golden brown on top, about fifteen minutes.

Yield: Six servings.

CAESAR SALAD

1 clove garlic
¾ cup olive oil
2 cups croutons, made from
  stale French bread
2 or three heads Romaine
  lettuce
Freshly ground black pepper
  to taste

½ teaspoon salt
2 eggs
Juice of one large lemon
6 to eight fillets of anchovy,
  diced
½ cup freshly grated
  Parmesan cheese

1. Crush the garlic and add the olive oil. Let stand overnight; discard the garlic.
2. Brown the croutons in one-quarter cup of the garlic-flavored oil. Stir the croutons carefully so they color on all sides. Drain them on paper toweling and reserve.

3. Break the lettuce into a large bowl. Sprinkle with the remaining half cup of the flavored oil and toss to coat. Grind a generous amount of black pepper over the salad and add the salt.

4. Cook the eggs in the shells in simmering water exactly one minute. Remove from the water and break the eggs over the salad.

5. Squeeze the lemon juice directly over the eggs and mix the salad so that there is a thick, creamy look to the lettuce.

6. Add the diced anchovies. Add more salt, pepper or lemon juice, if desired. Sprinkle the grated Parmesan cheese over the salad, mix and add the croutons at the last moment before serving.

Yield: About twelve servings.

PAN BANIA

1 long loaf French bread
1 clove garlic, split
1 cucumber, peeled and sliced
1 tomato, thinly sliced
3 pimentos, cut in half

1 two-ounce can flat anchovy fillets, drained
6 black olives (preferably Greek or Italian), pitted
Olive oil
Vinegar

1. Cut the bread in half lengthwise and rub the cut sides with garlic.

2. Arrange the cucumber, tomato, pimentos, anchovies and olives over half the loaf. Sprinkle with oil and vinegar.

3. Top with the other half of the loaf and press with a heavy weight thirty minutes or longer. Remove the weight, slice and serve.

Yield: Six servings.

AÏOLI SAUCE MADE IN A BLENDER

1 egg
½ teaspoon dry mustard
½ teaspoon salt

2 tablespoons lemon juice
1 cup olive oil
3 cloves garlic, split

1. Break the egg into the container of an electric blender. Add the mustard, salt, lemon juice and one-quarter cup of the olive oil.

2. Cover the blender and turn the motor on low speed. Immediately remove the cover and add the remaining oil in a steady stream. When the mayonnaise is ready, add the garlic and blend ten seconds.

3. This sauce is usually served with poached fish, hot or cold, but it also may be served with cold meat or a seasoning for salads and vegetables.

Yield: About one and one-half cups.

LAMB COUNTRY STYLE

4 pounds shoulder, breast or neck of lamb, cut into one- or two-inch pieces
Salt and freshly ground pepper to taste
2 tablespoons butter
2 tablespoons vegetable oil
2 cups finely chopped onion
¼ cup flour
2 bay leaves
2 sprigs fresh thyme or one teaspoon dried
3½ cups chicken broth
1 cup water
¼ cup chopped parsley
4 to 8 cloves garlic

1. Preheat the oven to 375 degrees.

2. Sprinkle the lamb pieces with salt and pepper.

3. Heat the butter and oil in a large skillet and brown the lamb pieces, a few at a time, on all sides. As they are browned transfer the meat to a kettle.

4. When all the pieces are browned, add the onion to the skillet and cook briefly. Transfer the onion to the kettle, using a slotted spoon. Pour off the fat from the skillet.

5. Sprinkle the lamb with the flour. Stir well with the spoon until all the pieces are coated. Add the bay leaves and thyme.

6. Meanwhile, add the chicken broth to the skillet and stir to dissolve the brown particles that cling to the bottom and sides. Pour this over the lamb and add the water. Place the kettle on top of the stove and bring to a boil. Cover, place in oven and bake for 45 minutes.

7. Uncover and, if the sauce seems too thin, cook it over medium-high heat to reduce. Skim off the fat. Cover again and bake for thirty minutes.

8. Chop the parsley and garlic together and add to the lamb. Serve hot with rice.

Yield: Six to eight servings.

Ginger

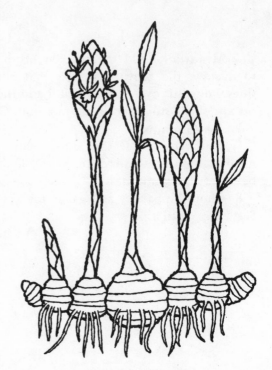

GINGER *has been called a spice lover's spice. It gives zest to anything with which it is linked whether the dish be sweet, meat, fish or fowl. It is coveted by Chinese cooks and revered in many American kitchens. It is the name ingredient in ginger snaps, gingerbread and ginger beer and it frequently is used in spice cakes. It is commonly used in curries. A little ginger would help the most pallid of pot roasts and ginger in syrup is delicious on plain ice cream.*

The recipes for preserved ginger are among the most fascinating. Here is one: "Wash ginger roots and boil them for twenty-four hours. Soak them for a day in salt water. Wash the roots again and dry them in the sun. Cook the roots half a day longer with an equal weight of sugar and let stand in jars for several days. Boil once more, then seal in jars." Very good commercial versions of preserved ginger are available in grocery stores. Fresh ginger roots (or "hands" as they are called) are available in oriental markets and those which cater to a Spanish-speaking clientele.

GINGER SOY SAUCE BEEF

2 tablespoons peanut or corn
  oil
2 slices fresh ginger root
1 scallion, cut into two-inch
  pieces

1 pound boneless beef, cubed
2 tablespoons sherry
¼ cup soy sauce
1 tablespoon sugar
1 cup water

1. Heat the oil over high heat in a saucepan with the ginger and scallion. Add the beef and cook, stirring, until the beef is lightly browned.

2. Add the sherry, soy sauce and sugar. Cook, stirring, five minutes.

3. Add the water, cover and cook over medium heat thirty minutes, stirring occasionally. Continue cooking thirty minutes longer.

Yield: Four to six servings.

HAMBURGERS WITH GINGER

2 pounds chopped round
  steak
2 teaspoons finely chopped
  ginger or one teaspoon
  powdered ginger
4 teaspoons freshly ground
  black pepper
Salt

4 teaspoons butter
Tabasco, Worcestershire sauce
  and lemon juice to taste
2 tablespoons cognac, warmed
  (optional)
Chopped parsley and chives

1. Mix the beef lightly with the ginger. Shape into four cakes and sprinkle each side with pepper. With the heel of the hand, press the pepper into the meat and let stand about twenty minutes.

2. Sprinkle a light layer of salt over the bottom of a heavy skillet. Place over high heat and, when the salt begins to brown, add the hamburgers. Cook until well browned on one side. Turn and, to produce a rare hamburger, cook thirty seconds over high heat then lower the heat to medium and cook one minute longer.

Adjust heat and time to cook hamburgers to a greater degree of doneness.

3. Place a teaspoonful of butter on each hamburger in the pan and add Tabasco, Worcestershire and lemon juice to taste. Ignite the cognac and add.

4. Transfer the patties to a warm platter and keep hot. Lower the heat and swirl the sauce in the skillet. Pour it over the meat and sprinkle with parsley and chives.

Yield: Four servings.

BARBECUED SPARERIBS

6 pounds spareribs
Boiling salted water
1 onion studded with cloves
1 teaspoon each rosemary, thyme, marjoram and orégano
1 cup dry red wine

⅓ cup tomato catchup or chili sauce
1 tablespoon soy sauce
½ teaspoon powdered ginger
2 tablespoons honey
1 teaspoon minced garlic

1. Cut the spareribs into generous serving pieces. Cover with boiling salted water and add onion and herbs.

2. Bring to a boil and simmer just until tender, about fifty minutes. Drain and place meat in a shallow pan.

3. Blend all remaining ingredients and pour over meat. Let stand in refrigerator until ready to barbecue.

4. Grill over hot charcoal or bake in a 350-degree oven, basting frequently with the sauce, until the ribs are browned and glazed, one hour or less.

Yield: Six servings.

SAUCE CHINOISE FOR SHRIMP

1 teaspoon chopped fresh ginger
3 teaspoons sugar

4 teaspoons vinegar or lemon juice
½ cup soy sauce

Combine all the ingredients and stir until the sugar is dissolved. Serve with two pounds of shrimp, cooked and deveined. As a serving idea, arrange the shrimp on a bed of fresh watercress surrounding the sauce.

Yield: About three-fourths cup of sauce.

BEET PRESERVES

2 pounds beets
Water
3 cups sugar
1 lemon, peeled and sliced
thin

⅓ cup chopped, blanched
almonds
1 teaspoon ground ginger

1. Cook the beets in water to cover until tender. Drain, peel and cut into thin strips or dice.
2. Bring three-quarters cup water and the sugar to a boil, stirring until the sugar has dissolved. Add the beets and cook one hour.
3. Add the lemon slices and simmer one hour longer or until liquid is jellied and the beets are transparent and slightly brown.
4. Add the nuts and ginger, stir and continue cooking fifteen minutes longer. Cool and store in jars or stoneware crocks.

Yield: About four cups.

MANGO CHUTNEY

6 medium mangoes
1 cup cider vinegar
2 two-inch cinnamon sticks
½ teaspoon ground cloves
½ teaspoon ground ginger

2 cups seedless raisins
1 cup sugar
½ cup water
⅓ cup diced preserved or
candied ginger

1. Peel and cube the mangoes. Measure them. There should be eight cups. Set aside.
2. Combine the vinegar, cinnamon sticks, cloves and ground ginger in a saucepan. Heat to the boiling point.

3. Add the mangoes, raisins, sugar and water. Cook, stirring frequently, until of medium thickness, about forty-five minutes. Add the diced preserved or candied ginger and cook one minute longer. Ladle into hot sterilized half-pint jars and seal at once.

Yield: Eight jars.

FRESH PEACH CHUTNEY

2 tablespoons salt
Water
7 cups sliced fresh peaches
3 cups sugar
1½ cups cider vinegar
2 large cloves garlic
1 cup chopped onions

1 teaspoon ground ginger
¼ teaspoon crushed red pepper
¾ cup lime juice
1 cup raisins
½ cup chopped candied ginger

1. Add the salt to a quart of water; pour over the peaches. Let stand one day. Drain.

2. Mix one-quarter cup water, the sugar, vinegar and garlic. Bring to a boil, add peaches and cook until they are clear, about forty-five minutes. Remove peaches from syrup.

3. Add onions, spices, lime juice and raisins to syrup. Cook until thickened, twelve to fifteen minutes. Add peaches and candied ginger; bring to boiling point. Ladle into hot sterilized half-pint jars. Seal at once.

Yield: Six jars.

GINGER CHEESE PIE

1½ cups graham cracker crumbs
¼ cup (one-half stick) butter, melted
11 ounces cream cheese
¾ cup sugar

2 eggs, well beaten
1 tablespoon freshly grated ginger
1 pint sour cream
2 tablespoons preserved ginger, chopped

1. Preheat the oven to 350 degrees.

2. Mix the crumbs with the melted butter and press into a nine-inch pie pan.

3. Blend the cream cheese with one-half cup of the sugar and the eggs. Beat until smooth. Add the grated ginger and pour the mixture into the prepared crust. Bake twenty minutes.

4. Mix the sour cream with the remaining sugar and spread over the surface of the pie. Sprinkle with the preserved ginger.

5. Return the pie to the oven with the heat turned off for three or four minutes. Cool and chill until set.

Yield: Six servings.

PUMPKIN PIE

Pastry for a one-crust nine-inch pie

3 eggs, lightly beaten

¾ cup brown sugar, packed

½ teaspoon salt

¾ teaspoon ground ginger

¼ teaspoon cinnamon

¼ teaspoon nutmeg

¼ teaspoon ground cloves

1¾ cups canned pumpkin or well-drained, mashed and sieved, home-cooked pumpkin

1½ cups undiluted evaporated milk

1 tablespoon molasses (optional)

1. Preheat the oven to 425 degrees with the rack near the bottom.

2. Prepare the pastry shell with standing fluted rim. Brush with a little of the beaten egg and chill while preparing the filling.

3. Mix the remaining beaten eggs with all the other ingredients.

4. Pour into the prepared pie shell and bake until a knife inserted near the center comes out clean, about thirty-five minutes. If served cold, the pie may be decorated with whipped cream.

Yield: Six to eight servings.

GINGER CREAM MOLD

1 envelope unflavored gelatin
¼ cup cold water
2 egg yolks
¼ cup sugar
⅛ teaspoon salt
2 cups milk

2 tablespoons syrup drained from preserved ginger
1 teaspoon vanilla
¼ cup finely diced preserved ginger
1 cup heavy cream, whipped

1. Soften the gelatin in the cold water.

2. Combine the egg yolks, sugar, salt and milk in the top of a double boiler. Mix well and cook over hot water until the mixture coats a metal spoon. Strain the mixture and stir in the softened gelatin, ginger syrup, vanilla and diced ginger. Chill until the mixture begins to thicken, stirring occasionally.

3. Fold in the whipped cream and turn the mixture into a one-quart ring mold. Chill until firm.

4. Unmold and serve with additional whipped cream sweetened and flavored with ginger syrup.

Yield: Four to six servings.

BRANDY SNAPS

¼ cup light corn syrup
¼ cup molasses
½ cup (one stick) butter
1 cup sifted flour

⅔ cup sugar
1 teaspoon ground ginger
2 teaspoons brandy

1. Preheat the oven to 300 degrees.

2. Heat the syrup and molasses to boiling. Remove from the heat and add the butter.

3. Sift together the flour, sugar and ginger. Add gradually, while stirring, to molasses mixture. Mix well and add the brandy.

4. Drop by half-teaspoonfuls three inches apart on a greased cooky sheet. Bake ten minutes.

5. Remove from oven, loosen one cooky at a time and roll over

the handle of a wooden spoon. Slip off carefully. Serve filled with whipped cream.

Yield: Eighteen cookies.

BAKED APPLES CANTONESE

6 large baking apples
1 cup coarsely chopped Brazil nuts
½ cup chopped pitted dates
⅓ cup chopped candied ginger

1 cup light corn syrup
1 teaspoon powdered ginger
Red food coloring
Boiling water
Sugar

1. Preheat the oven to 350 degrees.

2. Core apples almost through, leaving a little flesh at the blossom end. Pare about one-third of the way down from the stem end.

3. Combine Brazil nuts, dates and candied ginger and fill centers of apples with the nut-fruit mixture.

4. Combine the corn syrup and powdered ginger and tint red with food coloring. Simmer five minutes and brush apples thickly with this mixture.

5. Place the apples in a baking dish. Add enough boiling water to cover bottom of dish and bake until tender, about forty minutes, basting frequently with the syrup. Remove from oven.

6. Sprinkle the apples with sugar and broil, with surface of fruit four inches below source of heat, basting with remaining syrup and sprinkling with additional sugar, until glazed, about fifteen minutes.

Yield: Six servings.

GINGERED FRESH BLUEBERRY COMPOTE

1 pint fresh blueberries
1 cup orange juice
1 tablespoon lemon juice
¼ cup confectioners' sugar

2 tablespoons minced preserved ginger
Fresh mint leaves for garnish

1. Wash the blueberries and place them in a serving bowl.

2. Combine the remaining ingredients and pour over the blueberries. Chill one to two hours. Serve in sherbet glasses garnished with mint leaves.

Yield: Six servings.

BAKED CHICKEN GINGER

½ cup all-purpose flour
2 teaspoons salt
1 frying chicken (three pounds), cut into serving pieces
¾ cup butter

½ cup dry sherry
2 tablespoons soy sauce
2 tablespoons lemon juice
¼ cup finely chopped preserved ginger root

1. Preheat the oven to 350 degrees.

2. Combine flour and salt in a paper bag. Add the chicken pieces and shake well to coat each with flour.

3. Heat one-half cup of the butter and brown the chicken on all sides. Transfer the chicken to a baking dish with cover.

4. Meanwhile, combine the remaining butter, the sherry, soy sauce, lemon juice and ginger in a small saucepan. Bring to a boil, stir and pour the mixture over the chicken. Cover.

5. Bake the chicken for about one hour, turning the pieces once as they bake.

Yield: Four servings.

TONY CLARKE'S MANDARIN PORK

12 loin pork chops, each about three-quarters inch thick
1 cup apple juice
¾ cup soy sauce
½ cup honey
2 cloves garlic, crushed
2 tablespoons grated fresh ginger (or powdered ginger to taste)

1 tablespoon dry English mustard
2 dashes Worcestershire sauce
¼ teaspoon monosodium glutamate
½ cup amber-colored rum
12 ounces crab apple jelly
Juice of one lemon
Nutmeg

1. Carefully bone the meat from the chops, but reserve the bones. Place the meat in a mixing bowl.

2. Combine the apple juice, one-half cup soy sauce, honey, garlic, ginger, mustard, Worcestershire, monosodium glutamate and rum. Pour the mixture over the pork and stir to blend. Cover and refrigerate overnight.

3. Drain the marinade into a saucepan and add the crab apple jelly and the remaining soy sauce. Bring to a boil and simmer until reduced by about one-third. Add the lemon juice.

4. Meanwhile, make a hardwood or charcoal fire. When the coals have a white ash, grill the pork on both sides, basting with the marinade frequently. Cook until done and sprinkle pork lightly with nutmeg. Arrange the pieces on a serving dish and pour the remaining sauce over the meat.

Yield: Six to twelve servings.

Note: Mr. Clarke recommends throwing the reserved bones onto the fire and grilling until brown on all sides. Serve the next morning for breakfast.

BEEF WITH GINGER

2 pounds chuck, cut into two-inch cubes	½ cup diced salt pork
¼ cup all-purpose flour	2 cups finely chopped onion
1 teaspoon salt	1 garlic clove, finely minced
1 teaspoon freshly ground black pepper	1 cup canned Italian plum tomatoes
1 teaspoon ground ginger	1 cup fresh or canned beef broth
1 teaspoon turmeric powder	Tabasco to taste
½ teaspoon dried thyme	

1. Preheat the oven to 350 degrees.

2. Toss the meat in a mixture of flour, salt, pepper, ginger, turmeric and thyme.

3. Cook the salt pork in a heavy Dutch oven or casserole until rendered of its fat. Remove the bits of pork and brown the meat on all sides. Do not allow the meat or cooking fat to burn. When all browned, remove the meat.

4. Add the onion and garlic to the skillet and cook over low heat, stirring, until the onion is wilted. Return the meat to the casserole and add the remaining ingredients. Add salt to taste and bring to a boil. Cover closely and place in the oven. Bake about two and one-half hours or until the meat is fork tender.

Yield: Four to six servings.

EDWARD LOWMAN'S RASPBERRY GINGER CREAM

1 package (ten ounces) frozen raspberries	⅓ cup brown sugar
1 cup heavy cream	⅓ teaspoon ground ginger

1. Defrost the raspberries thoroughly and drain them.

2. Whip the cream and fold in the brown sugar and ginger.

3. Fold in the raspberries and chill one hour. Stir lightly and spoon into sherbet or parfait glasses.

Yield: Four servings.

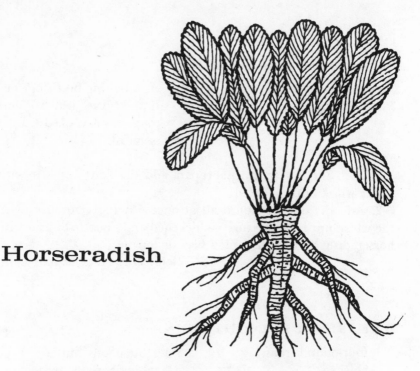

Horseradish

The name HORSERADISH has an inelegant ring to it and more's the pity. The root does not have a refined flavor but it is nonetheless admirable. Few things complement boiled beef or tongue better than a piquant horseradish sauce and grated horseradish is almost sine qua non in tomato cocktail sauces for shrimp, clams and other seafood. The root is used frequently in the making of pickles and it gives glory to a host of prepared mustards. Fresh horseradish, when grated, is fiery to the taste and it is capable of producing just as many tears as the most robust chopped onion.

HORSERADISH SAUCE

3 tablespoons butter
3 tablespoons flour

1½ cups boiling beef stock or liquid in which beef tongue was cooked
Horseradish to taste

1. Melt the butter in a saucepan, add the flour and stir with a wire whisk until blended.
2. Add the boiling liquid all at once, stirring vigorously with the whisk until the mixture is thickened and smooth. Season with horseradish. Serve with boiled beef or tongue.

Yield: One and one-half cups.

DANISH-STYLE CHICKEN

1 four-pound roasting chicken
12 cups chicken stock or cold water
5 ribs of celery with leaves
½ cup chopped carrots
½ cup chopped onion
6 sprigs parsley
12 black peppercorns
½ bay leaf
1½ teaspoons salt

3 tablespoons butter
3 tablespoons flour
3 egg yolks
3 tablespoons water
¾ cup (one and one-half sticks) butter, melted
Salt and freshly ground black pepper to taste
2 tablespoons freshly grated horseradish, or to taste
¼ teaspoon sugar

1. Combine the chicken, chicken stock, celery, carrots, onion, parsley, peppercorns, bay leaf and salt in a large kettle. Bring to a boil and simmer, covered, until the chicken is tender, forty-five minutes to one hour. Let the chicken stand while making the sauce.
2. Melt three tablespoons butter and blend in the flour. Add one cup strained hot broth in which the chicken cooked, stirring rapidly with a wire whisk. When the sauce is thickened and smooth, simmer over low heat about five minutes. Remove from the heat but keep hot.

3. Combine the egg yolk with the water and beat vigorously over hot water until the mixture begins to thicken. Gradually beat in the melted butter and, when it is thickened and smooth, add salt and pepper to taste. Combine the two sauces and blend them but do not boil. Stir in the horseradish, pepper to taste and sugar.

4. Remove the chicken from the kettle and remove the skin. Divide the chicken into serving pieces and serve with the sauce poured over it. Serve with rice.

Yield: Four servings.

BEETS WITH SOUR CREAM

2 bunches beets
  Boiling salted water
1 medium onion, finely
  chopped
¾ cup sour cream

¾ teaspoon salt
¾ teaspoon freshly ground
  black pepper
2 teaspoons grated horse-
  radish

1. Wash the beets and leave an inch of the stems attached. Cook the beets in boiling salted water to cover until tender. Cool, peel and slice. Arrange the slices in a bowl and top with the chopped onion.

2. Blend the remaining ingredients and spread this mixture over the beets and chopped onion. Serve chilled.

Yield: Four to six servings.

SEAFOOD COCKTAIL SAUCE

¼ teaspoon Tabasco
1 cup catchup or chili sauce
2 tablespoons lemon juice

½ teaspoon salt
1 tablespoon horseradish

1. Add the Tabasco to the catchup or chili sauce and mix well.
2. Stir in the remaining ingredients and chill before serving.

Yield: About one cup.

UNCOOKED CABBAGE RELISH

2 quarts shredded cabbage
2 green peppers, chopped
2 cups chopped onion
⅓ cup salt
¾ cup sugar
½ teaspoon cinnamon
½ teaspoon ground cloves
½ teaspoon ground allspice
1½ tablespoons dry mustard
1 tablespoon grated horse-radish
1 cup cider vinegar, approximately

1. Mix the cabbage, peppers, onion and salt; let stand overnight. Drain and rinse twice in cold water. Drain well.
2. Mix the sugar, spices and horseradish with the cabbage. Pack lightly into sterilized jars, leaving one inch headspace.
3. Add vinegar to fill the jars and seal. Let stand at least a day before using. Store the relish in the refrigerator.

Yield: About seven cups.

PETER DOHANOS' SWORDFISH SEVICHE

1½ cups coarsely chopped walnuts
3 pounds fresh swordfish steaks, each about one inch thick
1 tablespoon fresh lemon juice
6 tablespoons fresh lime juice
8 tablespoons olive oil
2 tablespoons soy sauce
1 tablespoon horseradish
2 teaspoons salt
1 teaspoon freshly ground black pepper
6 medium-size ripe tomatoes, peeled, cored and diced
1 medium-size red onion, chopped
Lettuce leaves
Fresh tomato slices

1. Preheat the oven to 350 degrees.
2. Scatter the walnuts over a baking sheet or a length of aluminum foil and bake five to ten minutes, stirring them around

occasionally. Cook only until they are crisp and lightly brown. Turn off the oven. Let cool.

3. Trim all the skin from the swordfish steaks and remove all bones. Cut the steaks into thin slices, then cut each slice into one-inch square. Transfer to a mixing bowl.

4. Combine the lemon and lime juices, olive oil, soy sauce, horseradish, salt, pepper, chopped tomatoes and onion. Pour the mixture over the raw fish and stir to blend. Refrigerate, stirring once in a while with a rubber spatula. Chill at least three hours. Before serving, stir in the walnuts.

5. Serve the seviche on the lettuce leaves with fresh tomato slices.

Yield: Sixteen servings as an appetizer.

CHICKEN WITH HORSERADISH

2 two-and-one-half-pound chickens, cut into serving pieces	2 tablespoons finely chopped shallots
Salt and freshly ground pepper to taste	2 sprigs fresh thyme or one-half teaspoon dried
2 tablespoons plus one teaspoon cold butter	½ clove garlic, finely minced
½ pound mushrooms, quartered	½ cup dry white wine
	2 cups heavy cream
2 tablespoons finely chopped onion	¼ cup horseradish, preferably freshly grated
	24 cherry tomatoes, peeled (see note), optional

1. Preheat the oven to 300 degrees.

2. Sprinkle the chicken pieces with salt and pepper.

3. Heat two tablespoons butter in a large skillet and add the chicken pieces, skin side down. Brown well on both sides. When brown, arrange the chicken symmetrically on an oven-proof platter. Place in the oven about 45 minutes while finishing the sauce.

4. Pour off the fat from the skillet. Add the mushrooms, onion, shallots, thyme and garlic to the skillet and stir with a wooden spoon. Add the remaining teaspoon of cold butter and stir it around in the skillet. Add the wine and stir to dissolve the brown particles that cling to the bottom and sides of the skillet. Simmer until most of the wine evaporates and add the cream. Bring to a boil and simmer about five minutes.

5. If commercial horseradish is used, dry it thoroughly in clean paper towels. Add the horseradish to the skillet and add salt and pepper to taste. If the cherry tomatoes are used, add them at the last minute and cook just to heat through. Pour the sauce over the chicken and serve hot with rice.

Yield: Six or more servings.

Note: To peel the tomatoes, drop them into boiling water and let them stand nine to 12 seconds. Do not overcook. Drain immediately and peel the tomatoes. The skin slips off easily when pulled with a paring knife.

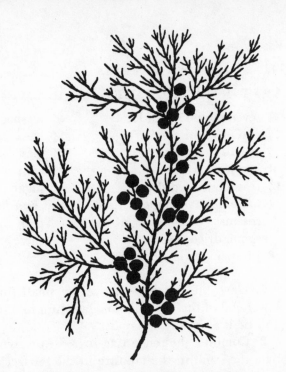

Juniper Berries

In the world of food and drink, JUNIPER BERRIES are most commonly associated with sauerkraut, game and gin. Almost if not all of the finest gins have a characteristic juniper flavor. Juniper berries are the dried fruit of an evergreen shrub, bush or tree and they have a dark bluish-purple cast. They are somewhat bittersweet to the taste and may be used in most game marinades.

Juniper symbolizes protection and, according to legend, when the Virgin Mary and the infant Jesus fled from Herod into Egypt they found refuge behind a juniper bush.

SPIT-ROASTED LEG OF LAMB

1 seven-pound leg of lamb
½ cup olive oil
½ cup dry red wine
1 bay leaf, crushed
¼ teaspoon dried thyme
1 tablespoon chopped fresh rosemary or one-half tablespoon dried rosemary
8 juniper berries, crushed
¼ teaspoon ground ginger
¼ teaspoon cayenne pepper
¼ teaspoon nutmeg
1 teaspoon confectioners' sugar
Salt and freshly ground black pepper to taste
1 clove garlic, cut into slivers

1. Have the butcher remove the small shank bone from the lower end of the leg of lamb. Have him fold back the shank meat and tie it as in a rolled roast.

2. Combine the remaining ingredients except the garlic. Marinate the lamb in the mixture in the refrigerator for twenty-four hours. Turn the meat occasionally.

3. When ready to cook, insert slivers of garlic between the fat and the meat of the leg of lamb.

4. Place the lamb fell side down. Insert the spit rod through the end where the shank meat is folded over and follow the underside of the bone. Adjust the rod to insure even balance. Insert the spit forks into each end of the roast and tighten the screws.

5. Cook the lamb on the revolving spit about twenty minutes a pound, basting frequently with the marinade. A seven-pound roast should cook about two hours or a little longer. Serve with flageolets en casserole page 23).

Yield: Six to eight servings.

CHOUCROUTE GARNIE

(GARNISHED SAUERKRAUT)

4 pounds sauerkraut
Water
1 tablespoon lard
¾ pound bacon, diced
1 large onion, studded with three cloves
1 Polish sausage, cut into two-inch pieces
1 pound smoked pork shoulder
¼ cup brandy
1 carrot, sliced

10 juniper berries and six peppercorns, tied in a cheesecloth bag
2 bay leaves
¼ teaspoon thyme
Salt to taste
2 cups dry white Alsatian wine
2 cups water
12 medium potatoes, peeled and boiled
12 frankfurters

1. Place the sauerkraut in a deep bowl. Loosen the shreds with the fingers. Fill the bowl with water and let stand fifteen minutes. Drain. Wash the sauerkraut under running water. Drain again and press in both hands until all the water is squeezed out.

2. Meanwhile, melt the lard in a Dutch oven or large, heavy pan. Add the bacon and onion. Cook until browned. Add the sausage and pork shoulder and cook until the meat is browned. Remove the meat and set it aside.

3. Add the sauerkraut to the pan and cook, stirring constantly, until it is slightly browned. Add brandy and continue cooking a few minutes. Add carrot, the bag of juniper berries and peppercorns, bay leaves, thyme, salt, wine and water. Bring to a boil.

4. Return the pork shoulder to the pan, cover and simmer over low heat three hours.

5. Return the sausage to the pan, cover and continue simmering forty-five minutes.

6. Add potatoes and frankfurters, cover and continue simmering fifteen minutes longer. Discard cheesecloth bag and serve piping hot with cold beer or champagne.

Yield: Eight to ten servings.

VEAL SAUMONÉE

1 five-pound leg of veal, boned
2 tablespoons saltpeter
4 onions, thinly sliced
½ lemon, sliced
2 bay leaves
4 cups white vinegar
4 sprigs parsley
4 whole cloves

12 peppercorns
1 sprig fresh tarragon or one-half teaspoon dried
Pinch of thyme
8 juniper berries
2½ quarts (ten cups) water
3 cups dry white wine
Salt

1. Pound the boned veal with a meat pounder or the bottom of a heavy skillet. Rub it well with saltpeter and roll it like a jelly roll. Tie the meat securely with a string.

2. Line the bottom of a large pan or casserole with the onion and lemon slices. Tie the bay leaves, parsley, cloves, peppercorns, tarragon, thyme and juniper berries in a cheesecloth bag and add to the casserole. Add the vinegar and let the meat marinate three or four days, turning it once a day.

3. Add the water, wine and salt to taste and simmer slowly three hours. Let the meat cool in the stock. Chill the meat and then remove the string.

4. The meat may be served sliced thin as a cold meat dish with parsley and mustard mayonnaise or in excellent open-faced sandwiches on rounds of rye bread. Top each sandwich with a dollop of the mayonnaise and a rolled fillet of anchovy.

Yield: Eight to ten servings.

VENISON CHOPS POLONAISE

6 venison chops
1 onion, sliced
2 carrots, sliced
4 shallots, chopped
4 sprigs parsley
½ teaspoon thyme
1 teaspoon salt
6 crushed peppercorns

6 juniper berries
½ cup vinegar
¼ cup olive or other vegetable oil
Red wine
¼ cup (one-half stick) butter
1 cup sour cream

1. Combine the venison chops, vegetables, seasonings, vinegar, oil and enough red wine to cover the chops. Let stand in the refrigerator twenty-four hours.

2. Drain the chops, reserving one-half cup of the marinade. Wipe the meat dry.

3. Heat the butter in a large skillet and cook the chops four minutes on each side, or to the desired degree of doneness. Remove the venison to a heated platter and keep warm.

4. Add the reserved marinade to the skillet and bring to a boil. Stir in the sour cream and heat thoroughly. Adjust seasonings and serve the sauce separately. Serve with wild rice.

Yield: Six servings.

VENISON STEW

½ cup vinegar
3 sprigs parsley
2 carrots
1 onion, peeled and chopped
2 leeks, trimmed, split down the center, washed and chopped
2 ribs celery, chopped
2 crushed cloves garlic
12 juniper berries
1 teaspoon each leaf sage, coriander, rosemary and marjoram

5 pounds venison cut into two-inch cubes
1 bottle dry red wine
Salt
Freshly ground black pepper
¼ cup vegetable or peanut oil
½ teaspoon thyme
1 cup flour
Water or stock to cover
½ pound small white onions, peeled
¾ cup diced salt pork
1 pound mushrooms, quartered

1. Combine the vinegar, parsley, carrots, onion, leeks, celery and garlic in a saucepan. Tie the juniper berries and spices in a small cheesecloth bag and add them. Bring to a boil.

2. Place the venison in an enamel or stainless steel container and pour the hot spice mixture over it. Add enough dry red wine to cover. Sprinkle with salt and freshly ground black pepper. Let stand in a cool place or in the refrigerator overnight or longer.

3. Preheat the oven to 325 degrees.

4. Drain the meat, discard the cheesecloth bag but reserve the chopped vegetables and the marinating liquid.

5. Heat the oil in a large skillet and brown the meat well, a few pieces at a time. As the meat browns transfer it to a large kettle.

6. Sprinkle the meat with thyme and salt and pepper. Place the kettle over moderate heat. Sprinkle the meat with the flour and stir until meat is evenly coated. Add the marinating liquid and vegetables and, if necessary, water or stock to cover. Bring to a boil, then transfer the kettle to the oven. Cook two to four hours depending on the age and tenderness of the meat. When done, the meat should be tender.

7. Meanwhile, peel the onions and cook them in water to cover until they are nearly tender. Drain.

8. Place the salt pork in a small saucepan and add water to cover. Bring to a boil and cook two minutes. Drain. Cook the salt pork in a small skillet until it is golden brown.

9. Add the mushrooms to the salt pork. Add the onions and cook briefly, stirring. Add the salt pork, mushrooms and onions to the stew and stir. Cook briefly and serve hot.

Yield: Eight to twelve servings.

Note: The wine and spice marinade in this recipe may be used for almost any game including pheasant, rabbit, etc.

ROCK CORNISH HENS WITH JUNIPER BERRIES

8 Rock Cornish hens or one-pound chickens
Salt and freshly ground black pepper
16 juniper berries
16 slices bacon, approximately

¼ pound butter, at room temperature
1½ cups gin
½ cup water

1. Preheat the oven to 500 degrees.

2. Wipe the birds with a damp cloth. Sprinkle them inside and outside with salt and pepper and add two juniper berries to the cavity of each. Truss or tie the birds with string.

3. Use two small or one large ovenproof baking dish. Line the dish or dishes with slices of bacon. Rub the birds with soft butter. Use the remaining butter to dot the bacon slices. Arrange the birds breast side up on the bacon and place in the oven. Bake fifteen minutes, basting frequently with a mixture of gin and water. Reduce the oven heat to 350 degrees and continue to cook, basting frequently, thirty minutes or longer. When done, the birds should be golden brown and the liquid in the cavity should run clear. If the birds are to be served on a picnic, wrap them while still hot in aluminum foil.

Yield: Eight to sixteen servings.

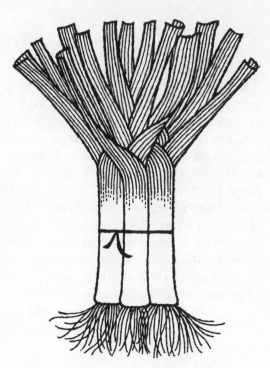

Leeks

LEEKS *are a cornerstone of French cuisine, particularly the bourgeois version. The lowly leek gives eloquence to soups and stews and leeks are eminently delicious in themselves when cooked and served with lemon butter or when cooked and chilled and served with a sauce vinaigrette.*

In Europe leeks have been called "the poor man's asparagus," but they are, in this country, unfortunately rare and therefore dear.

The leek is the national emblem of Wales. It is said that in former days when Cadwalader, a Welsh leader, was about to confront Edwin, King of Northumbria, in battle, he commanded his troops to adorn their headgear with leeks to distinguish them from their adversaries. The Welsh were victorious and thus the leek was given its position of esteem.

Leeks are somewhat sandy and they should be well washed before use.

SOUPE DE POISSONS AU VERMICELLE

(FISH SOUP WITH VERMICELLI)

3 pounds fish heads and bones
1 pound mussels
6 tablespoons olive oil
3 leeks, white part only, washed well and chopped
3 stalks celery, chopped
1 bulb fennel, chopped, or one-half teaspoon fennel seed
1 onion, peeled and quartered
½ clove garlic
3 sprigs parsley
4 tomatoes, peeled, seeded and crushed
½ teaspoon thyme
½ teaspoon saffron
1 bay leaf
2 cups dry white wine
4 cups water
Salt and cayenne pepper to taste
1 lobster, cleaned and cut into serving pieces (optional)
6 clams, scrubbed (optional)
12 raw shrimp, shelled and deveined (optional)
¼ cup vermicelli, cooked according to package directions

1. Wash the fish heads and bones under cold running water. Scrub the mussels well and wash them in cold water.

2. Heat the oil in a large kettle and add the leeks, celery, fennel, onion, garlic and parsley. Cook until the leeks are wilted but not brown.

3. Add the tomatoes, seasonings and wine; stir. Add the fish heads and bones, mussels and water; cook one hour. When nearly done, season with salt and cayenne.

4. Strain the liquid through a sieve lined with a double thickness of cheesecloth.

5. If desired, add the lobster, clams and shrimp to the strained liquid and simmer fifteen minutes. Add the vermicelli and serve at once.

Yield: Six to eight servings.

VICHYSSOISE À LA RITZ

4 leeks, white part only, sliced
1 medium onion, sliced
¼ cup (one-half stick) sweet butter
5 medium potatoes, thinly sliced

1 quart chicken broth
1 tablespoon salt, or less, to taste
3 cups milk
2 cups heavy cream
Chopped chives

1. In a deep kettle, brown the leeks and onion very lightly in the butter. Add the potatoes, broth and salt and boil thirty-five minutes, or until very tender. Crush and rub through a fine sieve or purée in an electric blender.

2. Return the sieved mixture to the kettle, add the milk and one cup of the cream and bring to a boil. Cool and rub again through a fine sieve. Chill.

3. Add the remaining cream. Chill thoroughly and serve garnished with chives.

Yield: Eight or more servings.

WATERZOOIE

¼ cup (one-half stick) butter
1 seven- to eight-pound capon, cut into large pieces
4 leeks, washed and trimmed
8 stalks celery, chopped
1 carrot, chopped
1 small onion, quartered
4 sprigs parsley
¼ teaspoon thyme

¼ teaspoon nutmeg
½ bay leaf
4 cloves
6 cups chicken broth
1 lemon, thinly sliced
1 tablespoon chopped parsley
4 egg yolks
¼ cup heavy cream

1. Heat the butter in a large skillet and brown the capon on all sides.

2. Place the capon with the vegetables and seasonings in a heat-proof casserole. Cover with chicken broth and bring to a

boil. Reduce the heat and simmer until tender, about forty minutes.

3. Remove the capon from the liquid. Remove and discard skin and bones. Cut the meat into large pieces; reserve.

4. Strain the liquid and skim off excess fat. Place over high heat. Add the lemon and chopped parsley.

5. Beat the egg yolks and cream together. Stir into the soup and allow to thicken slightly, but do not boil. Add pieces of chicken and heat briefly.

Yield: Six servings.

BOILED BRISKET OF BEEF

1 four-pound beef brisket
2 quarts cold water
1 tablespoon salt
1 bouquet garni (bay leaf, one-quarter teaspoon thyme, one-half teaspoon peppercorns, three cloves, four sprigs parsley, a few celery leaves, tied in a cheesecloth bag)
2 cups mixed chopped vegetables (onion, carrot, celery, turnip, parsnip)
6 leeks, white part only, quartered lengthwise
3 carrots, quartered
6 small cabbage wedges
6 potatoes, peeled

1. Place the meat in a large kettle. Add the water, salt, bouquet garni and chopped vegetables. Bring to a boil, reduce heat and simmer, covered, until the meat is almost tender, about three hours. Skim frequently.

2. Add the remaining vegetables and simmer until they are tender, forty-five minutes longer.

3. Remove the bouquet garni and serve the meat on a platter surrounded with the large pieces of vegetable. Serve with caper sauce (page 6) or horseradish sauce (page 7) and prepared mustard on the side. Remaining beef broth may be reserved for another use.

Yield: Six servings.

BOILED FRESH TONGUE

1 fresh beef tongue, about four pounds	4 sprigs parsley
	1 bay leaf
1 onion, studded with three cloves	Few whole black peppercorns
	1 tablespoon salt
1 leek	Water
1 rib celery	

1. Wash the tongue and place it in a large kettle with the remaining ingredients. Add cold water to cover. Cover the kettle and bring to a boil. Reduce the heat and simmer until tender, about three and one-half hours.

2. Let the tongue cool in the broth until it can be handled. Remove from the broth, cut off the bones, roots and gristle. Remove the skin by peeling, starting from the thick end. Return the tongue to the broth to reheat if it is to be served hot.

Yield: Eight to twelve servings.

Note: A smoked beef tongue should be covered with cold water and soaked six to twelve hours, drained and treated as above, but omit the salt.

LEEK AND SAUSAGE PIE

9 leeks	Grated fresh horseradish to taste
2 cups chicken stock	
6 tablespoons butter	1 baked nine-inch pie shell
6 tablespoons flour	½ pound pork sausage links, fully cooked
½ teaspoon salt	
¼ teaspoon freshly ground black pepper	1 baked eight-inch round of pastry
½ cup heavy cream	

1. Trim the top green leaves and roots from the leeks. Cut the leeks in half lengthwise down to but not through the root end. Wash thoroughly between the leaves under cold running water.

2. Cut the leeks into very thin julienne strips and simmer in the chicken broth in a covered pan until tender but not mushy. Drain and reserve the liquid.

3. Melt the butter, blend in the flour and stir in two cups of the reserved liquid slowly. Bring to a boil, stirring, and cook, covered, over boiling water for thirty minutes, stirring occasionally.

4. Preheat the oven to 375 degrees.

5. Season sauce with salt and pepper to taste. Add the cream and the drained leeks; season with freshly grated horseradish to taste.

6. Pour the leek mixture into the baked pie shell. Place the sausage links in position on top of the leek mixture, like spokes of a wheel, and top with the round of pastry. Reheat the pie for about ten minutes.

Yield: Six servings.

LEEKS VINAIGRETTE

8 to 12 leeks
Water to cover
Salt to taste

1 cup vinaigrette sauce (page 228)

1. Cut off the tops of the leeks, leaving one to two inches of green part. Use the leek tops for other purposes, such as in soup. Cut the stalks in half to within half an inch of the root end. Rinse leeks thoroughly in cold water to remove sand.

2. Make neat bundles of leeks and tie them with string to keep them from falling apart as they cook. Place them in a saucepan or kettle, cover with water and add salt. Simmer, partly covered, until the leeks are tender, twenty to forty minutes, depending on their size. Drain and chill until ready to serve.

3. Arrange leeks on chilled plates. Serve cold vinaigrette sauce separately or spooned over the leeks.

Yield: Four servings.

LEEKS AU GRATIN

4 tablespoons butter
4 tablespoons flour
2 cups milk
Salt and freshly ground black
    pepper to taste
Nutmeg to taste

1 egg yolk, slightly beaten
10 nice-sized leeks
Water
½ cup cubed Gruyère cheese
½ cup finely grated Gruyère
    cheese

1. Preheat the oven to 350 degrees.

2. Melt the butter and stir in the flour, using a wire whisk. When blended add the milk, stirring vigorously with the whisk. When the mixture is thickened and smooth, continue cooking, stirring frequently, for ten or fifteen minutes. Season with salt, pepper and nutmeg.

3. Remove the saucepan from the heat and, stirring rapidly, add the egg yolk. Set aside until ready to use.

4. Meanwhile, trim off the roots of the leeks. Trim off part of the green top. Cut through the leeks to within half an inch of the root end. Slit through but leave the half inch of root end intact. Carefully wash the leeks, separating the leaves, under cold running water to remove the sand. Dry briefly and tie the leeks into bunches, three or four to a bunch. Place them in a suitable kettle and cover with cold water. Add salt to taste and simmer until leeks are tender.

5. Drain the leeks. Remove the string and cut the leeks in half halfway between the root end and the leaf end.

6. Butter a casserole generously and cover the bottom with the cooked leaf ends.

7. Combine the cubed cheese with the sauce and spoon half the sauce over the casserole. Neatly arrange the cooked root ends over the sauce. Add the remaining sauce and sprinkle with the grated cheese. Bake until the casserole is bubbly and top is brown. If necessary, run the casserole under the broiler briefly to finish the browning.

Yield: Four to six servings.

POLENTA WITH LEEK GRAVY

1 cup finely chopped leeks
¼ cup (one-half stick) butter
½ cup fine soft bread crumbs
¾ pound salami, cut into six
  slices

2 cups water
Salt and freshly ground black
  pepper to taste
4 cups hot polenta

1. Sauté the chopped leeks in the butter until limp.

2. Add the bread crumbs, mix and add the salami. Brown lightly and add the water. Season with salt and pepper. Simmer, covered, forty-five minutes, adding more water if needed.

3. Turn the hot polenta onto a plate and cover with the leek gravy.

Yield: Four to six servings.

Mace

MACE is the outer coating, the aril as it were, of the nutmeg seed. In its natural state it is of a reddish hue but as it dries for commercial use it develops a light orange color.

The odor of mace, which is mild and fragrant, is not surprisingly like that of nutmeg and the uses of the two spices are similar. Mace complements cherry dishes and those made of chocolate in particular. It is a common ingredient for cakes and cookies, for pickles and preserves.

JELLIED VEAL

4 veal shanks, split
2 quarts plus one-quarter
  cup water
⅛ teaspoon freshly ground
  black pepper
1 teaspoon salt
1 bay leaf
1 blade of mace

1 envelope unflavored
  gelatin
2 ribs celery, minced
1 carrot, cooked and minced
1 tablespoon minced green
  pepper
8 sprigs parsley, minced
1 teaspoon cut chervil

1. Combine the veal shanks with two quarts of the water, the pepper, salt, bay leaf and mace. Bring to a boil and simmer slowly, covered, three hours.

2. Soften the gelatin in the quarter cup of water and stir it into the hot liquid in which the meat cooked. Remove the meat from the stock and cut it into shreds. Discard the bone. Let the kettle liquid cool but not jell.

3. Combine the shredded veal with the vegetables and herbs. Strain the cooled kettle liquid over the mixture and pour into a two-and-one-half-quart mold. Chill until jelled.

4. Unmold and garnish with salad greens. Serve with mayonnaise, if desired.

Yield: Eight to ten servings.

MACE-LEMON SOUFFLÉ PIE

4 eggs, separated
¾ cup sugar
½ teaspoon ground mace
¼ cup lemon juice

1 teaspoon grated lemon rind
1 teaspoon vanilla
Dash of salt
1 baked nine-inch pie shell

1. Preheat the oven to 325 degrees.

2. In the top of a double boiler mix the egg yolks, one-quarter cup of the sugar, the mace and lemon juice. Cook, stirring, over hot (not boiling) water until the mixture has thickened. Remove from the heat.

3. Mix in the lemon rind and vanilla. Add the salt to the egg whites and beat them until stiff but not dry. Gradually beat in the remaining half cup of sugar. Fold into the hot lemon mixture.

4. Turn into prepared shell and bake until golden brown, about thirty minutes. Cool.

Yield: Eight servings.

ALMOND-MACE CAKE

2 cups sifted all-purpose flour	1 cup sugar
1 teaspoon baking powder	3 eggs
¾ teaspoon ground mace	⅔ cup milk
¼ teaspoon salt	Almond-mace cream frosting
½ cup (one stick) butter	(recipe follows)

1. Preheat the oven to 350 degrees. Grease and lightly flour two round nine-inch cake pans.

2. Sift together the flour and baking powder. Set aside

3. Add the mace and salt to the butter and cream well. Gradually blend in the sugar. Beat in the eggs, one at a time. Add the flour mixture alternately with the milk. Beat half a minute.

4. Turn the batter into prepared pans and bake until a cake tester inserted in the center comes out clean, about twenty-five minutes.

5. Remove cake layers from the oven and cool in pans ten minutes. Turn out onto wire racks to finish cooling. Spread almond-mace cream frosting between layers and over top and sides of cake.

Yield: Eight to ten servings.

ALMOND-MACE CREAM FROSTING

⅛ teaspoon salt	½ cup chopped blanched almonds
2 egg whites	
¾ cup sugar	½ teaspoon ground mace
½ cup heavy cream, whipped	¼ teaspoon almond extract

Add the salt to the egg whites and beat until they stand in stiff peaks. Gradually beat in the sugar. Fold in the whipped cream, almonds, mace and almond extract.

BREAD PUDDING WITH RAISINS

3½ cups milk
¼ cup (one-half stick) butter, melted
2 cups dry bread crumbs or cubed stale bread
½ cup sugar
2 eggs, lightly beaten

½ cup sweet sherry
1½ teaspoons mace
1 teaspoon cinnamon
1 cup seedless raisins
½ cup thinly sliced citron (optional)

1. Preheat the oven to 375 degrees.
2. Scald the milk, add the butter and pour the hot liquid over the bread crumbs or cubes. Soak about five minutes, then add the sugar, eggs, sherry, spices, raisins and citron.
3. Pour the mixture into a buttered baking dish. Set the dish in a pan of hot water and bake until a knife inserted in the center comes out clean, about one hour.

Yield: Six servings.

MACE-PINEAPPLE CHARLOTTE

Ladyfingers, split
1 twenty-ounce can crushed pineapple, drained
Water
2 envelopes unflavored gelatin
3 eggs, separated
¾ cup plus two tablespoons sugar

1 teaspoon ground mace
¼ teaspoon salt
1 cup milk
½ teaspoon grated lemon rind
2 cups heavy cream
Additional ground mace for garnish

1. Line a nine-inch spring-form pan with ladyfingers. Set aside.

2. Drain the juice from the can of pineapple into a measuring cup. Set the pineapple aside for use later. Add water to the juice in the measuring cup to make one-half cup liquid. Add the gelatin to the liquid, mix well and let stand to soften.

3. Combine the egg yolks, three-quarters cup of the sugar, the teaspoon of mace and the salt in the top of a double boiler or in a saucepan. Blend in the milk. Cook, stirring, over hot (not boiling) water or low heat until the mixture coats a metal spoon. Remove from the heat and stir in the softened gelatin and grated lemon rind. Chill until the mixture begins to thicken. Fold in the drained pineapple.

4. Beat the egg whites until they stand in soft peaks, then gradually beat in the remaining two tablespoons sugar. Whip one cup of the cream. Fold the beaten egg whites and the whipped cream into the pineapple mixture. Turn into the ladyfinger-lined pan. Chill until firm.

5. Whip the remaining cup of cream and spread over the top of the charlotte. Garnish with ground mace.

Yield: Eight to ten servings.

Marjoram

The word MARJORAM (MAR-joram) derives from two Greek words which mean the "joy of the mountain." Isn't that a glorious thought? Marjoram is an aromatic herb and belongs to the mint family. Marjoram is enormously versatile and it enhances such dishes as soups, sauces, stuffings and stews; it also gives sum and substance to cooked vegetables and meat pies. One enthusiast states that marjoram should be used in all dishes made with lamb and mutton from a simple roast to a casserole.

Marjoram symbolizes blushes.

ROAST LAMB WITH HERBS

½ cup olive oil
Juice of one lemon
1 medium onion, chopped
¼ cup chopped parsley
1 teaspoon salt
½ teaspoon freshly ground black pepper

1 tablespoon marjoram
½ teaspoon thyme
½ teaspoon caraway seed
1 clove garlic, crushed
1 six-pound leg of lamb

1. Combine the olive oil, lemon juice, onion, parsley and seasonings. Cut slits in the lamb and rub the marinade into the meat. Wrap the lamb in heavy aluminum foil and marinate overnight in the refrigerator.

2. Preheat the oven to 325 degrees.

3. Open the foil and place the lamb in a roasting pan. Roast one and one-quarter hours, using the marinade and pan drippings for basting. For rare lamb a meat thermometer should register 140 degrees. If a well-done roast is desired, bake thirty minutes longer, or until thermometer registers 170 degrees.

Yield: Six to eight servings.

HOMEMADE KIELBASA (POLISH SAUSAGE)

3 pounds pork
1 pound veal
1 tablespoon crushed
    marjoram

2 cloves garlic, finely minced
4 teaspoons salt
1 teaspoon freshly ground
    black pepper

1. Coarsely grind together the pork and veal. Add the remaining ingredients and mix very thoroughly. Stuff into sausage casings.

2. Cover the sausage with water and bake in a preheated 350-degree oven until the water has completely evaporated. To serve, fry as any sausage. Often onion is fried with it.

Yield: Four pounds sausage.

BEANS À LA GRECQUE

1 pound dried white beans
Water
½ cup olive oil
3 or four cloves garlic,
    minced
4 or five medium onions,
    thickly sliced
½ teaspoon marjoram
¼ teaspoon thyme

1 bay leaf, crumbled
2 tablespoons minced fresh
    parsley
4 to six fresh tomatoes,
    peeled and diced, or one
    large can (one pound four-
    teen ounces) tomatoes
1 teaspoon salt, or more to
    taste

1. Soak the beans overnight in water to cover. Or boil two minutes, cover and let stand one hour. Drain thoroughly and wash with cold water.

2. Heat the olive oil in a heavy pot or Dutch oven. Add the garlic, onions and herbs and cook until the onions are soft but not brown. Add the tomatoes and simmer until well blended and saucelike.

3. Add the drained beans and enough water to reach just to the top of the beans. Bring to a boil, then turn the heat as low as possible and simmer, covered, one hour. Add the salt, remove the cover and simmer one hour longer.

Yield: Four to six servings.

Mint

To coin a phrase, MINT has more uses than money. It is excellent with vegetables, such as carrots and peas, it cools the palate when blended with yoghurt and it adds an interesting touch to mixed green salads. Some will contest the notion that mint jelly complements lamb but it surely is a question of taste.

Mint has several enchanting country names, including spearmint, heartmint, mackerel mint, spire mint, garden mint, lamb mint and sage of Bethlehem. With its fresh, mountain-spring flavor, small wonder that it symbolizes virtue.

ICED CUCUMBER AND MINT SOUP

3 cucumbers
Salt
3 tablespoons sweet butter
1 yellow onion,
  finely chopped
White pepper

3 tablespoons rice flour, or
  two tablespoons all-purpose flour
2 cups water
2 tablespoons finely chopped
  fresh mint
1¼ cups light cream
1 cup heavy cream, whipped

1. Peel the cucumbers and reserve half of one. Slice the remaining cucumbers fine, put them on a platter and sprinkle with salt. Let stand thirty minutes.

2. Melt the butter in a heavy pan. Add the onion and season to taste with salt and pepper. Cook slowly three minutes without browning.

3. Wash the salted cucumbers in cold water, drain and dry on paper towels. Add to the onion and cook slowly, covered, until the cucumbers are just soft.

4. Remove the pan from the heat and mix in the flour and two cups water. Return to the heat, stirring until the mixture comes to a boil. Simmer five minutes. Rub through a fine sieve. Add the mint and chill thoroughly.

5. Mix in the light cream and the whipped cream. Cut the reserved cucumber into fine shreds and add to the soup.

Yield: Four to six servings.

GREEN PEAS WITH MINT

1 package frozen green peas
  (preferably petits pois)
Butter

1 teaspoon chopped fresh
  mint or one-half teaspoon
  dried mint

Cook the green peas according to package directions and do not overcook. Season with butter and sprinkle with the mint. Cover and keep warm until ready to serve.

Yield: Four servings.

PERSIAN MUST

1 cup yoghurt
2 sprigs fresh mint, chopped,
   or one-half teaspoon dried
   mint
1 cucumber, peeled and
   grated

1 scallion, trimmed and
   chopped
1 tablespoon dried currants
Salt and freshly ground black
   pepper to taste

1. If desired, drain the yoghurt briefly in cheesecloth.
2. Combine yoghurt with remaining ingredients in a mixing bowl. Chill until serving time. Serve as a side dish with highly spiced foods.

Yield: About two cups.

FRESH MINT CHUTNEY

2 cups finely chopped fresh
   mint leaves
1/3 cup chopped onion
3 tablespoons lemon juice

3/4 teaspoon salt
1 tablespoon sugar
1/4 teaspoon cayenne

1. Combine the mint leaves, onion and lemon juice in the container of an electric blender. If a blender is not available, chop fine with a sharp knife.
2. Add seasonings and blend fifteen seconds or mix well with a spoon. Chill and serve.

Yield: Three-quarters cup.

Note: This chutney will keep several days if stored in the refrigerator.

MINTED CANTALOUPE AND BLUEBERRIES

1/2 cup sugar
1 cup water
1 tablespoon chopped fresh
   mint

1 cup fresh blueberries
2 cups cantaloupe balls (one
   and one-half cantaloupes)
Fresh mint sprigs

1. Combine the sugar, water and mint in a saucepan. Bring to the boiling point and boil three minutes. Strain and chill.

2. Add the blueberries and cantaloupe balls to the syrup. Serve in sherbet glasses, garnished with sprigs of fresh mint.

Yield: Six servings.

LIME-MINT SHERBET

12 sprigs mint	2 teaspoons grated lime rind
2 cups water	½ cup lime juice
¾ cup sugar	Green food coloring
½ cup light corn syrup	2 egg whites, stiffly beaten

1. Set the freezer control for fast freezing.

2. Pick mint leaves from the stems and chop. Add the water and sugar to the chopped leaves and boil, stirring, until the sugar has dissolved. Let stand and cool. Strain.

3. Add the corn syrup, lime rind and juice and enough coloring to give a delicate tint. Pour into the freezing tray and freeze until firm.

4. Remove the mixture to a bowl and break up the lumps with a wooden spoon. Beat until almost smooth but still a thick mush. Fold in the beaten egg whites, return to the tray and freeze until firm.

Yield: Six servings.

PINEAPPLE-MINT SHERBET

1 envelope unflavored gelatin	1 teaspoon grated lemon rind
1¼ cups water	1 cup milk
¾ cup sugar	1½ cups pineapple juice
½ cup light corn syrup	2 tablespoons lemon juice
½ cup lightly packed crushed mint leaves	Green food coloring
	2 egg whites

1. Soften the gelatin in one-quarter cup of the water.

2. Boil together for two minutes the remaining cup water, sugar, syrup, mint and lemon rind. Add the gelatin and cool to room temperature.

3. Add the milk, pineapple and lemon juices. Color a light green and freeze in a two-quart metal pan.

4. Beat the egg whites. Break up the frozen mixture, turn it into a mixer or other bowl and beat until very fluffy and soft but not melted. Fold in the egg whites. Return to the pan and freeze until firm.

Yield: About two quarts.

Whenever a recipe for mint julep appears in public print it is generally time to duck. There must be as many recipes for this traditional American drink as there are Kentucky thoroughbreds.

MINT JULEP

Wash well several sprigs of fresh mint.

By preference, select a fourteen- or sixteen-ounce silver julep cup or use a large Old-Fashioned glass. Place four or five sprigs of mint on the bottom and sprinkle with a teaspoon of sugar or more to taste. Add just enough (branch) water to dissolve the sugar. Muddle the mint until it is well bruised and until the sugar is dissolved. Remove the mint or not according to personal preference. Fill the glass three-fourths full with crushed ice and pour in two jiggers of Kentucky bourbon (some wayward souls have been known to use rye or cognac) and garnish with one or two additional bushy mint sprigs.

Mustard

The uses of MUSTARD are broad. Since earliest times it has been prized as a condiment as well as a digestive stimulant. It is said that more than two thousand years ago the Greeks dined on the tender leaves of the mustard plant and ground the seeds to a powder for use with roasts and seafood. Mustard seeds today are used principally in pickling and in salad dressings. Mustard powder gives piquancy to sauces and dressings and can be made into a sharp, delicious paste merely by the addition of water or milk, dry white wine or beer. When so made the paste should be allowed to stand fifteen minutes or so to let the flavor develop. In some minds steaks and chops become more interesting if they are sprinkled with powdered mustard before broiling.

There are dozens of kinds of prepared mustards now on the market and most connoisseurs consider the prepared mustards of Dijon or Düsseldorf to be among the finest.

Of all things, mustard symbolizes indifference.

CELERY ROOT RÉMOULADE

2 medium celery knobs   1 tablespoon Dijon or Düs-
¾ cup mayonnaise   seldorf mustard
                         Lemon juice to taste

1. Pare the celery knobs. Cut them into slices about one-six-teenth inch thick and cut the slices into strips as thin as or thinner than toothpicks.

2. Combine the mayonnaise, mustard and lemon juice. Add the celery knob strips and let stand in the refrigerator until serving time. Serve as an appetizer or first course.

Yield: Four to six servings.

PORK CHOPS CHARCUTIÈRE

6 lean pork chops   ¾ cup dry white wine
Salt and freshly ground black 1½ cups brown sauce (page
  pepper   4) or canned beef gravy
2 tablespoons vegetable or   2 tablespoons cold butter
  peanut oil   1 tablespoon Dijon or Düs-
¼ cup each finely chopped   seldorf mustard
  shallots and onion (or all 3 small sour gherkins, cut
  onion)   into julienne strips

1. Trim the pork chops, leaving a quarter-inch layer of fat. Sprinkle with salt and pepper.

2. Heat the oil in a skillet and brown the chops on all sides. Cook the chops twenty minutes, or until cooked through. Transfer to a warm platter and pour off and discard all but one table-spoon of fat from the skillet. Add the shallots and onion to the skillet and cook, stirring, two minutes.

3. Add the wine to the skillet and stir to dissolve brown parti-cles that cling to bottom and sides of pan. Cook until the wine is almost totally reduced. Add the brown sauce and cook about twelve minutes.

4. Turn off the heat and stir in the cold butter. Add the mus-tard and stir. Do not reheat. Add the gherkins. Spoon a little

sauce over each chop and serve the remainder in a sauceboat. Garnish, if desired, with additional gherkins and serve immediately.

Yield: Six servings.

GLAZED VIRGINIA HAM

1 Virginia ham	1 teaspoon dry mustard
Whole cloves	½ cup sweet pickle juice or
1½ cups brown sugar	dry white wine

1. If the ham is too long for a home-size kettle, have the shank end cut off. Scrub the ham thoroughly with a brush, cover it with water and let it stand twelve to eighteen hours.
2. Scrub the ham again and cover with fresh water. Cover the kettle and bring to a boil. Lower the heat and simmer until tender, about twenty minutes to the pound. (If water tastes too salty when ham is half done, change the water.) At the end of the cooking time, remove the ham. The liquid may be reserved for cooking snap beans, cabbage or dried legumes.
3. Preheat the oven to 350 degrees.
4. Skin the ham, score the fat in diamond shapes and stud with cloves. Place on a rack in an open roasting pan.
5. Mix the sugar, mustard and pickle juice and spread over the ham. Bake until well glazed, about forty-five minutes, basting several times with drippings in the pan.

Yield: One glazed ham.

KIDNEYS À LA MOUTARDE

2 or three veal kidneys	1 tablespoon finely chopped
Salt and freshly ground black	shallot
pepper to taste	¼ cup dry white wine
3 tablespoons peanut or	1 cup brown sauce (page
vegetable oil	4) or canned beef gravy
¼ cup (one-half stick) butter	1½ tablespoons Dijon or
	Düsseldorf mustard

1. Trim the kidneys but leave a thin layer of fat around them. Split them and trim away the tough center core. Slice thin and sprinkle with salt and pepper.

2. Heat the oil and cook the kidneys quickly, shaking the skillet. They should be browned but rare. Pour into a colander and drain.

3. Wipe the skillet with a cloth or paper towels and add two tablespoons of the butter. Add the shallot and cook briefly. Add the wine and cook until it is almost totally reduced. Add the brown sauce and bring to a boil.

4. Return the kidneys to the sauce and heat through. When the sauce returns to the boil, remove it from the heat and stir in the remaining butter. Add the mustard and, when it is thoroughly blended, serve immediately.

Yield: Three or four servings.

CHICKEN DIJON

2 tablespoons butter
1 two-and-one-half- to three-pound broiling chicken, quartered
1 cup each dry white wine and water
¼ teaspoon dried tarragon leaves
Pinch of thyme
1 bay leaf
½ teaspoon salt
¼ teaspoon freshly ground pepper
2 egg yolks
2 tablespoons prepared Dijon mustard
2 tablespoons sour cream
Pinch of cayenne pepper

1. Heat the butter in a heavy skillet. Add the chicken and brown it well on all sides. Add the wine and water, tarragon, thyme, bay leaf, salt and pepper. Bring to a boil, cover and simmer until the meat is tender, thirty to forty-five minutes. Remove the meat to a heated serving dish and keep it warm.

2. Remove sauce from heat. Discard the bay leaf. Add a little of the sauce to the egg yolks, then stir into the sauce in the skillet and blend well. Add the mustard, sour cream and cayenne. Heat, stirring briskly and constantly, but do not allow to boil. Pour the sauce over the chicken.

Yield: Four servings.

DEVILED OYSTERS

1 pint oysters
3 shallots or one small onion, minced
½ cup chopped mushrooms
3 tablespoons butter
3 tablespoons flour
½ cup light cream
Tabasco to taste
1 to two teaspoons prepared mustard
1 teaspoon Worcestershire sauce (optional)
1 teaspoon minced parsley
Salt and pepper to taste
1 egg yolk, slightly beaten
¼ cup fine bread crumbs, buttered

1. Pick over the oysters to remove any shell. Chop the oysters. Preheat the oven to 400 degrees.

2. Sauté the shallots or onion and mushrooms in the butter, stirring, for two to three minutes. Blend in the flour, add the cream and cook, stirring, until thickened.

3. Add the Tabasco, mustard, Worcestershire, parsley, oysters and salt and pepper to taste.

4. Simmer the mixture, stirring, for one minute. Add a little of the hot mixture to the egg yolk while stirring. Combine with the sauce and mix well.

5. Turn into scallop shells and cover with the buttered crumbs. Bake fifteen minutes.

Yield: Six to eight first-course servings.

SHRIMP IN MUSTARD SAUCE

36 raw shrimp, in the shell
Boiling water
Salt to taste
1 lemon slice
2 sprigs parsley
1 bay leaf
½ teaspoon dried thyme
1 tablespoon Dijon or Düsseldorf mustard
3 tablespoons lemon juice
¾ cup olive oil
1 tablespoon chopped fresh tarragon or one teaspoon dried tarragon

1. Place the shrimp in a saucepan and cover them with boiling water. Add salt, lemon slice, parsley, bay leaf and thyme. Bring

to a boil and cook four to six minutes, depending on the size of the shrimp. Drain and chill. Peel and devein the shrimp.

2. Place the mustard in a bowl and add lemon juice. Beat with a wire whisk, adding the oil a little at a time. Add salt to taste and tarragon. Pour over the shrimp and marinate one or two hours. Stir before serving.

Yield: Six servings.

DAL

1 pound dried split peas
5 cups water
2 teaspoons salt
½ to one teaspoon curry powder
1 cup canned Italian peeled tomatoes, or four medium fresh tomatoes, peeled and chopped
2 medium onions, chopped
2 tablespoons mustard seed
¼ cup vegetable oil
1 clove garlic, minced

1. Combine the peas, water, salt, curry powder, tomatoes and onions. Bring to a boil and simmer, covered, about forty-five minutes, or until the peas are tender and the consistency is that of thick pea soup.

2. Add the remaining ingredients and simmer ten minutes longer. This dish can be kept several days in the refrigerator and reheated, adding a little water each time. Serve as a side dish with curried foods.

Yield: Eight or more servings.

MUSTARD CABBAGE

2 pounds (one large head) Chinese cabbage
2 tablespoons dry mustard
½ teaspoon salt
2 tablespoons soy sauce
2 teaspoons vinegar

1. Discard any tough outer leaves of the cabbage. Cut the remainder into one-inch slices across the head and boil in water to cover one minute. Drain.

2. Mix the remaining ingredients, add the cabbage, toss to coat the vegetable evenly, cover and cool. Serve well chilled.

Yield: Five servings.

SPINACH SALAD WITH MUSTARD DRESSING

½ pound fresh spinach
1 teaspoon Dijon or Düsseldorf mustard
1 teaspoon grated onion
¼ teaspoon coarsely ground black pepper

½ teaspoon salt
½ cup olive oil
2 tablespoons wine vinegar
¼ teaspoon lemon juice

1. Wash the spinach gently but thoroughly in several changes of cold water. Remove the tough stems and discard them. Dry the leaves carefully and chill.

2. Combine remaining ingredients and beat vigorously with a wire whisk. When ready to serve, pour the sauce over the spinach and toss well.

Yield: Four servings.

HOT PREPARED MUSTARD

To prepare hot mustard combine dry mustard with just enough water, beer or dry white wine to make a smooth paste. Let stand ten minutes to develop flavor.

MUSTARD SALAD DRESSING

1 tablespoon dry mustard, or to taste
3 tablespoons dry white wine
1 egg yolk
½ cup olive or other salad oil

¼ teaspoon salt
1 teaspoon finely chopped chives
1 teaspoon finely chopped parsley
1 tablespoon lemon juice

1. Mix the mustard with the wine and allow the mixture to stand at room temperature ten minutes.
2. Beat the egg yolk into the mustard mixture by hand or electric mixer.
3. Add the oil very slowly while beating vigorously.
4. Fold in the salt, chives, parsley and lemon juice. Chill and use as a dressing for salad greens.

Yield: About one cup.

RÉMOULADE SAUCE

1 teaspoon dry mustard	1 tablespoon capers, drained and chopped
1 teaspoon paprika	
¼ teaspoon salt	2 tablespoons minced scallions
¼ teaspoon freshly ground black pepper	
	2 tablespoons minced chives
⅛ teaspoon cayenne pepper	2 tablespoons minced celery
1 teaspoon horseradish	3 tablespoons wine vinegar
4 anchovies, chopped	½ cup olive oil, or more

1. Combine the dry mustard, paprika, salt, black pepper and cayenne. Shake together in a covered jar to mix well.
2. Add the remaining ingredients and mix well to form a sauce. Add additional olive oil if necessary. Serve with cold shrimp

Yield: About one and one-half cups.

APPLE CHUTNEY

6 medium-size ripe tomatoes, peeled and quartered	2 cups vinegar
	¼ cup salt
2 cups green apples, cut into chunks	4 ounces white mustard seed
	2 ounces preserved ginger, coarsely chopped
2 cups seedless raisins	
1 cup minced onions	⅛ teaspoon cayenne pepper
3⅓ cups brown sugar, packed	

Combine all ingredients and cook slowly, stirring occasionally, three hours. Pack quickly into hot sterilized jars to within one-eighth inch of the top. Seal at once.

Yield: Three pints.

CHOWCHOW

2 cups finely chopped cucumbers
2 cups finely chopped onions
2 cups tiny onions, peeled
1 pound green tomatoes, quartered
2 cups tiny gherkins
8 red peppers, seeded and chopped

2 cups finely chopped celery
½ cup salt
Water
1½ quarts cider vinegar
¼ cup flour
1 cup sugar
1 teaspoon turmeric
3 tablespoons dry mustard

1. In a large mixing bowl combine the vegetables and salt. Add enough water to barely cover.

2. Let stand eight hours or overnight, then drain and rinse in cold water. Drain again.

3. Place vegetables in a preserving kettle and add vinegar. Bring to a boil.

4 Blend the remaining ingredients with enough water or vinegar to make a smooth paste. Stir the paste into the simmering vegetables. Cook five minutes longer, stirring constantly. Pour quickly into hot sterilized jars to within one-eighth inch of the top. Seal at once.

Yield: Two and one-half to three quarts.

CUCUMBER OIL PICKLES

⅓ cup salt
1 quart plus one-half cup water
12 six-inch cucumbers, thinly sliced
2 medium onions, thinly sliced

½ cup sugar
2 cups vinegar
2 tablespoons mustard seed
1 tablespoon celery seed
1½ teaspoons peppercorns
¼ cup olive oil

1. Dissolve the salt in one quart of the water, add the cucumbers and onions and let stand twelve to eighteen hours.

2. Drain the cucumbers. Taste them, and if they are too salty rinse them in cold water.

3. Boil in a six-quart kettle for three minutes the one-half cup water, sugar, vinegar, mustard and celery seeds and the peppercorns.

4. Add the cucumbers, onions and the oil and cook only until the cucumbers begin to look clear but are not soft.

5. Pack boiling hot into hot sterilized jars and seal at once.

Yield: About two quarts.

CUCUMBER RELISH

6 cups coarsely ground or chopped cucumbers	⅔ cup salt Water
2 cups coarsely ground or chopped green pepper	1 quart white or cider vinegar
2 cups coarsely ground or chopped red pepper	1 cup sugar, optional 2 tablespoons mustard seed
1 cup coarsely ground or chopped onion	1 tablespoon celery seed 2 hot red peppers

1. Mix the ground or chopped vegetables with the salt and six cups of water. Let stand about three hours. Drain, rinse in cold water and drain again well.

2. Bring the vinegar, sugar, mustard seed, celery seed and red peppers to a boil in a large pan, stirring until the sugar dissolves. Boil five minutes, add the drained chopped vegetables and return to a boil.

3. Remove from the heat immediately and turn into hot sterilized jars. Seal at once.

Yield: About three quarts.

I am indebted to Ann Seranne for the following outstanding recipe for mustard pickles, which she calls "Favorite Mustard Pickles." Tiny gherkins, which are sometimes difficult to obtain, are essential for perfect results.

MUSTARD PICKLES

2 quarts medium-size cu-
  cumbers
1 quart medium-size onions,
  peeled
6 red peppers, seeded
2 quarts tiny gherkins
2 quarts tiny pickling
  onions, peeled

2 heads cauliflower, broken
  into small flowerets
1½ cups salt
8 cups sugar
8 cups cider vinegar
1½ cups flour
½ cup dry mustard
3 tablespoons turmeric
2 tablespoons celery salt

1. Chop fine the medium-size cucumbers and onions and the red peppers, placing each in a separate bowl. If desired, each may be ground in a food chopper using the medium blade.

2. Also place in separate bowls the gherkins, tiny onions and cauliflower pieces. Sprinkle each vegetable with salt, using about one-fourth cup for each. Cover the gherkins, tiny onions and cauliflower with cold water. Let all vegetables stand overnight.

3. In the morning, drain the chopped vegetables in a sieve or colander. Drain the whole vegetables and dry them on a towel.

4. Combine all vegetables in a preserving kettle, add the sugar and six cups of vinegar and bring the mixture to a boil.

5. Blend the flour, mustard, turmeric and celery salt to a paste with the remaining vinegar. Stir this paste a little at a time into the vegetables and continue stirring until sauce is thickened slightly. Turn into hot sterilized jars and seal immediately.

Yield: About sixteen quarts.

SENFGURKEN

12 large ripe cucumbers
½ cup salt
1 quart cider vinegar
2 pounds sugar
⅓ cup sliced fresh horse-
  radish

4 hot red peppers
¼ cup mustard seed
2 bay leaves
2 pieces stick cinnamon
1 tablespoon whole cloves

1. Peel the cucumbers, cut them in half lengthwise and scrape out the seeds. If desired, cut into quarters. Sprinkle on the salt and let stand overnight.

2. Drain the cucumbers, rinse them in cold water, drain again and dry.

3. Boil for five minutes the vinegar, sugar, horseradish and the spices (which have been tied loosely in a cheesecloth bag). Stir until sugar dissolves.

4. Add cucumbers and return to boiling. Discard the spice bag. Pack the pickles at once into sterilized jars. Seal.

Yield: About two quarts.

Nutmeg

It is said that on the islands where the NUTMEG grows the aroma is so powerful the birds of the air become intoxicated with the scent. Nutmeg is one of the slyest and, used gingerly, most seductive of flavors. It can give stature to such a naïve item as a glass of cold, sweetened milk; yet it is an essential in some of the most glorious custards, pies and cheese dishes.

The nutmeg is a round, slightly oval affair about the size of a modest-size marble. The exterior is slightly furrowed. In her excellent book titled Herbal Delights, *Mrs. C. F. Leyel notes that "the silver graters our grandmothers wore on their chatelaines" were used to make nutmeg tea, which supposedly had restorative powers. There is no question that freshly grated nutmeg is far superior to the commercially ground variety.*

VEAL RONDELLES WITH EGG-AND-LEMON SAUCE

1 pound ground veal
¾ cup fresh bread crumbs
1 egg
1 tablespoon chopped
   parsley
½ teaspoon salt
Freshly ground black pepper
   to taste

½ teaspoon nutmeg, preferably freshly grated
⅓ cup heavy cream
Flour for dredging
2 tablespoons butter
2 tablespoons olive or peanut oil
2 cups egg-and-lemon sauce
   (page 6)

1. Combine the veal, bread crumbs, egg, parsley, salt, pepper, nutmeg and cream in a mixing bowl. Work the mixture lightly with the hands until well blended.

2. Shape the mixture into balls about one and one-half inches in diameter. Dredge with flour.

3. Heat the butter and oil in a large skillet and brown the meat balls on all sides over medium heat. Reduce the heat to low and cook, tossing the meat balls in the skillet occasionally, until done, ten to fifteen minutes. Serve with egg-and-lemon sauce.

Yield: Four to six servings.

Nutmeg does absolute wonders for many cheese dishes. To wit, the following.

CHEESE SOUFFLÉ

3 tablespoons butter
3 tablespoons flour
1 cup milk
Salt to taste
Cayenne pepper to taste
¼ teaspoon nutmeg

2 teaspoons cornstarch
3 tablespoons water
6 eggs, separated
¾ cup coarsely grated Swiss
   or Gruyère cheese, or half
   Swiss and half Parmesan

1. Preheat the oven to 375 degrees.

2. Melt the butter in a saucepan and stir in the flour. Add the milk gradually, stirring with a wire whisk until the mixture is thick and smooth. Add seasonings. Combine the cornstarch and water and add.

3. Beat yolks into sauce. Cook thirty seconds over low heat. Remove; stir in cheese.

4. Beat the egg whites until they stand in peaks. Add half the whites to the sauce and stir quickly. Gently fold in remaining whites.

5. Generously butter a two-and-one-half-quart soufflé dish. Pour in mixture. Bake until puffed and browned, thirty to forty minutes. Serve at once.

Yield: Five servings.

POULETTE CREAM SAUCE

1½ tablespoons butter	½ teaspoon salt
1½ tablespoons flour	⅛ teaspoon freshly ground
1 cup chicken stock	white pepper
1 egg yolk	¼ teaspoon nutmeg
⅓ cup heavy cream	1 teaspoon lemon juice

1. Melt the butter in a saucepan. Add the flour and chicken stock and cook over low heat, beating vigorously with a wire whisk, until the mixture begins to thicken.

2. Combine the egg yolk and cream and add. Continue to cook, stirring constantly, until thickened and smooth. Remove from the heat.

3. Add salt, pepper, nutmeg and lemon juice. Serve hot over cooked cauliflower, asparagus or steamed whole baby turnips.

Yield: About one cup sauce.

RUM CHOCOLATE PIE

1 cup milk	4 tablespoons rum
1/8 teaspoon nutmeg	1 nine-inch pie crust, baked
2 eggs, separated	and cooled
1/3 cup plus one tablespoon	1/2 pound milk chocolate
sugar	3 tablespoons cold water
1/8 teaspoon salt	1 1/2 cups heavy cream,
2 teaspoons unflavored gela-	whipped
tin, softened in two table-	1/2 teaspoon vanilla
spoons water	

1. Heat the milk and nutmeg in the top of a double boiler.

2. Beat the egg yolks, one-third cup sugar and salt until light. Pour the hot milk over the egg yolks, stirring well. Return to the double boiler and stir until thick. Remove from the heat and stir in the gelatin. Place the pan on cracked ice and cool the mixture.

3. Add three tablespoons rum. When the mixture thickens, fold in the beaten egg whites. Pour into pie shell.

4. Place the chocolate and water in a double boiler. Stir until the chocolate melts. Cool slightly. Add half the whipped cream and the remaining tablespoon rum.

5. To the remaining whipped cream, add the remaining table-spoon sugar and the vanilla. Spread over the pie. Cover this cream layer with the chocolate mixture. Chill.

Yield: Six to eight servings.

NUTMEG CAKE

2 cups brown sugar	1 cup sour cream
2 cups sifted flour	1 teaspoon baking soda
1/2 cup shortening	1/2 cup chopped walnuts, pe-
1 egg	cans or almonds
1 teaspoon nutmeg	

1. Preheat the oven to 350 degrees.

2. With the fingers, blend the sugar with flour and shortening until crumbs form.

3. Place half the crumbs in a greased nine-inch square pan one and one-half inches deep. Add the egg to the remaining crumbs along with the nutmeg and sour cream mixed with the soda. Pour this batter into the pan and sprinkle with nuts. Bake thirty-five to forty minutes. Serve hot or cold.

Yield: Ten to twelve servings.

RICE PUDDING

½ cup seedless raisins
2 tablespoons rum
1 teaspoon lemon juice
Grated rind of one lemon
¼ cup uncooked rice
2 cups milk

¼ teaspoon salt
2 tablespoons butter
2 eggs, separated
⅓ cup sugar
Nutmeg

1. Put the raisins in a bowl with the rum, lemon juice and rind. Let stand several hours or overnight.

2. Cook the rice, milk and salt in the top of a double boiler over gently boiling water until the rice is tender, about one hour, stirring frequently with a fork.

3. Remove the rice from the heat and stir in the butter.

4. Beat the egg yolks lightly. Pour the hot rice mixture into the yolks slowly, stirring vigorously. Cool. Add the raisins.

5. Preheat the oven to 325 degrees.

6. Beat the egg whites until stiff, adding the sugar gradually. Gently fold into the rice mixture.

7. Pour into a greased one-quart casserole and sprinkle generously with nutmeg. Set in a pan of hot water and bake thirty minutes.

Yield: Four servings.

The following is one of the most incredible of drinks, one of the richest of eggnogs. Many people who regard eggnog as a creation of the Borgias can tolerate this one. It is the recipe of Blanche Knopf, who attributes it to John Kilar.

BLANCHE KNOPF'S EGGNOG

12 eggs, separated	1 cup dark Jamaican rum
1½ cups powdered sugar	1 quart heavy cream,
1 quart milk	whipped
1 bottle (a standard fifth)	1 orange
cognac, bourbon or rye	1 lemon
whiskey	Powdered nutmeg

1. Combine the egg yolks and sugar and beat to the ribbon stage, which is to say until lemon colored and quite thick.

2. Stir in the milk and spirits.

3. Beat the egg whites until stiff and fold in. Chill in the refrigerator four hours.

4. Whip the cream and fold it into the eggnog.

5. Meanwhile, carefully peel the orange, discarding the white pulp but reserving the extreme outer rind. Cut this rind into tiny, needle-like strips. Grate the lemon rind. Stir both the orange and lemon rind into the eggnog and serve the drink sprinkled with nutmeg.

Yield: Thirty or more servings.

DAUPHIN POTATOES AU GRATIN

1 clove garlic, split	Salt and freshly ground pepper to taste
3 tablespoons butter, at room temperature	½ teaspoon nutmeg, or to taste
2 large Idaho or Maine potatoes	1 cup (approximately) heavy cream
Milk	

1. Preheat the oven to 300 degrees.

2. Rub a one-quart baking dish with the cut sides of the garlic, then discard. Butter the dish and set aside.

3. Peel the potatoes and cut them into thin, uniform slices less than one-quarter inch thick. As the potatoes are sliced, drop them into a basin of cold water. Drain and pat the slices dry on clean toweling.

4. Place potatoes in a large saucepan and add the milk to barely cover. Add salt, pepper and half the nutmeg and bring to a boil. Simmer, covered, until most of the milk is absorbed, about ten minutes.

5. Make one layer of potato slices in the prepared baking dish and sprinkle lightly with salt, pepper and nutmeg. Pour in half the cream. Add another layer of potatoes, salt, pepper and nutmeg. Add the remaining cream.

6. Bake until the cream is completely reduced and the top is golden brown. For a brown crust on the bottom of the dish, place the dish directly on a rack in the oven. If you wish the bottom to remain soft, place the dish in a larger utensil, pour boiling water around the dish and bake.

Yield: Six to eight servings.

CARROT PURÉE

8 medium-size or twelve small-size carrots, trimmed and scraped
Salt to taste

2 tablespoons butter
Freshly ground black pepper to taste
Nutmeg to taste

1. Cut the carrots in half or leave them whole. Place them in a saucepan with water to cover. Add salt and bring to a boil. Cook until just tender. Drain.

2. Put the carrots through a food mill or potato ricer and beat in the butter. Add salt, pepper and nutmeg to taste.

Yield: Four servings.

BROCCOLI PURÉE

2 bunches broccoli
Salt
3 tablespoons butter
½ teaspoon grated nutmeg,
  or to taste

3 tablespoons grated Swiss
  cheese
3 tablespoons grated Par-
  mesan cheese

1. Preheat the oven to 350 degrees.
2. Since the size of the broccoli stems varies, cooking time depends a lot on personal judgment. Trim the broccoli as necessary, separating the stems from the flowerets unless the broccoli is quite young and tender. If the stems are large, scrape them with a swivel-bladed knife. Rinse both tops and stems in cold water and drain.
3. Place the broccoli stems in a large saucepan or kettle and add cold water to cover. Add salt to taste. Bring to a boil and simmer five minutes. Add the flowerets and cook until tender. The cooking time will depend on the size and age of the broccoli. When cooked, drain.
4. Put the broccoli through a food mill.
5. Heat the butter in a large saucepan and add the broccoli. Season with nutmeg. Stir to blend. Pour the mixture into a casserole and sprinkle with cheese. Bake until golden on top and bubbling, about twenty minutes.

Yield: Six to eight servings.

BEEF AND MUSHROOMS FLORENTINE

2 tablespoons butter
2 tablespoons olive oil
2 cups finely chopped onion
1 clove garlic, finely minced
1 pound ground round steak
½ pound thinly sliced fresh
  mushrooms

1 pound fresh spinach,
  rinsed, drained well and
  coarsely chopped
2 eggs, well beaten
¼ teaspoon nutmeg
Salt and freshly ground pepper to taste

1. In a large skillet, heat the butter and oil. Add the onion and garlic and cook until the onion is wilted. Add the beef, breaking up the lumps with the side of a metal spoon. Add the mushrooms and cook until much of the moisture evaporates.

2. Stir in the spinach and when it wilts, add the eggs, nutmeg, salt and pepper. Cook, stirring, until they are blended throughout and set. Do not overcook.

Yield: Four servings.

Onions

One sage has noted that if the ONION were not quite so common it would be the most coveted of vegetables. It is probably true since it may be the groundwork for flavoring more main dishes than any other single ingredient barring butter, salt and pepper. Legend says that when the Pyramids were abuilding onions with the value of nine tons of gold were used to pay the laborers. Onions are delicious whether used raw in sandwiches, in a cream sauce or as a subtle ingredient in a thousand or more sauces and casseroles.

CHOPPED CHICKEN LIVERS

1 pound chicken livers
2 medium onions
2 eggs
1 very small piece of garlic

3 tablespoons rendered
chicken fat, homemade
or purchased
1 teaspoon salt
¼ teaspoon freshly ground
black pepper

1. Wash the livers and place in a pan with one onion and water to cover. At the same time, hard-cook the eggs in another pan. Bring the livers to a boil, lower the flame and cook ten minutes. Drain, discard the onion and peel the eggs.
2. Place the livers, eggs, garlic and remaining onion in a large wooden chopping bowl. Chop until smooth and blend in the fat, salt and pepper.
3. Serve immediately, without chilling, surrounded by watercress and cherry tomatoes.

Yield: Six servings.

ONION SOUP

¼ cup butter
4 large onions, sliced tissue
thin
4 cups beef stock
Freshly ground black pepper
to taste

1 teaspoon lemon juice
6 rounds of toast browned
in butter
6 tablespoons grated
Gruyère or Parmesan
cheese

1. Heat the butter in a large saucepan and cook the onions in it until tender, stirring frequently.
2. Add the stock and pepper and simmer five to ten minutes. Add the lemon juice.
3. To serve, ladle the soup into six individual casseroles, top

each with a toast round and sprinkle with cheese. Brown under the broiler until cheese bubbles.

Yield: Six servings.

BLANQUETTE OF LAMB

2½ pounds lamb shoulder, cut into two-inch cubes
1 onion studded with two cloves
Salt and freshly ground black pepper
¼ teaspoon thyme
Boiling water

15 to eighteen mushrooms
½ cup (one stick) butter
Lemon juice
24 small white onions, peeled
¼ cup flour
2 egg yolks, lightly beaten
½ cup heavy cream

1. Place the meat cubes in a deep kettle with the onion studded with cloves, one teaspoon salt, one-half teaspoon pepper and the thyme. Cover with boiling water, place a lid on the pan and simmer gently until the meat is tender, about one and one-half hours.

2. Meanwhile, remove the stems from the mushrooms and sauté the caps in one-quarter cup of the butter. Add a dash of lemon juice and salt and cook until the caps are just tender.

3. Cook the small white onions in just enough salted water to cover until they are barely done. Do not overcook.

4. When the meat is tender, remove it to a hot platter and keep it warm.

5. Let the broth from the meat cook down over high heat five minutes. Strain it. Add the liquid from the onions and any juice from the mushrooms. There should be two cups of stock. If not, add sufficient broth or consommé to make two cups.

6. Melt the remaining one-quarter cup butter in a saucepan. Blend in the flour and gradually stir in the stock. Continue cooking, stirring constantly, until it is thickened and smooth. Season to taste with salt and pepper.

7. Combine the egg yolks with the heavy cream. Add a little of the sauce to the egg-yolk mixture, then return the whole to

the saucepan and cook, stirring, until heated through. Do not allow the sauce to boil.

8. Add a dash of lemon juice to the sauce and pour over the meat. Surround with the onions and mushrooms and serve with buttered noodles.

Yield: Four servings.

EMS NIELSEN'S CHICKEN BREASTS

6 chicken breasts, skinned and boned whole	¼ cup cognac
1 quart boiling chicken broth	1 tablespoon flour
10 tablespoons butter	½ teaspoon salt
3 large onions, sliced as thin as possible	¼ teaspoon white pepper
	¼ to one-third cup thick cream, depending on thickness of sauce desired
	2 medium truffles, peeled

1. Place chicken breasts in heavy saucepan or kettle and cover with broth. Add six tablespoons of the butter. Cover and simmer thirty minutes, or until done. Drain; keep warm and reserve stock.

2. Meanwhile, in heavy saucepan cook onions with two tablespoons of butter for fifteen minutes. Cook over lowest possible heat to keep onions hot—they must not brown. Stir occasionally.

3. After ten minutes' cooking time, add cognac. Sprinkle with flour and cook three minutes longer. Stir in salt and pepper. Add three-quarters cup of reserved chicken stock and simmer from one to one and one-quarter hours, keeping the mixture as white as possible.

4. Rub onion mixture through fine sieve or purée in blender. Place into top of double boiler over hot water and add cream. Taste the mixture and correct the seasonings if necessary. Add remaining butter and stir until melted. Coat chicken breasts with part of the onion sauce and decorate with truffle cutouts.

5. Place breasts on platter and surround with baby peas and carrots and small browned potatoes. Serve remaining sauce separately.

Yield: Six servings.

BEANS À LA CHARENTE

1 pound dried white beans	¼ cup (one-half stick) butter
1 onion studded with two cloves	¾ cup chopped onion
	2 cups tomato purée
1 clove garlic	¼ cup chopped parsley
½ teaspoon thyme	2 teaspoons salt, or to taste
1 bay leaf	¼ cup cognac

1. Soak the beans overnight in water to cover. Or boil two minutes, cover and let stand one hour.

2. Add the onion studded with cloves, garlic, thyme and bay leaf to the beans. Bring to a boil and simmer until the beans are tender, one to three hours. Drain the beans but reserve one cup of the cooking liquid. Discard the onion, garlic and bay leaf.

3. Melt the butter and cook the chopped onion in it until tender. Add the tomato purée, parsley, salt, cognac and reserved bean liquid. Simmer thirty minutes, then combine with the beans. Bring to a boil and serve hot. Leftover beans may be refrigerated and reheated.

Yield: Six servings.

ONIONS WITH CHICKEN-LIVER STUFFING

6 large onions	½ cup cream
Salted water	2 cups cooked rice
1 pound chicken livers	Salt and freshly ground black pepper
4 tablespoons butter	
1 small onion, grated	6 strips bacon, halved
1 egg, lightly beaten	

1. Peel the large onions and cut a slice from the top of each. Boil the onions in salted water until almost tender, about twenty minutes. Drain and remove centers to make shells about one-half inch thick. Invert to drain. Chop the centers and drain.

2. Preheat the oven to 375 degrees.

3. Brown the livers in half the butter; chop them.

4. Cook the grated and chopped onion, egg, cream, rice, salt and pepper to taste in remaining butter two minutes. Mix with the liver.

5. Fill the onion shells with the liver mixture and cross bacon strips on top. Bake thirty minutes.

Yield: Six servings.

ONION SOUFFLÉ

6 tablespoons butter	½ teaspoon freshly ground
4 tablespoons flour	pepper
1 cup milk	8 egg yolks
1 teaspoon salt	½ cup chopped onion
	10 egg whites

1. Preheat the oven to 375 degrees.

2. Melt four tablespoons (one-half stick) of the butter in a saucepan and stir in the flour. When the mixture is blended add the milk, stirring vigorously with a wire whisk. Season with salt and pepper. When the mixture is thickened and smooth, remove from the heat and cool slightly. The sauce should be fairly stiff.

3. Beat the egg yolks lightly and stir them into the sauce. Return to the heat briefly but do not boil.

4. Meanwhile, cook the onion in the remaining butter until wilted. Put the onion through a food chopper or food mill, then stir into the sauce.

5. Beat the egg whites until stiff. Stir half the egg whites into the sauce with a wire whisk. Fold the mixture into the remaining egg whites with a rubber spatula or wooden spoon.

6. Generously butter a two-quart soufflé dish and pour the mixture into it.

7. Bake the soufflé for thirty to thirty-five minutes, until well puffed and browned. Serve immediately.

Yield: Six servings.

STEAMED ONIONS IN VINAIGRETTE SAUCE

Boiling water
30 small white onions, unpeeled

Chicken broth or bouillon
Vinaigrette sauce (page 228)

1. Pour boiling water over the onions and let stand five minutes.
2. Peel the onions and place them in a saucepan with stock one inch deep. Bring to the boiling point and cook uncovered six minutes.
3. Cover and continue cooking until the onions are crisp tender, about fifteen minutes. Drain and serve with vinaigrette sauce.

Yield: Six servings.

ORANGE-AND-ONION SALAD

2 large oranges
2 large red Italian onions
¼ cup olive oil
1 tablespoon orange juice

1 tablespoon lemon juice
Salt and freshly ground black
    pepper to taste
Dash of rosemary

1. Peel the oranges and onions and cut them into thin slices. Arrange the sliced oranges alternately with the sliced onions on a large platter or salad plate.
2. Mix the olive oil, fruit juices, salt, pepper and rosemary. Pour over the salad.

Yield: Four servings.

BACON-AND-ONION BREAD

1 package yeast
1¼ cups lukewarm water
6 teaspoons sugar
4½ cups flour, approximately
⅓ cup non-fat dry milk solids

½ cup minced onion
½ cup (four ounces) minced bacon
1 clove garlic (optional)
¾ teaspoon salt

1. Dissolve the yeast in one-quarter cup of the lukewarm water with one teaspoon of the sugar.

2. Combine the remaining cup of water, the remaining sugar, two cups of the flour and the milk. Add the yeast and mix.

3. Sauté the onion, bacon and garlic, without browning, until almost done. Cool to lukewarm. Discard the garlic.

4. Add the bacon and onion to the sponge. Add the salt and enough of the remaining flour to make a soft dough.

5. Turn onto a floured board and knead until dough is smooth and not sticky. Place in a greased bowl and grease the surface of the dough. Cover and let rise in a warm place (80 to 85 degrees) until double in bulk, about one hour.

6. Shape into two loaves and place in two greased 8 x 4 x 2-inch pans. Grease the tops of the loaves, cover and let rise until double in size, about forty-five minutes.

7. Bake the loaves near the bottom of a preheated 400-degree oven ten minutes. Lower the oven temperature to 350 degrees and bake thirty minutes longer, or until the bread shrinks from the sides of the pans and is well browned.

Yield: Two small loaves.

SHRIMP PROVENÇALE

6 tablespoons olive oil
1 tablespoon red wine
vinegar
½ cup fresh lemon juice
2 cloves garlic, finely
chopped
1 tablespoon Dijon mustard
1 teaspoon salt
1 teaspoon freshly ground
black pepper

2 pounds shrimp, cooked,
shelled and deveined
1 Bermuda onion, thinly
sliced
½ cup black olives, sliced
2 tablespoons chopped
pimento
1 lemon, thinly sliced with
rind
Capers for garnish
Chopped parsley for garnish

1. In a mixing bowl combine the olive oil, wine vinegar, lemon juice, garlic, mustard, salt and pepper and blend well.

2. Add the shrimp, onion slices, olives, pimento and lemon slices. Spoon into an hors d'oeuvre dish and garnish with capers and chopped parsley.

Yield: About twelve appetizer servings.

PINTO BEANS VINAIGRETTE

1 cup dried kidney beans
1 carrot, scraped and sliced
1 small onion, stuck with
four cloves
2 cloves garlic, finely minced
Salt and freshly ground pepper to taste

½ cup finely chopped onion
1 tablespoon coarsely
chopped parsley
9 tablespoons olive oil
3 tablespoons wine vinegar
1 seven-ounce can tuna
packed in oil

1. Soak the beans overnight in cold water to cover.

2. Drain the beans and place them in a large saucepan. Add water to cover to one inch over the top of the beans. Add the carrot, onion stuck with cloves, half the garlic, salt and pepper. Bring to a boil and simmer one to one and one-half hours or until the beans are tender but not mushy. Chill.

3. Drain the beans and place them in a mixing bowl. Add the chopped onion, parsley, salt, pepper, remaining garlic, oil and vinegar. Toss. Cut tuna into bite-size pieces and toss it with the beans. Serve cold.

Yield: Six servings.

Orégano

ORÉGANO (or-AY-gano) is frequently called wild marjoram but savants claim that it is different from the other marjorams in the world of cuisine. Whatever its botanical status it is probably true that orégano has in recent years enjoyed the most profound sudden fame of any herb or spice in America. It has been reckoned that the annual sale of orégano has increased nearly two thousand percent in the past two decades. This may be attributable, at least in part, to the recent popularity of the pizza. Orégano is all but indispensable in Italian, Spanish and Mexican kitchens. The Italians spell it origano. *The herb, a handsome, leafy perennial, complements almost all tomato dishes and can be used to advantage in robust, savory dishes of Mediterranean inspiration.*

EGGPLANT ANTIPASTO

3 cups peeled and cubed eggplant

⅓ cup chopped green pepper

1 medium onion, coarsely chopped

¾ cup sliced fresh mushrooms or one four-ounce can mushroom stems and pieces

2 cloves garlic, crushed

⅓ cup olive or other salad oil

1 cup canned tomato paste

¼ cup water

2 tablespoons wine vinegar

½ cup stuffed green olives

1½ teaspoons sugar

1 teaspoon orégano

1 teaspoon salt

⅛ teaspoon freshly ground black pepper

1. Put the eggplant, green pepper, onion, mushrooms, garlic and oil in a skillet. Cover and cook gently ten minutes, stirring occasionally.

2. Add the remaining ingredients and mix well. Simmer, covered, until the eggplant is tender, about thirty minutes.

3. Put in a dish, cover and chill in the refrigerator overnight to blend flavors. Serve on lettuce leaves.

Yield: About one quart.

CHICKEN NAPOLITANA

1 three-pound broiling chicken, cut into serving pieces

3 tablespoons olive oil

1 clove garlic, finely chopped

1 small onion, finely chopped

1 teaspoon salt

Freshly ground black pepper to taste

4 mushrooms, sliced and cooked in butter until wilted

1 teaspoon orégano

1 bay leaf

1½ cups canned Italian plum tomatoes

6 to eight thin slices mozzarella cheese

Chopped parsley

1. Brown the chicken on all sides in the olive oil. Add the garlic and onion to the skillet and cook briefly.

2. Transfer the contents of the skillet to a heat-proof casserole and add salt, pepper, mushrooms, orégano, bay leaf and tomatoes. Cover and simmer until the chicken is tender, about forty-five minutes to one hour.

3. Fifteen minutes before the chicken is done, preheat the oven to 400 degrees.

4. When the chicken is tender, uncover the casserole and arrange the slices of mozzarella on top of the chicken. Place in the oven only long enough for the cheese to melt. Serve immediately, sprinkled with chopped parsley.

Yield: Four servings.

HERB-BROILED SWORDFISH

1 tablespoon butter	¼ teaspoon freshly ground
2 tablespoons lemon juice	black pepper
1 teaspoon orégano	1½ pounds swordfish steaks
2 teaspoons salt, or to taste	

1. Preheat the broiler.

2. Melt the butter. Add the lemon juice and seasonings and rub over all sides of the fish.

3. Place in a buttered baking pan and broil until the fish is brown and flakes easily when tested with a fork, about ten minutes. Baste occasionally.

Yield: Four or five servings.

HERBED CREOLE CABBAGE

1 medium head cabbage	2 cups canned tomatoes
Boiling water	¾ teaspoon orégano
¼ cup chopped onion	2½ teaspoons salt
1 cup chopped green pepper	1½ teaspoons sugar
3 tablespoons butter	2 teaspoons lemon juice

1. Shred the cabbage, cover and cook ten minutes in a small amount of boiling water.

2. Cook the onion and green pepper in the butter until they are wilted. Add the tomatoes and simmer, uncovered, fifteen minutes.

3. Drain the cabbage, if necessary. Add the tomato sauce and the remaining ingredients and serve hot.

Yield: Eight servings.

EGGPLANT PIZZA

2 tablespoons cooking oil
1 small clove garlic, minced
¾ cup finely chopped onion
¾ cup finely chopped green pepper
4½ tablespoons tomato paste
3 tablespoons water
1 teaspoon orégano
¾ teaspoon basil leaves
¾ teaspoon sugar
2¾ teaspoons salt
1 medium eggplant
1 egg
1 tablespoon milk
½ cup fine dry bread crumbs
¼ cup freshly grated Parmesan cheese
¼ teaspoon freshly ground black pepper
Flour for dredging
Hot fat for frying
Sliced mozzarella cheese, anchovies, sliced stuffed olives or chopped basil leaves

1. Heat the oil in a one-quart saucepan. Add the garlic, onion and green pepper. Cook, stirring, three minutes or until the onions and green pepper are limp.

2. Add the tomato paste and water. Cover and cook, stirring frequently, over low heat until very thick, about ten minutes. Add the orégano, basil, sugar and three-quarters teaspoon of the salt two minutes before the end of the cooking time.

3. Remove from the heat and set aside while preparing the eggplant.

4. Wash, peel and cut the eggplant into crosswise slices one-half inch thick.

5. Beat the egg with the milk and set aside. Mix the bread

crumbs with the grated cheese, the remaining two teaspoons of salt and the pepper.

6. Dip the eggplant slices in the flour, then in the beaten egg, then in the seasoned bread crumbs.

7. Sauté the eggplant slices in hot fat until golden, turning to brown both sides. Remove from the skillet and drain on paper toweling.

8. Place the eggplant slices on cooky sheets and spread them with the cooked tomato mixture. Top with sliced mozzarella cheese, anchovies, sliced stuffed olives or chopped basil leaves. Place under a broiler until the cheese has melted and is lightly browned. Serve at once.

Yield: Six servings.

EGGPLANT PARMIGIANA

1 large eggplant
¼ cup flour
1 egg, lightly beaten
2 tablespoons water
½ teaspoon salt
¾ cup dried bread crumbs
3 to four tablespoons olive oil

½ pound mozzarella or Swiss cheese, sliced
1 eight-ounce can tomato sauce
½ teaspoon orégano
½ cup freshly grated Parmesan cheese

1. Slice the eggplant one-half to three-quarters-inch thick; do not peel. There should be six center slices. Dredge them with flour.

2. Mix the egg, water and salt. Dip the floured pieces of eggplant in this mixture, then coat them with the bread crumbs. If time permits, refrigerate the slices thirty minutes or longer to set the coating.

3. Preheat the oven to 400 degrees.

4. Heat two tablespoons of the oil in a large skillet until hot but not smoking. Cook the eggplant slices slowly in the fat until they are tender, turning to brown both sides. Add more oil as needed.

5. Arrange the eggplant in a single layer in a greased shallow pan or in individual baking dishes. Distribute cheese slices over the top, add two tablespoons tomato sauce to each slice and sprinkle orégano and grated Parmesan cheese over the surface.

6. Bake until the cheese melts, about ten minutes.

Yield: Six servings.

Note: If desired, the dish may be assembled in advance and refrigerated before baking.

HERBED ESCAROLE

2 pounds escarole	1¼ teaspoons salt
2 cloves garlic, split	¼ teaspoon freshly ground
¼ cup olive oil	black pepper
½ teaspoon orégano	

1. Wash the escarole and trim off all outside leaves. Separate and drain. Cut the leaves into quarters.

2. Brown the garlic in the olive oil. Remove the garlic and discard it. Add the escarole and orégano to the olive oil. Cover and cook over medium heat until tender, about ten to fifteen minutes, depending on the age of the greens. Season with salt and pepper. Serve hot as a vegetable.

Yield: Four or five servings.

TOMATO-AND-EGGPLANT CASSEROLE

1 medium eggplant (one and one-half pounds)	1 teaspoon finely chopped onion
Boiling water	½ teaspoon orégano
1½ teaspoons salt	½ cup dry bread crumbs
2 tablespoons butter	6 medium-size tomato slices
2 eggs, beaten	½ cup grated Cheddar cheese
¼ teaspoon freshly ground black pepper	

1. Preheat the oven to 375 degrees.

2. Peel the eggplant and cut it into slices one-quarter inch thick. Place in a saucepan with boiling water one-half inch deep and the salt. Cover, bring to the boiling point and cook until tender, about ten minutes. Drain and mash.

3. Blend in the butter, eggs, pepper, onion, orégano and bread crumbs. Turn into a buttered one-quart casserole and cover the surface with tomato slices. Sprinkle with the grated cheese and additional salt and pepper. Bake until lightly browned, about twenty-five minutes.

Yield: Six servings.

ZUCCHINI-TOMATO CASSEROLE

¼ cup oil
1 clove garlic, finely minced
4 medium zucchini, cut into one-quarter-inch slices
¼ teaspoon orégano
¼ teaspoon basil
½ cup grated Cheddar cheese
¼ cup freshly grated Parmesan cheese
4 medium tomatoes, peeled and sliced
Salt and freshly ground black pepper
½ cup bread crumbs
2 tablespoons melted butter

1. Preheat the oven to 350 degrees.

2. Heat the oil in a skillet. Add the garlic and cook just long enough to flavor the oil, five or six minutes. Remove the garlic and discard it. Sauté the zucchini slices in the flavored oil.

3. Combine the orégano, basil, Cheddar and Parmesan cheeses. Place alternate layers of zucchini and sliced tomatoes in a buttered one-and-one-half-quart casserole. Sprinkle each layer lightly with salt and pepper and with the cheese mixture.

4. Combine the bread crumbs and the melted butter. Sprinkle on top of the casserole and bake, uncovered, until the crumbs are browned, about twenty to twenty-five minutes.

Yield: Six servings.

Paprika

It is ruefully true that American cooks by and large have only the most pallid conception of what PAPRIKA is. The innocuous powder which most merchants pass on to their customers as paprika has slightly more character than crayon or chalk.

Any paprika worthy of its name has an exquisite taste and varies in strength from decidedly hot to pleasantly mild but with a pronounced flavor.

The finest paprika is imported from Hungary and logically enough it is called Hungarian paprika or rose paprika. This is available packaged in the food shops of most first-rank department stores and fine food specialty shops. It is also available in bulk in Hungarian markets.

Paprika is the ground powder of a pepper plant. The color of the highest-quality paprika is a vibrant red.

PORK CHOPS HONGROISE

6 very large, lean pork chops	Pinch of thyme
Salt and freshly ground black pepper	1 bay leaf
	¾ cup chicken stock or dry white wine
3 tablespoons butter	1 cup sour cream
½ cup chopped onion	1 tablespoon paprika
1 clove garlic, finely minced	

1. Trim the fat from the chops. Sprinkle the meat with salt and pepper and sauté in the butter in a skillet.

2. Add the onion, garlic, thyme and bay leaf and sauté over medium-high heat until the chops are well browned on both sides.

3. Lower the heat and add the chicken stock or wine. Cover and cook thirty minutes. Remove the chops to a warm serving platter and keep them warm. Reduce the pan liquid by half by boiling rapidly. Discard the bay leaf.

4. Add the sour cream and paprika to the skillet and heat thoroughly but do not boil. Pour the sauce over the meat and serve hot.

Yield: Six servings.

SZEKELY GOULASH

3 pounds sauerkraut	3 pounds pork shoulder or boned fresh ham, cut into one-and-one-half-inch cubes
3 large onions, finely chopped	
2 cloves garlic, crushed	
¼ cup corn oil	Salt and freshly ground black pepper to taste
1 tablespoon caraway seeds	
2 tablespoons imported Hungarian rose paprika	1 teaspoon monosodium glutamate
2 cups canned tomatoes, finely chopped	2 tablespoons flour
	1 cup water
	1 cup sour cream

1. Rinse the sauerkraut and let drain in a colander two to three hours.

2. Sauté the onions and garlic in the oil until the onion is golden. Add the caraway seeds and paprika, stirring well. Add the tomatoes and simmer three minutes.

3. Add the pork, salt, pepper and monosodium glutamate to the onion mixture and simmer slowly until the meat is tender, about one hour.

4. Add the sauerkraut to the meat and mix carefully without breaking the meat. Continue to simmer until the sauerkraut is tender but not mushy.

5. Mix the flour, water and sour cream well with a wire whisk. Pour over the entire goulash and cook two minutes. Serve the goulash immediately with small boiled new potatoes.

Yield: Six to eight servings.

ELEANOR STEBER'S CHICKEN PAPRIKA

1 two- to three-pound frying chicken, disjointed and with giblets	1 bay leaf
	¼ cup finely chopped onion
	4 tablespoons butter or oil
2 cups water	1 cup flour
1 small onion, sliced	6 teaspoons paprika
3 or four sprigs parsley	⅓ cup cream
2 teaspoons salt	⅓ cup strong coffee
4 whole peppercorns	1½ cups thick sour cream

1. Place the giblets in a saucepan with the water, sliced onion, parsley, one teaspoon of the salt, the peppercorns and the bay leaf. Simmer, covered, one hour.

2. Sauté the chopped onion in a skillet in two tablespoons of the butter until soft but not brown. Remove the onion, leaving the butter in the skillet.

3. Combine the flour, reserving two tablespoons for use later, the remaining teaspoon salt and two teaspoons of the paprika in a paper bag. Shake the chicken pieces in the bag until coated with the flour mixture. Brown the meat well in the butter in

the skillet. Add two tablespoons of the giblet broth and cook, covered, over low heat until the chicken is tender, about thirty-five to forty minutes.

4. In a saucepan heat the remaining two tablespoons butter and blend in the reserved two tablespoons flour. Add the remaining giblet broth, the cream, coffee and remaining paprika. Stir over low heat until smooth and thickened. Add the sour cream gradually, stirring vigorously.

5. Pour the sauce over the chicken in the skillet and cook over low heat three minutes, turning the chicken and stirring the sauce. Do not boil.

Yield: Four servings.

MUSHROOMS PAPRIKASH

1 tablespoon finely chopped shallot or onion	1 teaspoon flour
2 tablespoons butter	½ teaspoon salt
1 pound fresh mushrooms, sliced	2 teaspoons paprika, or to taste
1 teaspoon lemon juice	Dash of ground red pepper
	¼ cup sour cream

1. Sauté the shallot in the butter three minutes. Add the mushrooms and lemon juice and cook five or six minutes, or until the mushrooms are tender.

2. Combine the flour, salt, paprika and red pepper. Add to the mushrooms and cook, stirring, one minute. Add the sour cream and heat but do not boil.

Yield: Six servings.

CUCUMBER SAUCE

1 large cucumber	⅓ teaspoon salt
¾ cup heavy cream	⅛ teaspoon paprika
2 tablespoons lemon juice	

1. Peel, seed and finely chop the cucumber. Drain it well and reserve while preparing the cream.

2. Whip the cream until it is stiff, slowly adding the lemon

juice. Season with salt and paprika.

3. Add the chopped cucumber and serve the sauce with cold meat or fish.

Yield: About one and one-half cups.

LOBSTER AND SHRIMP IN PAPRIKA CREAM

Salt
1 bay leaf
15 peppercorns
½ teaspoon cayenne pepper
2 ribs celery, broken
3 sprigs fresh parsley
2 one-and-one-half-pound
   live lobsters

2 pounds shrimp in the shell
4 tablespoons butter
2 teaspoons paprika
Freshly ground pepper
¼ cup cognac
4 cups heavy cream
3 egg yolks
Tabasco to taste

1. Pour into a kettle two quarts of water, or enough to cover the lobsters when they are added. Add salt to taste, bay leaf, peppercorns, cayenne pepper, celery and parsley to the water and when it is boiling vigorously, add the lobsters and cover. Cook fifteen minutes and add the shrimp. Simmer five minutes longer. Drain. When cool enough to handle, shell the shrimp and remove the meat from the lobsters. Cut the lobster meat into bite-size pieces. Leave the shrimp whole.

2. Heat half the butter in a skillet and add the shrimp, lobster, paprika, salt and pepper to taste. Shake and stir briefly. Add the cognac and ignite it. Remove the shellfish with a slotted spoon and cover with foil to keep warm.

3. Add the cream to the skillet and cook, stirring frequently with a wooden spoon. Simmer thirty minutes to reduce. Remove three-quarters cup of the sauce to a small mixing bowl.

4. Beat the egg yolks lightly and add them to the sauce in the bowl.

5. Return the seafood to the skillet. Heat thoroughly and add the egg mixture, stirring constantly. Cook briefly without boiling until the sauce thickens slightly. Add the salt and Tabasco to taste. Stir in the remaining butter.

Yield: Six to eight servings.

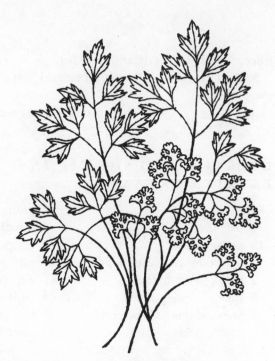

Parsley

*PARSLEY has a dual symbolism. It is said to signify both
revelry and victory. In mythology parsley supposedly
sprang from the blood of Archemorus, a Greek hero, and
subsequently garlands of parsley were used to crown
champions at the Isthmian games.*

*Parsley is most frequently used either chopped or in
the leaf as a garnish for dishes, but it is delicious when
used in large quantities as a pronounced seasoning. Like
mint, it is one of the easiest of herbs to grow. Generally,
there are two kinds of parsley available, the curly variety and the flat leaf, which is also called Italian parsley.*

Raw parsley is said to sweeten the breath.

*There is a beguiling expression, no longer current,
which says, "We are at the parsley and the rue." This
meant being at the beginning of a project, derived from
the Greek habit of bordering their gardens with parsley
and rue.*

FRESH MUSHROOM SALAD

1 pound fresh mushrooms
½ cup lemon juice
2 tablespoons tarragon
  vinegar
¼ cup chopped parsley

Salt and freshly ground black
  pepper to taste
½ cup vegetable oil
½ teaspoon sugar

1. The mushrooms should be stark white. Trim off the end of each stem and slice the mushrooms as thinly as possible with a sharp knife.

2. Place the mushroom slices in a mixing bowl. Pour over them the remaining ingredients, then adjust the ingredients to taste. This recipe produces a very tart flavor. Chill the mushrooms well and serve on chilled plates as an appetizer.

Yield: Four to six servings.

MEAT BALLS ALLA ROMANA

Meat Balls

½ pound ground beef
½ pound ground fresh pork
½ pound ground veal
4 slices whole-wheat bread,
  trimmed of crusts
½ cup milk
1 medium onion, chopped
½ green pepper, chopped
1 clove garlic, finely minced
1 cup finely chopped parsley

Grated rind of half a lemon
2 eggs
1 teaspoon salt
1 teaspoon freshly ground
  black pepper
Pinch each of cloves and nutmeg
Salad or olive oil
2 bay leaves

1. Grind the meats together twice. Soak the bread five minutes in the milk.

2. Place the meat in a mixing bowl and add all remaining ingredients except the oil and bay leaves. Squeeze the bread and add it to the meat. Mix well and let stand one hour or longer.

3. Preheat the oven to 450 degrees.

4. Shape the meat into twelve large balls. Grease the bottom of a roasting pan with oil and add the bay leaves and meat balls. Bake, uncovered, fifteen minutes. Brush with additional oil and bake fifteen minutes longer.

SAUCE

¼ pound salt pork, chopped
1 clove garlic, finely minced
¼ pound round steak, cubed
¼ cup dry white wine
Salt and freshly ground black pepper to taste
¾ cup chopped parsley
¼ cup chopped fresh basil
3½ cups plum tomatoes
1 four-ounce can tomato paste
½ cup water

1. Heat the salt pork in a kettle and brown the garlic lightly. Brown the beef and add the wine. Let simmer ten minutes. Season with salt, pepper, parsley and basil.

2. Stir in the tomatoes. Add tomato paste and water; cook thirty minutes. Add the meat balls and cook over medium heat one hour longer, stirring occasionally.

Yield: Six servings.

HERBED VEAL LOAF

2 pounds ground veal
2 eggs
½ cup fine bread crumbs
¾ cup chopped parsley
¼ cup finely chopped chives
2 tablespoons fresh basil, finely chopped, or one tablespoon dried basil (optional)
¼ cup green pepper, coarsely chopped (optional)
1½ teaspoons salt
½ teaspoon freshly ground black pepper
Bacon slices to cover top

1. Preheat the oven to 350 degrees.
2. In a mixing bowl combine all the ingredients except the

bacon slices. Using the hands, blend well; do not overwork the meat or it will produce a meat loaf that is too tightly packed.

3. Line a nine-inch pie plate with aluminum foil and shape the meat mixture into an oval loaf. Place the loaf on the foil and cover with bacon slices.

4. Bake one and one-half hours. Serve with tomato sauce.

Yield: Six servings.

BOILED TONGUE VINAIGRETTE

1 four-pound beef tongue	1 bay leaf
1 onion, studded with three cloves	3 peppercorns
	1 tablespoon salt
1 leek	Cold water to cover
1 rib celery with leaves	1¼ cups vinaigrette sauce
4 sprigs parsley	(page 228)

1. Place tongue in kettle with onion, leek, celery, parsley, bay leaf, peppercorns and salt. Add water to cover. Cover tightly, bring to a boil, lower heat and simmer until tender, about three and one-half hours. Cool in broth.

2. Remove tongue from kettle, reserving broth. Cut off bones and gristle at thick end of tongue. Slit skin from thick end to tip on underside. Using a paring knife, loosen skin at thick end and peel off skin from thick end to tip.

3. Reheat tongue in broth. Discard broth and place tongue on a serving dish. Heat vinaigrette sauce and serve separately or spooned over meat.

Yield: Eight servings.

SMOTHERED SHAD ROE

Melt one-half cup (one stick) butter in a skillet. When hot and foaming, add three pairs of shad roe. Cover and simmer ten to fifteen minutes, depending on size. Turn once. Season with salt and freshly ground black pepper and sprinkle with chopped parsley. Serve with lemon wedges and, if desired, crisp bacon slices and boiled potatoes.

Yield: Six servings.

STUFFED EGGPLANT WITH CLAMS

1 large eggplant
3 tablespoons olive oil
2 tablespoons butter
⅓ cup finely chopped onion
⅓ cup finely chopped green pepper
½ cup finely chopped fresh mushrooms (optional)
1½ cups fresh bread crumbs

1 seven-ounce can minced clams or one cup minced steamed clams with their juice
¼ cup finely chopped parsley
2 egg yolks, well beaten
2 tablespoons cold butter, cut into bits, or two strips raw bacon, finely minced

1. Cut the eggplant in half lengthwise. Using a sharp paring knife, carefully trim around the inside edges, leaving a quarter-inch rim. Score the center flesh almost but not down to the skin.

2. Heat the oil in a large skillet and place the eggplant halves, scored side down, in it. Cover the skillet with a close-fitting lid or aluminum foil. Cook eggplant over low heat until tender.

3. Preheat the oven to 350 degrees.

4. While the eggplant is cooking, heat the butter in another skillet and cook the onion, green pepper and mushrooms in it until the onion is tender. Stir in half the bread crumbs, the clams with their juice and the parsley.

5. Scoop the flesh from the cooked eggplant and add it to the skillet. Reserve the eggplant skins. Blend the eggplant with the remaining ingredients in the skillet, stirring over low heat.

6. Cool the mixture slightly and add the beaten egg yolks. Use this mixture to fill the eggplant shells. Sprinkle with the remaining bread crumbs and dot with butter or bacon. Bake until golden brown, about fifteen minutes.

Yield: Four servings.

MACARONI WITH ANCHOVIES

1 two-ounce can flat an-
   chovy fillets, drained
¼ cup olive oil or butter
2 cups tomato sauce
½ cup chopped parsley

1 pound macaroni, cooked
   until tender in boiling
   salted water
Freshly grated Parmesan
   cheese
Butter

1. Preheat the oven to 400 degrees.
2. Chop the anchovies and cook them in the oil or butter, stirring to make a paste.
3. Add the tomato sauce and parsley; bring to a boil.
4. Combine the sauce with the macaroni in a heat-proof dish and sprinkle with grated Parmesan cheese. Dot with butter and bake until thoroughly heated. Serve immediately with additional grated Parmesan cheese.

Yield: Four servings.

ASPARAGUS WITH PARSLEY SAUCE

2 tablespoons butter
2 tablespoons flour
1 cup chicken stock
½ cup light cream
¾ teaspoon salt
⅛ teaspoon freshly ground
   black pepper

2 egg yolks
¾ cup finely chopped fresh
   parsley
2 to two and one-half
   pounds fresh asparagus,
   cooked

1. Melt the butter in a saucepan. Remove from heat and blend in the flour. Stir in the chicken stock and one-quarter cup of the cream.
2. Return to the heat and cook, stirring, over medium heat until the mixture begins to thicken, about five minutes. Add salt and pepper.
3. Beat egg yolks, mix with the remaining cream and stir into the sauce. Cook over low heat only until hot, about two minutes.
4. Just before serving, add parsley and heat about thirty seconds. Serve over the hot asparagus.

Yield: Six servings.

BEETS WITH PARSLEY BUTTER

6 medium-sized fresh beets
(about one and one-
quarter pounds)
Boiling water
2 tablespoons butter
½ teaspoon crumbled basil
leaves

½ teaspoon salt
⅛ teaspoon freshly ground
black pepper
1½ tablespoons chopped
fresh parsley

1. Leave the beets whole with root ends and about two inches of the tops attached. Cook in boiling water to cover until tender, twenty-five to thirty-five minutes.

2. Remove the beets from the heat, slip off the skins and trim off tops. Slice one-quarter inch thick and place in a saucepan with the butter, basil, salt and pepper. Cook until hot. Turn into a serving dish and sprinkle with chopped parsley.

Yield: Four servings.

PARSLEY-STUFFED PEPPERS

6 large green peppers
1 cup boiling water
2¾ teaspoons salt
½ clove garlic, finely chopped
2 tablespoons finely chopped
onion
¼ cup (one-half stick) butter

1¾ cups fine bread crumbs
¾ teaspoon ground thyme
⅛ teaspoon freshly ground
black pepper
4 cups finely chopped fresh
parsley

1. Wash the peppers. Cut a thin slice from the stem end of each and remove seeds. Place in a saucepan with boiling water and one and one-half teaspoons of the salt. Cover and boil five minutes. Remove from the water and drain.

2. Sauté the garlic and onion in butter until limp and transparent, about five minutes. Add bread crumbs, remaining salt, thyme and black pepper. Toss lightly. Blend in the parsley.

3. Spoon into the drained peppers. Arrange in a close-fitting casserole, cover and bake thirty minutes in a 375-degree oven;

remove cover and bake ten minutes longer. Or, if desired, simmer thirty minutes in a covered Dutch oven.

Yield: Six servings.

POTATOES AND ANCHOVIES VINAIGRETTE

1 pound small new or waxy potatoes (see note)	8 anchovy fillets, flat or rolled with capers
Water to cover	¾ cup vinaigrette sauce (page 228)
Salt	

1. Wash the potatoes and place them in a saucepan. Add cold water to cover and add salt. Bring to a boil and cook until potatoes are tender but still firm. Drain and cool.

2. Peel potatoes and cut into slices one-quarter inch thick. Arrange on chilled plates and garnish with anchovies. Chill. Serve cold sauce separately or spooned over the potatoes.

Yield: Four servings.

Note: Potatoes, in general, are of two types: those that are mealy when cooked and those that have a firm, waxy texture when cooked. For this dish, select firm potatoes.

POTATO DUMPLINGS

6 medium potatoes	1 slice bread, crust removed, cut into one-quarter-inch cubes
Water	
2 eggs	
1½ teaspoons salt	2 tablespoons butter
½ cup flour	½ cup (one stick) butter
	¼ cup dry bread crumbs
	¼ cup chopped parsley

1. Scrub the potatoes and place them in a saucepan. Cover with water and boil, uncovered, in their jackets until tender, about thirty minutes.

2. Chill the potatoes well for twelve hours or longer. Peel and rice. Add the eggs, salt and flour to the potatoes and beat with a fork until fluffy. Roll into one-inch balls, placing a bread cube, which has been sautéed in two tablespoons of butter, in the middle of each. Roll the balls in flour.

3. Drop the balls into two quarts of salted boiling water a few at a time. Boil gently for four minutes after they rise to the surface, about eight minutes in all. Remove from the pot with a slotted spoon and drain on paper toweling. Pile into a serving dish.

4. Melt the half cup of butter, stir in the bread crumbs and parsley and pour over the dumplings.

Yield: Eight to ten servings.

One of the most excellent and unusual of salads in the Arab world is tabbouleh, made with parsley, mint and cracked wheat. It is generally served with hearts of lettuce or cabbage and these are used as scoops.

Cracked wheat (or burghul) is available from many sources in New York including the Middle Eastern stores on Atlantic Avenue in Brooklyn (near Court Street); Trinacria Importing Company, 415 Third Avenue; Atlas Importing Company, 1109 Second Avenue, and Kassos Brothers, 570 Ninth Avenue. Most of these sources also carry sesame paste or tahini.

TABBOULEH

(PARSLEY AND MINT SALAD)

1 cup cracked wheat
Boiling water
½ cup finely chopped fresh mint
1½ cups finely chopped parsley
1 cup finely chopped onion or scallion
¾ cup peeled, chopped tomatoes
¾ cup olive oil
1 cup lemon juice
Salt and freshly ground black pepper to taste

1. Place the cracked wheat in a mixing bowl and add boiling water barely to cover. Let stand thirty minutes, or until all the liquid is absorbed. The wheat should become tender yet still be somewhat firm to the bite. If the wheat is too dry, add a little more boiling water. If excessive water is added it may be necessary to drain the wheat and press it.

2. Let the cracked wheat become thoroughly cool, then mix well with the remaining ingredients. If desired, garnish with additional chopped tomatoes.

Yield: Six to eight servings.

PARSLEY CHEESE NOODLES

8 ounces noodles
3 quarts rapidly boiling salted water
1 cup cream-style cottage cheese
1 cup grated Cheddar cheese
¼ cup melted butter
½ cup finely chopped parsley
¼ cup finely chopped green onions
3 eggs, well beaten
Salt and freshly ground black pepper to taste

1. Preheat the oven to 350 degrees.

2. Cook the noodles until tender in the boiling salted water; drain.

3. Combine the noodles with the remaining ingredients and turn the mixture into a one-and-one-half-quart casserole. Bake thirty minutes.

Yield: Four servings.

TARTAR SAUCE

1 cup mayonnaise
2 tablespoons finely chopped parsley
1 tablespoon finely chopped chives
1 tablespoon finely chopped tarragon
1 tablespoon finely chopped chervil (optional)
1 teaspoon finely chopped onion (optional)
1 tablespoon finely chopped capers
1 small sour pickle, finely chopped

Combine all ingredients and blend well. If desired, add a little finely minced garlic.

Yield: About one and one-fourth cups.

VINAIGRETTE SAUCE

3 tablespoons wine vinegar
¾ cup olive oil
½ cup chopped parsley
1 tablespoon finely chopped chives
1 tablespoon chopped, drained capers
½ teaspoon finely chopped onions
1 teaspoon finely chopped cornichon or sour pickle (optional)
Salt and freshly ground black pepper to taste

1. Combine all the ingredients and beat with a fork until well blended.
2. Chill the sauce if it is to be used with chilled vegetables or shrimp. Heat sauce to lukewarm if it is to be used with hot boiled beef, fish or chicken, pigs' feet or calves' head.

Yield: About one and one-quarter cups sauce.

Note: If desired, ingredients such as chopped shallots, chopped hard-cooked eggs or dry mustard may be added.

Pepper

Throughout recorded history, PEPPER has been the most precious of spices. During the Middle Ages it was a form of wealth. Taxes, tributes and dowries are said to have often included levies of pepper. In Good Queen Bess's day, the dockmen who unloaded cargoes of pepper wore uniforms without pockets as a measure against theft. During the reign of Henry II there was a pepper guild whose members were known as pepperers.

The commonest form of table pepper in the United States is black pepper, although large quantities of white pepper are also available. White pepper is preferred by some chefs for making white sauces since the pepper is less conspicuous to the eye. Black pepper and white pepper are harvested from the same tree and are, basically, the same. White pepper is made by soaking peppercorns and removing the dark outer coating of the seed. Pepper is a stimulant and is said to aid digestion by helping the gastric juices to function. For thousands of years, pepper has been used as a preservative for meats as well as a spice to enhance their flavor.

ANTICUCHOS

1 beef heart
Red wine vinegar
1 bay leaf
2 cloves
10 whole peppercorns, crushed slightly

½ teaspoon dried hot red pepper flakes
Salt to taste
Peanut or olive oil
Tabasco or other hot sauce

1. Trim the beef heart, remove the skin and fat. Cut the heart into small, bite-size pieces.
2. Place the meat in a mixing bowl and add vinegar to cover. Add the bay leaf, cloves, peppercorns, pepper flakes and salt. Chill overnight (if desired, the meat may be left standing in the refrigerator two or three days).
3. Drain the meat and dry it on absorbent toweling. Place the meat on individual skewers and brush well with oil.
4. Grill the meat over hot charcoal or under the broiler, turning once. Cook to desired degree of doneness and serve with hot sauce. Serve as an appetizer.

Yield: Four to six servings.

HERB-FARM ROAST LAMB

1 five-pound leg of lamb, trimmed
1 clove garlic, crushed
1 teaspoon salt
2 teaspoons coarsely cracked black pepper
½ teaspoon powdered ginger

1 bay leaf, crumbled
½ teaspoon thyme
½ teaspoon sage
½ teaspoon marjoram
1 tablespoon soy sauce
1 tablespoon salad oil

1. Preheat the oven to 300 degrees.
2. Cut small slits in the lamb. Combine the remaining ingredients and rub the sauce thoroughly over and into the meat. Place the meat on a rack in a roasting pan and roast, uncovered, eighteen minutes a pound for well done (170 degrees on a meat thermometer), twelve minutes a pound for rare (140 degrees).

3. Transfer the lamb to a warm serving tray and let stand twenty minutes before carving. Serve with pan gravy.

Yield: Six servings.

The following is an astonishingly good veal loaf heavily accented with coarse black pepper. It is a classic example of how a spice or herb can assert itself to advantage in an unexpected manner.

HENRY CREEL'S VEAL AND PEPPER LOAF

3 or four tablespoons whole peppercorns
2 slices white bread, preferably the end pieces, torn into pieces
2 cups parsley, stems removed
3 ribs celery, chopped
½ cup water
2 pounds ground veal
1 egg, slightly beaten
1 teaspoon salt
6 to eight bacon strips

1. Preheat the oven to 325 degrees.
2. Crush the peppercorns in a mortar with a pestle or on a board with the bottom of a heavy skillet.
3. Blend the bread in a blender or grate it to make fine crumbs.
4. Place the parsley, celery and water in the container of an electric blender and blend on high speed until ingredients are chopped and blended but not mushy.
5. Place the meat in a mixing bowl and add the peppercorns, the parsley mixture, the egg, bread crumbs and salt. Blend with the fingers and shape into a round or oval loaf on a baking dish. Cover with bacon strips and bake two hours. Serve with basil and tomato sauce (page 18).

Yield: Six to eight servings.

PURÉED CELERY ROOT AND POTATOES

3 large potatoes
3 large celery roots (knob celery)
Water
Salt to taste
4 tablespoons butter
½ cup heavy cream
Freshly ground white pepper

1. Pare the potatoes and celery roots. Cut into quarters and place in a kettle. Cover with water and add salt to taste. Bring to a boil and simmer, covered, until the vegetables are tender. Drain.

2. Put the vegetables through a food mill or potato ricer and return to the kettle. Using a wooden spoon or an electric mixer, whip the puréed vegetables, adding the butter a little at a time.

3. Add the cream and beat to the consistency of mashed potatoes. Adjust the seasonings with salt and pepper to taste. Keep hot until ready to serve.

Yield: Six servings.

CHEESE-AND-PEPPER BREAD

1 package yeast	½ cup nonfat dry milk solids
1¾ cups lukewarm water	5½ cups sifted all-purpose
6 teaspoons sugar	flour, approximately
1 teaspoon salt	2 tablespoons soft butter or
1 teaspoon freshly ground	shortening
black pepper	1 large egg, lightly beaten
½ teaspoon dried basil,	1 cup (four ounces) grated
crumbled	sharp cheese

1. Dissolve the yeast in one-quarter cup of the water with one teaspoon of the sugar.

2. Mix the remaining sugar, the salt, pepper, basil, dry milk and one and one-half cups of the flour. Add the remaining one and one-half cups water, the butter and egg. Add the dissolved yeast and mix until smooth.

3. Add enough of the remaining flour to make a moderately stiff dough. Turn out onto a floured board and knead until smooth and elastic.

4. Place in a greased bowl and grease the top surface of the dough. Cover with a towel and let rise in a warm place (80 to 85 degrees) until double in bulk, about one hour.

5. Turn out onto a very lightly floured surface, press to flatten and cover with half the cheese. Knead in the cheese and repeat with remaining cheese.

6. Shape into two loaves and place in two greased 9 x 5 x 3-inch loaf pans. Grease the top surfaces of the loaves, cover and let rise until double in size, about one and one-half hours.

7. Bake the loaves in a preheated 400-degree oven fifteen minutes. Lower the oven temperature to 350 degrees and bake thirty-five minutes longer, or until the bread shrinks from the sides of the pan and is well browned.

Yield: Two loaves.

AVGOLEMONO SAUCE

2 tablespoons lemon juice
2 tablespoons flour
¼ teaspoon salt
⅛ teaspoon white pepper

2 cups vegetable water or broth
2 egg yolks, well beaten

1. Mix the lemon juice, flour, salt, pepper and enough water to thin the mixture.

2. Bring the broth to a boil and add the lemon mixture. Bring to a boil again and cook, stirring, until slightly thickened.

3. Stir the hot broth slowly into the egg yolks. Return to the heat and cook, stirring, over low heat until thickened. Pour over cooked vegetables.

Yield: Six servings.

Pepper Pods
or Flakes

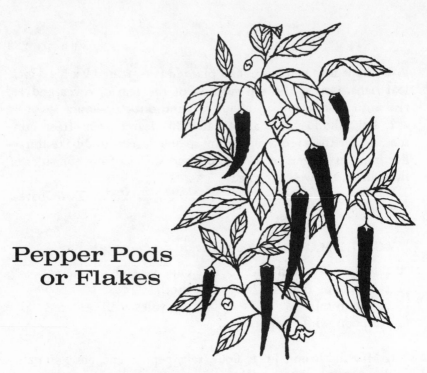

*The hot peppers which are sold in pods or flakes are
unrelated to the peppercorns of the spice trade which
yield white and black pepper. The hot peppers are frequently finger-shaped, they are red when ripe and should
be used according to palate and conscience. They are
important in Indian and Mexican cuisines and, oddly
enough, in almost all countries where the climate is
markedly warm.*

PERUVIAN SEVICHE

1 pound haddock, red
snapper or bay scallops
3 long hot green chili
peppers or canned hot
green chili peppers
3 long hot red chili peppers
or one teaspoon dried hot
red pepper flakes

1 medium onion, cut into
wafer-thin, almost trans-
parent slices
1 cup lime juice
1 teaspoon salt, or to taste
Finely chopped cilantro
(optional)

1. Slice the raw fish into thin strips. If scallops are used, leave them whole.

2. Split the peppers down the side, remove and discard the seeds. Cut the peppers crosswise into thin strips.

3. Combine the fish, peppers, onion, lime juice and salt. Chill overnight or longer. Add seasonings to taste and serve sprinkled with cilantro, if desired. Serve with buttered toast.

Yield: Four to six servings.

PHILADELPHIA PEPPER POT

3 pounds honeycomb tripe
Water
10 cups chicken broth, approximately
1 small but meaty veal knuckle, cut in half
1 bay leaf
1 leek, split nearly to the root end and thoroughly washed
3 sprigs parsley
1 sprig thyme or one-half teaspoon leaf thyme

1 whole red pepper pod
2 stalks dill or one-half teaspoon dried dill weed
Salt and freshly ground black pepper
4 medium potatoes, peeled and cut into half-inch cubes
2 Bermuda onions, peeled and chopped
Cayenne pepper to taste
Chopped fresh parsley

1. Wash the tripe thoroughly in several changes of water. Cut it into large squares and place in a kettle with water to cover. Bring to a boil and drain immediately.

2. Add the chicken broth to the tripe. It should cover the tripe generously. If not, add more broth. Add the veal knuckle. Tie the bay leaf, leek, parsley sprigs, thyme, red pepper and dill in a cheesecloth bag and add it to the kettle. Add salt and pepper to taste. Bring to a boil and simmer until the tripe is fork tender, about two hours.

3. Strain the liquid in the kettle and place it in a clean kettle.

Cut the meat from the veal bone, shred it and add it to the kettle along with the potatoes and onions. Cut the tripe into half-inch strips, then into half-inch cubes and add to the kettle. Bring to a boil and simmer until the potatoes are tender.

4. Add cayenne pepper to taste. Serve very hot, sprinkled with chopped parsley.

Yield: Eight to twelve servings.

SPANISH OMELET SAUCE

¼ cup olive oil
1 cup chopped onion
2 cloves garlic, finely minced
2 green peppers, peeled, seeded and cut into half-inch cubes
4 cups Italian peeled tomatoes
½ teaspoon hot red pepper flakes, or to taste
¾ teaspoon thyme
2 bay leaves

1 teaspoon sugar
¼ cup capers, drained and coarsely chopped
½ cup finely chopped parsley
1 cup cooked green peas
½ cup pimentos, cut into small cubes (optional)
Salt and freshly ground black pepper to taste
1 cup shredded sharp Cheddar cheese (optional)

1. Heat the olive oil in a large skillet and cook the onion and garlic until wilted.

2. Add the green peppers, cook three minutes, stirring, and add the tomatoes. Add the pepper flakes, thyme, bay leaves and sugar and simmer thirty minutes, stirring occasionally. The sauce should be reduced and thickened.

3. Add the capers, parsley, peas and pimentos and season to taste with salt and pepper. Simmer five minutes longer. Use as a filling for six omelets. Serve sprinkled with grated cheese, if desired.

Yield: Six servings.

PICKLED WHITE ONIONS

3 pounds tiny white onions
2 tablespoons coarse salt
Water
3 cups white vinegar
½ cup sugar

½ teaspoon whole cloves,
   tied in a bag
6 dried red pepper pods
6 small bay leaves

1. Soak onions and one tablespoon salt two hours in water to cover. Remove onions, peel. Soak forty-eight hours in water to cover, adding the remaining salt. Drain and rinse.

2. Bring to a boil the vinegar, one cup water, sugar and cloves. Add onions and boil three to five minutes. Remove bag.

3. Ladle into hot sterilized jars, covering onions with boiling vinegar mixture. Add a pepper pod and bay leaf to each jar. Seal at once. Let stand six weeks before using.

Yield: Six pints.

Pickling Spice

When it comes to pickling spices, it almost goes without saying that every packager has his own formula. A common combination might include allspice, bay leaves, cloves, chilies, cardamom, coriander, cinnamon, mustard, peppercorns and mace. Pickling spices are used principally for pickles and relishes but they also find their way into a lazy cook's kettle of fish.

ITALIAN SHRIMP

1 cup wine vinegar	1 tablespoon mixed pickling
½ cup olive or salad oil	spices
3 cups water	1 teaspoon salt
1 large onion, sliced	2 pounds shrimp, shelled
	and deveined

1. Combine all ingredients but the shrimp in a saucepan and bring to a boil.

2. Add the shrimp and cook five minutes. Pour into hot sterilized jars, cool and store in the refrigerator at least twenty-four

hours. Serve on food picks with cocktails or as a first course nested in lettuce. If desired, mayonnaise or sour cream may accompany the shrimp. These will keep a week or longer in the refrigerator.

Yield: Four to six generous servings.

BREAD-AND-BUTTER PICKLES

24 medium cucumbers, thinly sliced
3 medium onions, thinly sliced
¾ cup coarse salt
1 cup olive oil
Powdered or lump alum
4 whole hot red peppers

4 to eight cloves garlic
1 quart cider vinegar
⅓ cup yellow mustard seed
¼ cup black mustard seed
1 tablespoon mixed pickling spices
2 tablespoons celery seed

1. Arrange the cucumber and onion slices in layers in a large crock or bowl, sprinkling each layer with some salt. Let stand five hours.

2. Drain, rinse in ice water and drain again well. Add the olive oil and toss until all the slices are coated.

3. Put one-half teaspoon powdered alum or one lump of alum into each of four sterilized one-quart jars and fill the jars with the vegetables. Add one red pepper and one or two cloves garlic to each.

4. Bring the vinegar and spices to a boil. Pour over the vegetables in the jars. Seal and let stand one week before using.

Yield: Four quarts.

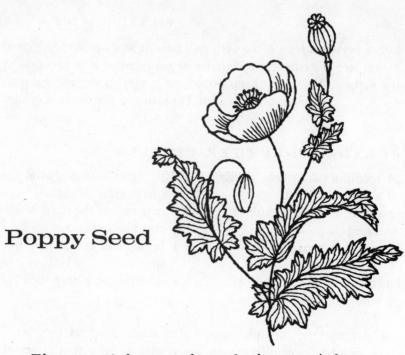

Poppy Seed

The name of the man who made the count is lost to posterity but it is claimed that there are 900,000 POPPY SEEDS to the pound. These delectable seeds, incidentally, do not come from the plant that yields opium. They hail from another variety altogether.

The texture of poppy seeds is one of their most cunning attributes. They do, however, have a mild flavor that seems vaguely related to that of walnuts. Poppy seeds have infinite uses in desserts and pastries. They make an admirable addition to buttered noodles.

CHICKEN LIVERS WITH POPPY SEEDS

4 medium onions, peeled and sliced
6 tablespoons butter
1½ teaspoons marjoram
Salt
1 pound chicken livers
1 tablespoon poppy seeds

1 clove garlic, minced
3 tablespoons flour
½ teaspoon freshly ground black pepper
1 teaspoon paprika
⅔ cup sherry

1. In a covered skillet, sauté the onions in three tablespoons of the butter for ten minutes. Add one teaspoon of the marjoram and one-quarter teaspoon salt. Stir well, cover and keep warm.

2. Wipe the livers with a damp cloth and leave them whole. Bruise the poppy seeds.

3. Heat the remaining butter in a second skillet. Add the livers, poppy seeds, garlic and remaining marjoram. Stir well and cook for five minutes at high heat, stirring often.

4. Sift in the flour, pepper and paprika. Stir and cook five minutes longer. Add salt to taste and lift out the livers and place atop the onions.

5. To the skillet in which the livers have cooked, add the sherry and heat to boiling, stirring to loosen and blend the residue from the frying. When boiling, pour over the liver and onions, cover the skillet and cook at low heat for thirty minutes, leaving the cover off part of the time so that the wine reduces slightly. Do not stir.

Yield: Four servings.

POPPY SEED NOODLE RING WITH CREAMED TUNA

4 tablespoons (one-half stick) butter
3 tablespoons flour
1½ cups milk
2 six-ounce cans tuna fish
¾ teaspoon salt
¼ teaspoon ground thyme
⅛ teaspoon freshly ground black pepper
1 tablespoon poppy seeds
½ pound noodles, cooked according to package directions
Parsley (optional)
Pimento (optional)

1. Melt three tablespoons of the butter in a saucepan. Blend in the flour. Stir in the milk and cook, stirring constantly, until of medium thickness.

2. Drain the tuna fish, flake and add to the white sauce. Add the seasonings and mix well. Heat, stirring as little as possible to avoid mashing the fish.

3. Add the poppy seeds and remaining tablespoon butter to the drained, cooked noodles. Toss lightly and turn into a buttered one-and-one-half-quart ring mold. Place briefly in a pan of hot water to keep warm.

4. Turn out the noodle ring on a hot platter. Fill the center with the creamed tuna. Garnish with parsley and pimento, if desired.

Yield: Six servings.

POPPY SEED NOODLES

½ pound medium noodles
Boiling salted water

3 tablespoons butter, at
    room temperature
1 tablespoon poppy seeds

1. Cook the noodles in boiling salted water according to package directions. Drain immediately.

2. Add the butter to the utensil in which the noodles were cooked and quickly toss the noodles in the butter. Just before serving, sprinkle with the poppy seeds.

Yield: Four to six servings.

ASPARAGUS WITH POPPY SEED SAUCE

1 tablespoon olive oil
2 tablespoons butter
2 tablespoons buttered,
    toasted bread crumbs
1 heaping teaspoon toasted
    poppy seeds

Juice of one lemon
Salt and cayenne pepper to
    taste
12 to sixteen hot cooked
    asparagus spears

1. Heat the oil and butter in a small skillet. Add the bread crumbs and poppy seeds. Stir well and cook slowly two to three minutes.

2. Add the lemon juice and seasonings, stir and pour over hot asparagus.

Yield: Four servings.

Asparagus: To cook asparagus, trim the main part of the stalks with a swivel-bladed potato cutter. Slice off the tough ends of the asparagus, leaving them of uniform size. Rinse the tops of the asparagus and lay them flat in a large skillet. Add water and salt to taste. Bring to a boil and cook until asparagus is just tender, three to ten minutes, depending on size of the asparagus stalks. Drain on clean toweling or paper towels and serve immediately.

POPPY SEED CAKE

2 cups sifted cake flour
1/8 teaspoon salt
2 teaspoons baking powder
1/2 cup poppy seeds
1 1/2 cups sugar
1/2 cup (one stick) butter

1 cup milk
1 teaspoon vanilla extract
4 large egg whites
Confectioners' sugar or
  vanilla frosting

1. Preheat the oven to 350 degrees.
2. Sift together the flour, salt and baking powder. Mix with the poppy seeds and set aside.
3. Gradually blend one and one-quarter cups of the sugar with the butter, mixing well after each addition. Stir in one-quarter cup of the milk and the vanilla. Add the flour mixture alternately with the remaining milk.
4. Beat the egg whites until they stand in soft peaks, then beat in the remaining sugar. Fold into the cake batter. Turn into a well-greased, lightly floured, nine-inch tube cake pan.
5. Bake until a cake tester inserted in the center comes out clean, about fifty minutes. Cool in the pan ten minutes. Remove from the pan onto a wire rack to finish cooling. If desired, dust with sifted confectioners' sugar or frost with a creamy vanilla frosting.

Yield: One nine-inch tube cake.

POPPY SEED STRUDEL

2 cups ground poppy seeds
½ cup sugar
½ cup white raisins
Pinch of cinnamon
Grated lemon rind

2 leaves strudel dough
(purchased)
Melted butter
Dry bread crumbs

1. Preheat the oven to 400 degrees.

2. Mix together the poppy seeds, sugar, raisins, cinnamon and lemon rind.

3. Place one leaf of strudel dough unfolded on a damp cloth. Brush the dough with melted butter and sprinkle with bread crumbs.

4. Place the second leaf of dough directly over the first. Brush with butter and sprinkle with bread crumbs.

5. Place the poppy seed mixture on one edge of the dough and roll the leaves slowly jelly-roll fashion. Place in a buttered baking pan and brush the top with butter. Mark individual portions with a knife.

6. Bake the strudel until golden brown, twenty-five to thirty minutes.

Yield: Four to six servings.

Note: Leaves of strudel dough may be purchased at Paprikas Weiss, 1504 Second Avenue and H. Roth & Son, 1577 First Avenue, New York.

Rocket

ROCKET symbolizes deceit. As to flavor it is one of the most unusual of salad greens and it goes by many names in various sections of the United States. In some Italian markets, for example, greengrocers will boast of their fine arugula or rugula; the French will speak of roquette. It is also called rocket cress or garden rocket.

Rocket is not well known and it is not widely available but it is cordially recommended for the salad bowl. The flavor is pungent, however, and the herb should be used sparingly at first. It is said to be easy to grow in home gardens and seeds are available from professional nurserymen. A popular canapé of the McIlhenny family, the makers of Tabasco in New Iberia, Louisiana, is made with rocket.

Many years ago it is recorded that rocket seeds were mixed with vinegar as a lotion that was thought to cure freckles.

ROCKET CANAPÉS

1 bunch rocket (arugula)
½ cup chopped watercress
3 tablespoons or more
   mayonnaise
Tabasco to taste
Lemon juice to taste

¼ teaspoon finely minced
   garlic or one scallion,
   finely chopped
Salt to taste
Thinly sliced white bread

1. Trim the ends from the rocket and wash the green in several changes of cold water. Dry it gingerly with linen or paper towels.

2. Place the green on a chopping board and chop it fine. This should yield about one cup.

3. Combine the chopped rocket with the watercress, mayonnaise, Tabasco, lemon juice, garlic and salt. Mix well.

4. Prepare rounds of the white bread by trimming the slices and cutting with a small biscuit cutter. Spread the mixture on the bread rounds and chill until ready to serve.

Yield: About twenty-four canapés.

ITALIAN SALAD

1 large head Romaine
   lettuce
4 rocket leaves
¼ cup peanut oil
¼ cup plus two tablespoons
   olive oil
3 tablespoons wine vinegar
1 tablespoon dry mustard

1 egg yolk
1 tablespoon anchovy paste
2 slices dry toast
1 clove garlic, split
3 tablespoons or more
   freshly grated Parmesan
   cheese

1. Separate the lettuce leaves and rocket leaves and wash them well under cold running water. Dry with a towel and cut into bite-size pieces. Wrap in clear plastic and let stand in the refrigerator until ready for use.

2. In a large mixing bowl combine the oils, vinegar, mustard,

egg yolk and anchovy paste. Stir vigorously with a fork or wire whisk until well blended. Chill until ready to use.

3. Trim the toast and rub both sides with garlic. Cut the toast into small cubes.

4. When ready to serve, stir the salad dressing once more and add the lettuce. Toss with a large fork and spoon and add the toast cubes and cheese. Toss once more and serve immediately.

Yield: Four to six servings.

Rosemary

That splendid British herbalist Mrs. C. F. Leyel once wrote that ROSEMARY, like lavender and peppermint, grows better and smells sweeter in England than anywhere else. Mrs. Leyel, bless her, had doubtless not been to Provence.

The good woman also observed, properly perhaps, that rosemary grows well only in gardens where mistress is master.

Rosemary is one of the most fragrant of herbs and it has many unexpected uses. A little freshly chopped rosemary is interesting with orange sections; it is appealing in dumplings and biscuits and it has few equals for poultry stuffings. Rosemary is notable with lamb and pork. Rosemary is for remembrance.

LOMBARDY MEAT LOAF

2 pounds ground beef
½ pound ground pork
½ pound ground veal
2 teaspoons dried basil
1 tablespoon salt
½ cup freshly grated
Parmesan cheese
2 cups bread crumbs
1 clove garlic, minced
¼ cup minced onion

¼ cup minced parsley
1 teaspoon crushed
rosemary
1 teaspoon freshly ground
black pepper
3 eggs
2 tablespoons softened
butter
2 cups beef broth or water

1. Preheat the oven to 425 degrees.

2. Mix thoroughly all the ingredients except the butter and broth. Form into a large loaf and spread with the butter.

3. Place the loaf in a pan lined with buttered aluminum foil and bake one-half hour. Add one cup of the broth and reduce the oven temperature to 350 degrees. Continue to bake thirty minutes to one hour longer, adding more broth as necessary.

Yield: Six servings.

VEAL MAISON WITH ROSEMARY

1½ pounds veal shoulder
¼ cup shortening
2 medium onions, chopped
1½ cups tomato juice
1 teaspoon salt

1 teaspoon chopped fresh
rosemary or one-half
teaspoon dried Cayenne
pepper to taste
2 tablespoons flour
¼ cup water or chicken stock

1. Remove any fat or bone from the meat. Cut the meat into strips about one and one-half inches by one-half inch.

2. Melt the shortening and lightly brown the meat in it, stirring frequently. Add the onions and cook until golden. Add tomato juice and seasonings. Cover and simmer until the meat is tender, twenty to twenty-five minutes.

3. Combine the flour and water and stir into the meat. Heat, stirring constantly, until thickened. Serve over hot buttered noodles.

Yield: Four servings.

CHICKEN ROSEMARY

1 teaspoon dried or one tablespoon fresh rosemary
2 teaspoons white wine vinegar
¼ cup (one-half stick) butter
2 tablespoons olive oil
3 medium onions, finely minced
1 small clove garlic, crushed

1 three-pound frying chicken, cut into serving pieces
Salt and freshly ground pepper to taste
½ cup dry white wine
½ cup chicken broth
2 teaspoons finely minced parsley
½ cup chopped cooked ham

1. Soak the rosemary in the vinegar.
2. Melt the butter and olive oil in a skillet. Heat slowly until foamy. Add the onions and garlic and sauté until golden.
3. Add the chicken to the skillet and sauté over medium heat until golden brown. Add the vinegar and the soaked rosemary, salt and pepper, wine and chicken broth. Sprinkle with the minced parsley. Cover and cook until done, twenty to thirty minutes. Five minutes before the chicken is ready, add the ham.

Yield: Three or four servings.

RED SNAPPER À LA FRANEY

1 one-and-one-half to two-pound red snapper
1 teaspoon dried rosemary
Salt and freshly ground black pepper

6 tablespoons butter
2 tablespoons capers
2 tablespoons chopped lemon

1. Preheat the oven to 425 degrees.

2. Have the fish thoroughly cleaned and scaled but leave the head and tail intact. Dry the fish with a paper towel.

3. Sprinkle the rosemary in the cavity of the fish and salt and pepper the outside of the fish generously.

4. Melt the butter in a skillet or ovenproof casserole. When the butter is hot, put in the fish and sauté on one side only for about five minutes, tilting the pan and spooning the hot butter over the fish.

5. Place the pan in the oven and bake until the fish flakes easily when tested with a fork, about twenty-five minutes.

6. Remove from the oven and sprinkle with the capers and chopped lemon. Garnish with lemon slices, if desired.

Yield: Two or three servings.

MINESTRA DI PASTA

¾ cup olive oil
3 large cloves garlic, finely chopped
8 canned anchovy fillets, drained and chopped
1 cup finely chopped parsley
2 twenty-ounce cans Mexican chick peas

3 medium tomatoes, peeled, seeded and chopped
2 teaspoons dried rosemary
1 quart water
1 pound ditalini or elbow macaroni, cooked according to package directions
Freshly grated Parmesan or Romano cheese

1. Heat the olive oil in a saucepan. Add the garlic, anchovies and parsley. Cook over low heat five minutes.

2. Add the undrained chick peas, tomatoes, rosemary and water. Cover and cook over low heat, stirring frequently, thirty minutes.

3. Add the cooked macaroni to the anchovy-chick pea mixture and heat five to ten minutes, stirring occasionally. Serve hot with grated Parmesan or Romano cheese to be sprinkled to taste over the top.

4. Serve the soup accompanied by a hot loaf of crusty Italian bread with butter.

Yield: Six to eight servings.

RIVIERA SALAD

1 two-ounce can flat
anchovy fillets
3 seven-ounce cans tuna
fish, drained
¾ cup chopped hearts of
celery
1 clove garlic, finely minced
¼ cup finely chopped onion,
or to taste
⅓ cup chopped green
pepper
½ cup finely chopped
parsley
½ teaspoon thyme
1 bay leaf, finely chopped,
or one-quarter teaspoon
ground bay leaf

1 teaspoon chopped fresh
rosemary or one-half
teaspoon dried
2 tablespoons wine vinegar
½ cup olive oil
Salt and freshly ground black
pepper
3 red, ripe tomatoes, cut
into wedges
12 black olives (preferably
Greek or Italian)
3 hard-cooked eggs, cut into
quarters
Black olives, chopped

1. Coarsely chop the anchovy fillets with a knife and fork in a large mixing bowl.

2. Cut the tuna fish into large chunks and add the chunks to the mixing bowl.

3. Add the celery, garlic, onion, green pepper, parsley, thyme, bay leaf and rosemary. Toss gently but thoroughly.

4. Sprinkle the salad with the vinegar and olive oil and salt and pepper to taste. Toss the salad again and spoon it into a serving dish or salad bowl.

5. Garnish the salad with tomato wedges, black olives and quartered hard-cooked eggs. Sprinkle the top with additional chopped black olives and chill the salad until serving time.

Yield: Six to eight servings.

ROSEMARY WINE

⅔ cup fresh rosemary sprigs
2 cups dry red or white wine

Combine the rosemary with the wine and store, tightly sealed, in a cool, dark corner of the pantry. Do not refrigerate. Let stand one week, then strain through a clean filter paper. Use for basting broiled fish or in any recipe for chicken, veal or lamb calling for a dry wine.

Yield: Two cups.

BEEF WITH ROSEMARY

3 pounds lean bottom round of beef	½ teaspoon dried rosemary
2 tablespoons olive oil	Pinch of dried thyme
1 tablespoon butter	½ bay leaf
½ cup chopped onion	¼ cup freshly chopped parsley
2 garlic cloves, finely minced	1 cup (1 eight-ounce can) tomato purée
2 teaspoons salt	½ cup beef stock
Freshly ground black pepper to taste	

1. Preheat the oven to 350 degrees.
2. Brown the meat on all sides in the olive oil. Meat should be dark brown all over. Transfer meat to a Dutch oven or heavy kettle.
3. Meanwhile, melt the butter and cook the onion and garlic lightly in butter until onion is translucent. Spoon the vegetables over the meat and add the remaining ingredients. Cover closely and bake for two and one-half to three hours, or until meat is tender.

Yield: Six servings.

ROAST RACKS OF LAMB

3 two-pound racks of lamb
(seven ribs each and with
the ribs neatly trimmed,
French style)
Salt and freshly ground pepper to taste
1½ cups coarsely chopped
carrots
¼ cup coarsely chopped
parsley
1 onion, finely chopped
1 teaspoon coarsely
chopped rosemary
½ teaspoon chopped fresh
or dried thyme
½ cup coarsely chopped
celery
1 cup chicken broth
¾ cup fresh bread crumbs
½ cup finely chopped shallots
½ cup finely chopped parsley

1. Preheat the oven to 500 degrees.

2. Sprinkle the meat all over with salt and pepper.

3. Arrange the racks of lamb, fat side down, in a large, flat baking pan. Place in oven and, after about eight minutes when the meat starts to brown well, turn the racks over, fat side up. Continue baking, turning occasionally, until the racks of lamb are handsomely browned, about twenty minutes.

4. Reduce the oven heat to 400 degrees.

5. Pour off the fat from the pan and scatter the chopped vegetables and seasonings around the racks of lamb. Continue cooking, turning the lamb, about ten minutes longer. Add the chicken broth and cook five minutes longer.

6. Pour off and save the broth from the pan. Strain it and keep it hot. Discard the vegetables.

7. Place the racks of lamb fat side up. Blend well the bread crumbs, shallots and finely chopped parsley. Coat the tops of the racks of lamb with the mixture, patting the mixture down so it will adhere. Run the lamb quickly under the broiler until the tops are brown.

8. Slice the racks into rib portions and serve hot with the strained broth.

Yield: Six to ten servings.

ROAST PORK AU VIN BLANC

1 four-pound pork roast	1 clove garlic, peeled
¼ cup butter	1 teaspoon freshly chopped
Salt and freshly ground black	rosemary
pepper to taste	Pinch of thyme
1 onion, studded with four	¾ cup dry white wine
cloves	

1. In a Dutch oven, brown the pork on all sides in the butter. Sprinkle with salt and pepper and add the onion, garlic, rosemary and thyme.

2. Add the wine. Cover and simmer over low heat one and one-half to two hours. Strain the sauce and serve with the pork.

Yield: Four to six servings.

Roses

In many minds, the use of ROSES in cuisine is a gastro-nomic conceit, on a par perhaps with the use of crystal-lized violets. Nonetheless roses have played a part in cuisine for centuries. Roses originated in Persia and a rose-water trade was carried on by the Persians as far back as the eighth century. Some people still make rose wine and Indians, in particular, are fond of rose petal preserves. Rose water has widespread uses to this day in the desserts and foods of the near and Middle East.

The rose, by the way, symbolizes love.

ANN SERANNE'S ROSE PETAL JAM

1 pound petals from fresh red roses	2 cups sugar
	½ cup water

1. Rinse the petals gently and dry them.

2. Dissolve the sugar in the water and stir into the petals. Place the petals and sugar in a shallow pan, cover with a sheet of glass and place under clear sun for eight hours.

256

3. Place in a kettle. Bring the mixture to a boil and simmer twenty minutes, stirring constantly. Pour into jars and seal.

Yield: One and one-half to two pints.

ROSE HIP JAM

About two pounds rose hips
Water to cover
1 cup finely diced pine-
apple

1 lemon, thinly sliced
½ cup water
5 cups sugar

1. The rose hips should be bright red; chill after picking. Remove the blossom and stem ends. Slit the hips in two and discard the seeds and any tough flesh. Cover with water and simmer until soft. Press them through a sieve and measure the purée.

2. There should be about four cups of purée. If not, adjust the recipe accordingly. For each four cups of purée add one cup finely diced pineapple.

3. Meanwhile cook the lemon in the half cup of water for ten to fifteen minutes. Drain it and add it to the purée. Add the sugar, bring to a boil and simmer slowly until thick. Pour into hot sterilized jars and seal at once.

Yield: About three pints.

SICILIAN CASSATA

1 ten-inch spongecake,
homemade or purchased
1½ pounds ricotta cheese
⅓ cup sugar
½ cup milk or cream
2 to three tablespoons rose
water
½ ounce bitter chocolate,
chopped

½ cup chopped toasted
almonds
⅔ cup finely diced candied
fruit
¼ cup rum
Cassata frosting (recipe
follows)

1. Cut the spongecake into two or three layers. Chill.

2. Mix the ricotta, sugar, milk and rose water. Rub through a sieve or whip until smooth.

3. Add the chocolate, almonds and candied fruit and mix well. Chill.

4. Place a spongecake layer on a serving plate and spread with half the ricotta filling for three layers, all if only two layers are used. Top with final cake layer. Sprinkle with rum. Refrigerate until shortly before serving time.

5. Frost the cake, reserving a small amount of frosting.

6. Beat enough additional confectioners' sugar into remaining frosting to give stiff peaks when the beater is withdrawn. Color a delicate pink with red food coloring and use in a pastry tube to decorate the cassata as desired.

Yield: Twelve servings.

Cassata Frosting

1 egg white	1 teaspoon almond extract
2 cups or more confectioners' sugar	1 tablespoon lemon juice

Mix all ingredients until smooth. If necessary, add a little water.

MELON DELIGHT

1 medium Persian melon or cantaloupe	2 tablespoons lemon juice
2 ripe peaches	½ teaspoon salt
⅓ cup sugar	2 tablespoons rose water
	Crushed ice

1. Cut the melon in half and scoop out as many melon balls as possible. Put them in a crockery bowl and pour the melon juice over them.

2. Peel the peaches and slice them thin. Add to the melon balls. Add sugar, lemon juice and salt. Let stand in the refrigerator several hours.

3. One-half hour before serving, add the rose water and return to the refrigerator. Just before serving, place the fruit mixture in individual serving dishes and top with finely crushed ice.

Yield: Five or six servings.

The following is a recipe of Dr. Moritz Jagendorf, folklorist, winemaker and bon vivant.

ROSE PETAL WINE

Enough red roses to fill eight
  glass quart jars
Water
5 to eight pounds sugar

2 lemons, washed and dried
½ ounce powdered yeast
4 or more clean eggshells

1. Cut off and discard the white bottoms of the petals. Let cold water run over the petals for about ten minutes.

2. Drain the petals and place them in a three-gallon stone crock or enamel pot.

3. Pour two gallons of water into an enamel pot and bring to a boil. While the water is heating add the sugar and stir until sugar is dissolved. The amount of sugar will depend on the desired sweetness of the wine. The more sugar, of course, the sweeter the resulting wine will be. It is necessary to use a minimum of four pounds of sugar for proper fermentation. When the water boils, pour it over the petals.

4. Peel the lemons and reserve the rinds. Place the rinds in the crock of petals. Squeeze the lemon juice over the petals. Let the mixture cool to room temperature.

5. Dissolve the yeast in one-half cup lukewarm water. Pour it into the petals and stir briefly.

6. Cover the crock and within a day or two the fermentation should begin. As the mixture ferments, stir it with a wooden spoon once a day. The fermentation will stop in approximately two weeks. When there is no more visible fermentation, strain

the wine into half-gallon or gallon jars. Squeeze every drop from the petals. Place two eggshells into each jar to help clear the wine. Seal the jars. Let the wine stand quietly and still for at least two or three weeks. Then siphon off the clear wine into clean wine bottles.

> **Yield: Ten or more bottles of wine depending on quantities of ingredients used.**

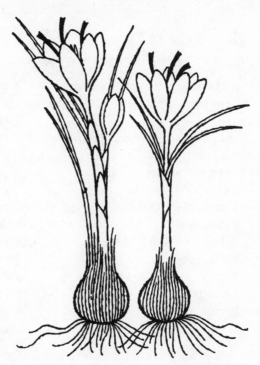

Saffron

SAFFRON is probably the most expensive spice on earth and it has reasons. Saffron is made from the dried stigmas of the autumn crocus and the blossoms must be picked by hand. Each blossom has three stigmas and it has been reckoned that seventy-five thousand blossoms are necessary to yield a pound of saffron. Saffron is most widely used in the kitchens of Spain, Italy and the South of France.

What with its cost, there is small wonder that saffron symbolizes the necessity of guarding against excess.

CHICKEN, VALENCIA STYLE

3 chickens, cut into serving
pieces
Salt
Freshly ground black pepper
Paprika
Cayenne pepper
Ground ginger
1 rib celery, finely chopped
1 bay leaf
2 large onions, finely
chopped
1 cup (two sticks) butter,
melted
2 cups rice
½ cup olive oil

2 green peppers, finely
chopped
2 cloves garlic, minced
2 tomatoes, peeled, seeded
and chopped
1 pound fresh mushrooms or
one cup canned mush-
rooms, drained
Water
⅛ teaspoon saffron
1 cup chicken stock
1 hard-cooked egg, chopped
¼ cup minced parsley
2 packages frozen peas,
cooked and drained
2 pimentos for garnish

1. Preheat the oven to 400 degrees.

2. Rub the chicken pieces with salt, pepper, paprika, cayenne and ginger. Place in a greased baking pan with the celery, bay leaf, onions and melted butter. Place in the oven and brown quickly.

3. Reduce the oven temperature to 300 degrees, cover the baking pan and cook forty-five minutes, basting frequently.

4. Meanwhile, wash the rice; add the olive oil, green peppers, garlic, tomatoes and mushrooms. Cook briefly, stirring. Add water to barely cover and cook slowly, covered, ten minutes.

5. Boil the saffron in the chicken stock three minutes. Add to the rice and season to taste. Continue cooking twenty minutes longer.

6. Place half the rice mixture in a large casserole, add the chicken and cover with the remainder of the rice mixture. Sprinkle with the chopped hard-cooked egg and minced parsley. Return to the 300-degree oven and bake twenty minutes.

7. Aften ten minutes, stir in the peas. Serve garnished with additional chopped parsley and the pimentos.

Yield: Six generous servings.

JEAN DALRYMPLE'S ARROZ CON POLLO

½ cup (one stick) butter

6 tablespoons olive or other oil

4 cloves garlic, or to taste, minced

2 three-pound chickens, disjointed

Salt and freshly ground black pepper to taste

3 cups long-grain rice

8 cups chicken stock

1 chorizo (hot Spanish sausage) or one pepperoni (hot Italian sausage), cut into half-inch pieces

1 tablespoon saffron, or to taste

2 cups large fresh or frozen lima beans

2 cans pimentos

3 cups hot cooked peas

1. Preheat the oven to 350 degrees.

2. Melt the butter in a flameproof casserole. Add the oil and garlic and sauté the chicken in it until golden brown. Season with salt and pepper. Remove the chicken and keep it warm.

3. Add the rice to the casserole and stir it in the fat until golden. Add the stock and stir well. Add the chorizo, saffron and lima beans. Return the chicken to the casserole and stir thoroughly.

4. Cover the casserole with aluminum foil and bake in the oven until the chicken is tender and the liquid has been absorbed by the rice, about forty-five minutes. Serve garnished with pimentos and green peas.

Yield: Six to eight servings.

PAELLA

1 teaspoon orégano
2 peppercorns
1 clove garlic, peeled
1½ teaspoons salt
6 tablespoons olive oil
1 teaspoon vinegar
1 one-and-one-half-pound chicken, in serving pieces
2 ounces ham, cut into thin strips
1 chorizo (hot Spanish sausage), sliced
1 ounce salt pork, finely chopped
1 onion, peeled and chopped
1 green pepper, seeded and chopped
½ teaspoon ground coriander
1 teaspoon capers
3 tablespoons tomato sauce
2¼ cups rice
4 cups boiling water
1 teaspoon saffron
1 pound shrimp, shelled and deveined
1 one-and-one-half-pound lobster, cooked
1 can peas, drained
1 quart mussels, scrubbed
1 dozen or more small clams
1 can pimentos

1. Combine the orégano, peppercorns, garlic, salt, two tablespoons of the olive oil and the vinegar and mash with the back of a kitchen spoon or in a mortar. Rub the chicken with this mixture.

2. Heat the remaining olive oil in a deep, heavy kettle and brown the chicken lightly over moderate heat. Add the ham, chorizo, salt pork, onion, green pepper, coriander and capers.

3. Cook ten minutes over low heat. Add tomato sauce and rice and cook five minutes.

4. Add the boiling water, saffron and shrimp. Mix well and cook rapidly, covered, until the liquid is absorbed, about twenty minutes. Turn rice from top to bottom.

5. Remove the meat from the lobster. Add the lobster meat and peas to the kettle, cover and cook five minutes longer.

6. Steam the mussels and clams in a little water until the shells open. Strain both through cheesecloth over the rice. Heat pimentos. Use mussels, clams and pimentos as a garnish.

Yield: Six to eight servings.

PERSIAN RICE

½ teaspoon saffron leaves
¼ cup cold water
3 cups rice
1 quart boiling salted water
6 tablespoons melted butter

1 medium onion, thinly
  sliced
1 medium potato, peeled and
  thinly sliced
Salt and freshly ground black
  pepper to taste

1. Soak the saffron in the cold water thirty minutes.

2. Add the rice gradually to the boiling salted water. Return to a boil and cook until the rice is half done, about ten minutes. Drain the rice in a colander.

3. Add the butter to the kettle in which the rice cooked. Arrange the onion and potato slices in a flat layer on the bottom. Cook briefly, then spoon the rice over the vegetables to make a pyramid. Season with salt and pepper.

4. Sprinkle the saffron over the rice and cover with a damp tea towel. Cover the kettle and steam the rice over very low heat until done, thirty to forty-five minutes. Add more melted butter or water if necessary to prevent burning. Note, however, that the vegetables and bottom layer of rice turn the color of amber. This is desirable and this part is served with the dish.

5. When the rice is done, place the bottom of the kettle in cold water and let stand three to five minutes. This helps extricate the brown layer from the kettle.

Yield: Six servings.

SAFFRON CAKE

½ cup milk
½ package yeast
2 cups flour, sifted
1 cup plus one teaspoon
  sugar
½ cup (one stick) butter, softened

2 eggs, separated
1 teaspoon cinnamon
½ teaspoon cloves
½ teaspoon mace
½ teaspoon powdered saffron
1 tablespoon caraway seed
1 teaspoon rose water

1. Heat the milk to boiling, then cool to lukewarm. Dissolve the yeast in the milk. Add one-half cup of the flour and one teaspoon sugar. Cover and let rise one hour in a warm place, until the sponge doubles in bulk.

2. Cream the butter with the remaining cup of sugar. Add the egg yolks and beat well, preferably with an electric mixer, until light and creamy. Add to the sponge.

3. Sift the remaining flour twice more, adding the spices the second time. Add to the sponge, along with the caraway seeds and rose water.

4. Fold in well-beaten egg whites and pour the batter into a one-quart tube pan that has been lightly greased with oil and floured. Smooth the batter with a knife to make as even as possible.

5. Set the batter aside to rise four hours in a warm place.

6. Bake the cake in a preheated 375-degree oven ten minutes. Reduce the heat to 350 degrees and cook until the cake tests done, about forty minutes longer.

7. Remove the pan from the oven and let the cake cool a few minutes in the pan before turning out onto a wire rack to finish cooling. Dust with confectioners' sugar and serve with fruit or custard.

Yield: One cake.

Note: The cake will keep well if stored in a covered tin box.

Sage

Without SAGE where would homemade sausage be? And how many childhood memories are inextricably linked to the warm, homelike odor of sage in the stuffing for a Thanksgiving turkey or a Christmas goose?

Sage seems to have an affinity for poultry, pork and veal, because, perhaps, of the bland nature of these meats. It also has its virtues in cheese, and the sage cheese of Vermont is among the best.

Through the ages, many healing properties have been ascribed to sage. Its name probably derives from this fact, for botanically sage is called salvio, which means to save. Understandably, sage symbolizes domestic virtue.

SAUSAGE-STUFFED BREAST OF VEAL

1 three- to four-pound boneless breast of veal, with a
pocket for stuffing
Salt and freshly ground black
pepper
8 ounces pork sausage meat
½ teaspoon crushed sage
1 cup fresh white bread
crumbs

1 cup chopped tart apple
2 tablespoons chopped onion
½ cup chicken stock
¼ teaspoon salt
⅛ teaspoon freshly ground
black pepper
½ pound thinly sliced bacon

1. Preheat the oven to 325 degrees.

2. Sprinkle the inside of the veal pocket with salt and pepper.

3. Sauté the sausage meat gently, breaking it into pieces and leaving the fat in the pan.

4. Add the remaining ingredients, except the bacon, to the sausage and mix together lightly.

5. Stuff the pocket with the sausage mixture. Secure the edges together with skewers and string or by sewing.

6. Place the meat on a rack in a shallow roasting pan. Place the strips of bacon over the top of the veal roast.

7. Roast, uncovered, until the meat is tender, about three hours.

Yield: Six servings.

FARM-STYLE HOMEMADE SAUSAGE

2 pounds ground lean pork
1 pound ground salt pork
1 large onion, finely minced
1 clove garlic, ground
1 tablespoon salt
1 tablespoon rubbed sage

1 teaspoon each of ground
cloves and mace
2 teaspoons coarsely ground
black pepper
1 tablespoon minced parsley
1 bay leaf, crushed
¼ teaspoon ground allspice

Combine all ingredients and mix thoroughly. Use to stuff sausage casings or form into patties. In either case, pan-fry or bake on a rack until crisp but not dry.

Yield: About three pounds sausage.

SAGE CHICKEN WITH POLENTA

1 four-pound chicken, cut into serving pieces
Salt and freshly ground black pepper
¼ cup salad oil or other shortening
½ cup chopped onion

1 clove garlic, minced
2½ cups canned tomatoes
1 six-ounce can tomato paste
½ teaspoon ground sage
3 cups hot polenta

1. Sprinkle the chicken pieces with two teaspoons salt and one-quarter teaspoon black pepper. Heat the oil or shortening and in it brown lightly the chicken, onion and garlic. Add the tomatoes, tomato paste, sage and salt and pepper to taste. Cover and simmer until the chicken is tender, forty to fifty minutes.

2. Place the polenta on a large platter. Arrange the chicken on top and spoon the tomato gravy over it. Serve hot.

Yield: Four to six servings.

POLENTA RING WITH CHICKEN LIVERS AND SAGE

4 cups hot polenta
2 slices bacon, chopped
1 small onion, chopped
2 tablespoons butter
1 pound chicken livers, halved

½ pound mushrooms, sliced
3 tablespoons dry white wine
¼ teaspoon sage
Salt and freshly ground black pepper to taste

1. Turn the polenta into a one-quart buttered ring mold and keep it warm in a pan of hot water.

2. Sauté the bacon with the onion. Add the butter, livers and mushrooms and cook, stirring often, until the livers are brown, about two minutes.

3. Add the wine, sage, salt and pepper and cook two minutes longer.

4. Unmold the polenta and fill the center with the liver mixture.

Yield: Five or six servings.

PINTO BEANS WITH SAGE

2 cups pinto beans	1 teaspoon salt
Water	¼ teaspoon freshly ground
½ pound bacon or salt pork,	black pepper
cubed	½ teaspoon dry mustard
1 large onion, chopped	1½ teaspoons sage
1 clove garlic, minced (op-	2 teaspoons brown sugar
tional)	

1. Wash and pick over the beans. Cover with six cups water and soak overnight. Or boil two minutes; remove from the heat, cover and let stand one to two hours.

2. Cook the bacon or salt pork until brown. Add pork to beans. Pour off all but four teaspoons fat from the skillet, add the onion and brown lightly. Add to beans. Add garlic.

3. Mix salt, pepper, mustard, sage and sugar with enough water to form a thin mixture. Add to beans. Add enough water, if needed, to cover beans. Cover and boil gently until tender, about two hours.

Yield: About five cups.

EGGPLANT WITH MACARONI-SAUSAGE STUFFING

2 medium eggplants
Salt
1 pound sausage meat
1 medium onion, chopped
2 cloves garlic, minced
1 teaspoon sage
1 cup elbow macaroni, cooked

¾ cup freshly grated Parmesan cheese
3 cups canned or cooked tomatoes, chopped
¼ teaspoon freshly ground black pepper

1. Preheat the oven to 400 degrees. Place unpeeled eggplants in a pan with one-quarter inch water and bake about twenty minutes. Cut each in half lengthwise; scoop out centers. Salt the shells; drain them. Chop the centers and reserve.

2. Lightly brown the sausage, onion and garlic. Drain off excess fat and reserve.

3. Add chopped eggplant and sage to sausage meat. Cook until eggplant is tender.

4. Mix the macaroni, one-quarter cup cheese, half the sausage mixture and about three-quarters cup of the tomatoes. Add salt and pepper to taste; fill the eggplant shells.

5. Sprinkle remaining cheese on tops. Brush tops and sides with reserved fat. Turn remaining tomatoes and sausage into a baking dish. Stand eggplants in it. Bake fifteen minutes.

Yield: Eight servings.

SAGE-STUFFED ONIONS

6 large onions, peeled
Water
Salt
1 cup finely diced cooked veal or pork
1 cup bread crumbs

⅛ teaspoon freshly ground black pepper
1 teaspoon ground sage, or to taste
4 tablespoons (one-half stick) butter, melted
¼ cup grated Cheddar cheese

1. Preheat the oven to 350 degrees.

2. Boil the onions in salted water to cover until barely tender. Drain. Scoop out the centers, leaving enough outside layers to make a substantial wall. Chop enough onion centers to make one cup.

3. Mix the chopped onions with the diced meat, one-third cup of the bread crumbs, one tablespoon water, one teaspoon salt, pepper and sage. Fill the onion cavities, mounding up the stuffing. Brush with two tablespoons of the melted butter. Place in a shallow baking dish, cover and bake fifteen minutes.

4. Remove the cover from the baking dish and sprinkle the onions with the remaining two-thirds cup bread crumbs, remaining melted butter and the grated cheese. Bake, uncovered, until brown.

Yield: Six servings.

HERB BREAD

1 package yeast	1 tablespoon salt
¼ cup warm water	6 to seven cups sifted flour
¼ cup sugar	1 teaspoon dried sage leaves
1½ cups milk, scalded and cooled to lukewarm	¾ teaspoon dried thyme leaves
½ cup shortening, melted	¾ teaspoon dried marjoram leaves
2 eggs, beaten	

1. Dissolve the yeast in the warm water along with one tablespoon of the sugar. Add the milk, remaining sugar, shortening, eggs, salt and two cups of the flour. Mix well. Cover and let rise in a warm place (80 to 85 degrees) until bubbly, about one hour.

2. Mix the herbs and crumble them. Add to the yeast mixture.

3. Stir in enough of the remaining flour to make a stiff dough. Knead on a floured board until satiny and elastic. Place in a bowl, cover and let stand in a warm place (80 to 85 degrees) until double in bulk.

4. Punch down the dough and let it rest ten minutes.

5. Shape into two loaves and place in two greased 9 x 5 x 3-inch bread pans. Brush the tops with milk and let rise until double in bulk.

6. Bake in a preheated 375-degree oven until done, about fifty minutes.

Yield: Two loaves.

SOUTHERN CORNBREAD STUFFING

1½ cups (3 sticks) butter
1½ cups chopped celery
1½ cups chopped onion
2 quarts day-old white bread, cubed
1½ quarts stale cornbread, cubed or broken into coarse crumbs

1 tablespoon salt
1 tablespoon sage
½ teaspoon freshly ground black pepper
½ pound crisp cooked bacon, crumbled (optional)
1 cup turkey giblet stock or chicken broth (optional)

1. Heat the butter in a large skillet. Add the chopped celery and onion and cook until the vegetables are yellow.

2. Combine the bread cubes, butter and vegetables, salt, sage, pepper and bacon for a dry stuffing. For a moist filling, add the stock or broth.

Yield: Stuffing for a sixteen-pound turkey.

Savory

SAVORY, whether of the summer or winter variety, is, as one connoisseur put it, "comforting in salads." The herb, which is distinctly aromatic, is excellent in chilled vegetable juices and in meat loaves. Savory has been called the "bean herb" because of the compelling character it lends to dishes whose base is peas, beans or lentils.

Bees dote on savory and if their hives are situated near a blooming savory plant their honey will be all the better for it. Savories are said to be the chosen plants of the Satyrs.

NAVY BEANS WITH SAVORY

2 cups navy beans	1 onion, peeled
Water	½ teaspoon fresh or dried
Salt to taste	savory

1. Soak the beans overnight in two quarts water. Or boil two minutes, cover and let stand one hour.

2. Drain the beans and add fresh water to cover and salt to taste. Add the onion and savory and bring to a boil. Lower the flame and simmer gently until beans are tender, two to three hours.

Yield: Four to six servings.

CREAMED CABBAGE WITH SAVORY

1 medium-size head of cabbage
Water to cover
Salt to taste
2 tablespoons butter

2 tablespoons flour
1 cup milk or half milk and half cream
½ teaspoon or more chopped fresh or dried savory

1. Remove the core and coarse outer leaves from the cabbage. Shred it fine.

2. Drop the cabbage into rapidly boiling water seasoned to taste with salt. Cook eight to ten minutes or until cabbage is crisp-tender. Drain.

3. Meanwhile, melt the butter and stir in the flour. Add the milk, stirring rapidly with a wire whisk. When the sauce is thickened and smooth add the savory. Continue cooking, stirring frequently, for five minutes. Combine the cabbage with the sauce, heat through and serve.

Yield: Four to six servings.

BAKED WHOLE ONIONS

6 large onions
¼ teaspoon salt
2 tablespoons butter

1 tablespoon chopped savory or one teaspoon ground savory

1. Wipe the onions without peeling them and bake in a 350-degree oven until tender, about one to one and one-quarter hours.

2. Take the onions from the oven and remove the skins. Season with butter, salt and savory.

Yield: Six servings.

SQUASH WITH CHICKEN STUFFING

4 medium-size, tender yellow squash
2 cups chopped cooked chicken
1 cup soft bread crumbs
1 medium onion, grated
1 egg, lightly beaten
½ teaspoon salt
1 teaspoon savory
⅓ cup olive oil
1 clove garlic, crushed
1 cup tomato sauce

1. Preheat the oven to 375 degrees. Cut the ends from the squash and then cut each squash into pieces about two and one-half inches long. Use an apple corer to remove seedy portion from centers, making tubes.

2. Mix the chicken, crumbs, onion, egg, salt and savory. Fill tubes with the mixture.

3. Pour the oil into a casserole and add garlic and tomato sauce. Add the squash, cover and bake until tender, about twenty minutes, turning once. Serve the squash with the tomato sauce.

Yield: Six to eight servings.

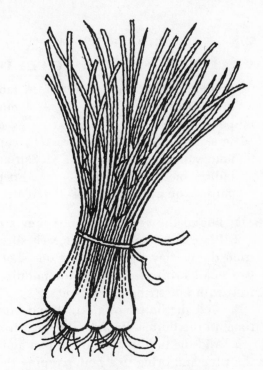

Scallions

SCALLIONS, otherwise known as green onions or spring onions, are among the most delicate members of the onion family. They are in fact merely the tender seedlings of onion and, when garden fresh, edible from green tip to root base.

Raw scallions with a touch of salt are perfect fare for the picnic basket and they are delicious when chopped and mixed in salads whether the salads are made with potatoes, tossed greens or beans. The uses of chopped scallions are legion, adding as they do both color and flavor to such dishes as cream cheese, mayonnaise sauces and herb butters.

VEAL BIRDS WITH SCALLIONS

1 pound veal, cut into thin,
even slices
1/4 pound sliced boiled ham
6 to eight scallions, trimmed
and washed
2 ounces mozzarella cheese,
cut into quarter-inch strips

6 tablespoons butter
4 ounces mushrooms, thinly
sliced (optional)
1/2 cup dry white wine
Salt and freshly ground black
pepper
Watercress or parsley

1. Pound the veal slices until they are very thin.

2. Place a piece of ham on each slice of veal. Roll the veal from the narrow end, enclosing one short length of scallion and two small strips of cheese in the middle of each roll. Secure the rolls with fine string or food picks.

3. Melt the butter in a skillet and brown the rolls, a few at a time, in the butter. Remove the meat from the pan.

4. Add the mushrooms to the pan and cook five minutes. Add the wine and bring to a boil, scraping the bottom of the pan.

5. Return the rolls to the skillet. Add salt and pepper to taste. Cover and simmer gently until the meat is tender, about five to ten minutes.

6. Arrange the rolls on a hot platter and pour the sauce over. Garnish with watercress or parsley.

Yield: Three or four servings.

VIRGINIA CRAB CAKES

1 pound crabmeat, fresh,
frozen or canned
3 eggs
1/2 cup mayonnaise
1/4 cup minced scallions, including green part
2 tablespoons minced celery
with leaves

1 teaspoon Worcestershire
sauce
1 tablespoon lemon juice
1/2 cup fresh bread crumbs
3/4 cup flour
Fine fresh bread crumbs
Oil
Butter

1. Pick over crabmeat; drain if canned. Mix the crabmeat, one egg, mayonnaise, scallions, celery, Worcestershire sauce, lemon

juice and the half cup of bread crumbs. Place in a sieve and drain.

2. Place the flour on one sheet of wax paper, fine bread crumbs on another. Beat two eggs lightly. Heat equal parts of oil and butter to a depth of one-quarter inch in a large, heavy skillet.

3. Shape the crab mixture into rounded teaspoonfuls and drop into the flour. Coat with flour, then with egg and finally with crumbs.

4. Brown on both sides in hot fat.

Yield: Six servings.

RICE PARMIGIANA

2 cups cooked rice
1 cup finely chopped parsley
½ cup chopped green onions, green part and all
1 cup grated Parmesan cheese
3 eggs, well beaten
¼ cup milk
Salt and pepper to taste

1. Preheat oven to 350 degrees.
2. Combine the rice, parsley, onions and cheese.
3. Combine the eggs, milk, salt and pepper. Fold the egg mixture into the rice mixture and pour it into a generously buttered casserole. Place the casserole in a pan of hot water. Bake twenty-five to thirty minutes or until firm.

Yield: Four servings.

COTTAGE CHEESE NOODLES WITH SCALLION BUTTER

⅔ cup soft butter
1 cup creamed cottage cheese
1 teaspoon salt
2 eggs
2½ cups sifted flour, approximately
Boiling salted water
2 bunches scallions, tops and all, chopped
Freshly grated Parmesan cheese

1. Cream one-quarter cup of the butter, the cottage cheese and salt until smooth and fluffy. Add the eggs and mix well. Add the flour, mix and knead on a floured surface until smooth and non-sticky.

2. Cut in half and roll each half very thin. Dry the sheets on cooling racks or kitchen towels until just dry enough to fold without breaking. Fold and cut into any desired width. Unfold the strips and complete the drying.

3. Cook the noodles in a large quantity of boiling salted water for ten minutes and drain.

4. While the noodles are cooking, sauté the scallions in the remaining butter until wilted. Pour over the noodles and toss gently. Serve with grated Parmesan cheese.

Yield: Six servings.

SCALLION QUICHE

Pastry for a one-crust, nine-inch pie
4 strips bacon
½ cup finely chopped scallions
1 cup cubed Swiss cheese (Gruyère or Emmentaler)
¼ cup freshly grated Parmesan cheese

3 eggs, lightly beaten
1½ cups cream or three-fourths cup each milk and cream
¼ teaspoon nutmeg
½ teaspoon salt
¼ teaspoon freshly ground white pepper

1. Preheat the oven to 450 degrees.

2. Line a nine-inch pie pan or shallow, scalloped soufflé dish with pastry and bake five minutes.

3. Cook the bacon until crisp and remove it from the skillet. Pour off all but one tablespoon of the fat in the skillet.

4. Sauté the scallions in the fat in the skillet until tender but not browned.

5. Crumble the bacon and sprinkle it over the bottom of the

partly baked pie shell. Sprinkle the scallions and the cheeses over the bacon.

6. Combine the eggs, cream, nutmeg, salt and pepper; strain over the cheese mixture.

7. Bake the quiche fifteen minutes, reduce the oven temperature to 350 degrees and bake until a knife inserted one inch from the pastry edge comes out clean, about ten minutes longer. Serve immediately.

Yield: Six to eight servings.

CUCUMBERS IN CREAM

6 cucumbers
3 tablespoons butter
3 tablespoons finely chopped
 scallion
⅛ teaspoon freshly ground
 black pepper

1 cup heavy cream
Salt and additional pepper
 to taste
2 teaspoons chopped parsley

1. Preheat the oven to 375 degrees.

2. Peel the cucumbers, cut them into quarters lengthwise and remove the seeds. Cut into one-and-one-half-inch lengths and trim each piece into an oval shape.

3. Place the cucumber pieces in boiling salted water and simmer three minutes; drain.

4. Melt the butter in a baking dish and add the scallion and pepper. Toss the cucumber pieces in the butter mixture. Bake until almost tender, about fifteen minutes, tossing two or three times during baking.

5. Reduce the cream to half its volume and the consistency of a cream sauce by boiling it in a small saucepan. Season with salt and pepper, then fold in the hot, baked cucumbers. Sprinkle with parsley.

Yield: Four servings.

MARINATED LENTILS

2 cups lentils
1 quart water
1½ teaspoons salt
½ cup olive oil
3 tablespoons vinegar

⅓ cup chopped scallions
¾ cup chopped parsley
Salt and freshly ground black
  pepper to taste

1. Pick over and wash the lentils. Boil them gently in the water with the salt until tender, thirty to forty minutes. Cool.

2. Add the oil, vinegar, scallions, parsley, pepper and additional salt to taste. Chill. Serve on lettuce or other greens and garnish with sliced hard-cooked egg.

Yield: About six cups.

CREAMED POTATOES WITH SCALLIONS

2 pounds potatoes
Salted water
½ cup (one stick) butter, at
  room temperature
3 egg yolks
Salt and freshly ground
  pepper to taste

1 cup cream, scalded
1 cup chopped trimmed
  scallions
Paprika or finely chopped
  parsley (optional)

1. Peel the potatoes and place them in salted water to cover. Bring to a boil and simmer until tender but still firm. Force the potatoes through a food mill or potato ricer into a warm mixing bowl.

2. Add the butter and beat with a wooden spoon or electric mixer until thoroughly blended. Beat in the egg yolks, one at a time, and season to taste with salt and pepper.

3. Continue beating while adding the cream. Keep potatoes warm in the top of a large double boiler until ready to serve. Just before serving, fold in the scallions. Place in a hot serving dish and dust with paprika or parsley, if desired.

Yield: Six servings.

MUSHROOMS MARYLAND

12 to sixteen large mushrooms
½ cup (one stick) butter, melted
1½ cups crabmeat
2 eggs
3 tablespoons mayonnaise

¼ cup minced scallions
2 teaspoons lemon juice
½ teaspoon Worcestershire sauce
½ cup fresh bread crumbs

1. Preheat the oven to 375 degrees.

2. Wash and stem the mushrooms. Dip the caps into melted butter and place upside down in a buttered baking dish.

3. Combine crabmeat, eggs, mayonnaise, scallions, lemon juice, Worcestershire and half the bread crumbs. Fill mushroom caps with mixture, sprinkle with remaining crumbs and butter. Bake fifteen minutes.

Yield: Four to six servings.

ZUCCHINI PURÉE

2 pounds zucchini
1 bunch scallions
1 tablespoon water, if necessary
Salt and freshly ground black pepper to taste

⅛ teaspoon nutmeg
1 tablespoon butter
1 tablespoon heavy cream
Paprika

1. Trim off the ends and any rough spots from the zucchini, but do not peel it. Slice the squash and scallions very thin.

2. Place half the sliced squash in a saucepan. Add the scallions and then the remaining squash. Cover tightly and place over moderate heat, shaking the pan frequently the first five minutes of cooking to prevent sticking. If necessary, add the water. After it has started to cook well, reduce the heat to low and let steam until done, fifteen to eighteen minutes.

3. To serve, mash the mixed vegetables with a potato masher, stir in the salt, pepper, nutmeg and butter. Cover again for a

few minutes to reheat. Add the cream just before serving. Turn into a serving dish and garnish with paprika.

Yield: Four servings.

TOMATO AND SCALLION SALAD

3 large ripe tomatoes, chilled
½ cup chopped scallions
¼ cup finely chopped parsley
½ cup olive oil

3 tablespoons wine vinegar
½ teaspoon salt, or to taste
Freshly ground black pepper to taste

1. Slice the tomatoes and arrange them symmetrically on a chilled serving dish. Sprinkle with scallions and parsley.
2. Just before serving, pour the oil, vinegar, salt and pepper over the tomatoes.

Yield: Six servings.

HUSH PUPPIES

2 cups white cornmeal
2 teaspoons baking powder
1 teaspoon salt
½ cup coarsely chopped scallions

⅔ cup milk
1 egg
Fat for deep frying

1. Combine the cornmeal, baking powder and salt. Stir in the chopped scallions, then the milk, beaten with the egg. The mixture should be thick enough to mold in the fingers. Mold the hush puppies into the shape and size of ladyfingers.
2. Heat the fat in a skillet to a depth of one inch. The fat and skillet in which fish has been fried may be used.
3. Drop the hush puppies into the heated fat. Cook about three minutes, turning so as to brown evenly. Serve hot.

Yield: About sixteen hush puppies.

Note: The cornmeal mixture may also be shaped into very small balls, deep-fried until golden brown and used as a cocktail appetizer.

PICKLED SCALLIONS

18 bunches of scallions
1 cup salt
Water
¼ cup sugar
6 cups white vinegar
6 tablespoons whole allspice

1 tablespoon white mustard
seed
2 tablespoons whole peppercorns
6 small hot peppers
6 bay leaves
6 cloves garlic (optional)

1. Trim the scallions to fit into half-pint Ball jars. Wash the scallions thoroughly and remove the outer layer, if it is tough or discolored. Wash the vegetable again.

2. Place the scallions in layers in a large bowl, sprinkling each layer lightly with some of the salt. Cover with cold water and let stand twelve hours or overnight, making sure that the scallions remain submerged.

3. Drain the scallions, rinse them in fresh cold water and drain again.

4. Combine the sugar and vinegar. Add the allspice, mustard seed and peppercorns, tied together in a cheesecloth bag. Bring to a boil and simmer fifteen minutes. Discard the spice bag.

5. Pack the scallions, standing upright, into six sterilized jars. Add one hot pepper, one bay leaf and one clove of garlic, if desired, to each jar.

6. Fill the jars to within one-half inch of the top with the boiling liquid and place the covers on loosely.

7. Place the jars on a wooden rack in a kettle half filled with boiling water. Boil fifteen minutes, remove the jars with tongs and tighten the covers. Store in a cool place.

Yield: Six half-pint jars.

Sesame

SESAME SEEDS were introduced into the United States during the days of slave trading but they did not achieve their extraordinary and deserved status in this country until a decade or so ago. One of the first uses for the seeds in America was as an ingredient in benne wafers, which are closely associated with the South. Today, of course, sesame seeds play an important commercial role in pastry making.

It is the toasted-nut flavor of baked or roasted sesame seeds that gives them their principal appeal. Toasted sesame seeds make an excellent addition to green salads and to French dressings in general. Toasted sesame seeds blended with butter makes a most palatable spread. Sesame oil is notable as a frying medium and is available in many grocery stores which handle oriental products; sesame paste, known as taheeni *or* tahini, *has many tantalizing uses and is available in tins in Near Eastern grocery outlets.*

SESAME EGGPLANT APPETIZERS

2 tablespoons sesame seed
1 medium eggplant
½ clove garlic, finely chopped
1 teaspoon salt

⅛ teaspoon freshly ground
   black pepper
2 tablespoons sour cream
Lemon juice
Dash of ground red pepper

1. Preheat the oven to 400 degrees. Put sesame seeds in a small heavy pan and roast in the oven until slightly brown.

2. Wash the eggplant and prick the skin in one or two places with a fork. Bake the unpeeled vegetable until it is very soft and partly collapses, about one hour and fifteen minutes. Cool slightly, open it and remove the soft pulp. Mash and beat until very smooth. Discard the skin.

3. Add the garlic, salt, black pepper, sour cream, one tablespoon of the toasted sesame seed, one-half teaspoon lemon juice and red pepper to the mashed pulp. Chill thoroughly.

4. To serve, cut off a slice from the top side of an uncooked eggplant. Scoop out the pulp and reserve it for another use. Brush the inside of the eggplant shell with lemon juice and fill the shell with the mashed eggplant mixture. Sprinkle with the remaining sesame seed and serve as an appetizer with crackers or toast.

Yield: About one and two-thirds cup.

The following is less a recipe than a grand luxe production where each guest serves himself. It is called a Chinese chrysanthemum pot and is generally made in an oriental chafing dish. It may be made with excellent results in an electric saucepan. All of the oriental foods needed for a Chinese hot pot are available in the Chinatowns of New York and San Francisco and in many shops that specialize in Chinese foods. The necessary ingredients include fresh ginger, sesame paste (taheeni), bean curd and shrimp paste. An acceptable version of the hot pot may be made, however, without using all of these ingredients.

Oriental chafing dishes are available in New York from the Cathay Hardware Corporation, 49 Mott Street, and the Vibul Phanich Company, 857 Second Avenue. They are also available from the East Norwich House, Huntington, L. I.; Frost Brothers, San Antonio, Tex., and the Emporium in San Francisco.

This is the recipe of Mrs. Emily Kwoh, the owner of New York's Mandarin House and Mandarin East restaurants.

CHINESE CHRYSANTHEMUM POT

2 pounds lean meat (lamb, beef, pork or chicken)
¾ cup finely chopped scallions
¼ cup finely chopped garlic
½ cup finely chopped fresh ginger
½ cup wine vinegar
1 cup sesame paste (available in Middle Eastern grocery stores)
½ cup imported Chinese soy sauce
½ cup dry sherry
½ cup sesame oil
½ cup red bean curd
½ cup shrimp paste

½ cup finely chopped cilantro (Chinese parsley, available in Chinese and Spanish-American markets)
2 quarts meat broth or water
1 head Chinese cabbage chopped, cooked briefly with boiling water and squeezed dry
½ package cellophane noodles, covered with boiling water and drained
1 pound tender, fresh spinach, trimmed, well-washed and drained

1. Have the meat or chicken partly frozen so it is easy to slice. Slice the meat as thinly as possible and arrange it on chilled plates. Allow it to defrost, then chill until ready to use.

2. Place the scallions, garlic, ginger, vinegar, sesame paste, soy sauce, sherry, sesame oil, bean curd, shrimp paste and cilantro in small, individual containers, such as Chinese lacquered serving dishes.

3. Pour the broth into either a traditional chrysanthemum pot, a heatproof earthenware casserole or a deep electric casserole or

saucepan. Bring the broth to a boil. The broth must continue to simmer during the time the dish is prepared and eaten.

4. Arrange the various dishes of condiments around the broth container and allow each guest to prepare his own seasonings, using a spoonful or so of each condiment. Furnish each guest with a small dish for preparing his own sauce.

5. Pass the plates containing the meat slices around the table and allow each guest to serve himself with chopsticks or long forks. The object is to dip the thin slices of meat into the boiling broth and let the meat cook to the desired degree of doneness. The cooked meat is then dipped into the prepared sauces and eaten while hot.

6. After all the meat has been eaten, have each guest ladle a little of the remaining broth into his individual serving of sauce and drink it as a soup.

7. Then drop the Chinese cabbage, cellophane noodles and spinach into the remaining broth. Cook them briefly and eat while warm.

Yield: Eight to ten servings.

TARATOUR BI TAHEENI

(SESAME SAUCE)

6 tablespoons sesame paste (taheeni)	⅓ cup lemon juice
Water	1 clove garlic, finely minced
	1 teaspoon salt

Spoon the sesame paste into a mixing bowl and add a little water. Beat with a whisk and continue adding a little water until the paste becomes somewhat stiff and white. Continue beating and add the lemon juice, garlic and salt. Serve as a dip with bread or use in the following recipe for baba ghanouj.

Yield: About three-quarters cup.

BABA GHANOUJ

(EGGPLANT AND SESAME SAUCE)

2 medium eggplants   ¾ cup sesame sauce (see above)

1. Place the eggplants over hot charcoal or under a medium broiler flame. If the broiler is used, line it first with aluminum foil. Broil the eggplants, turning occasionally, until they are somewhat charred and collapse. The skin will burst.

2. Let the eggplants cool slightly, then peel off the skin, leaving bits of the charred portion to flavor the dish. Beat the eggplant pulp with a whisk or spoon or in an electric mixer. Add the sesame sauce and continue beating until smooth. Garnish with parsley and serve cold with toast or sesame seed crackers.

Yield: Six servings.

PARSLEY AND SESAME PASTE SAUCE

3 cloves garlic

1¼ teaspoons salt

1 cup lemon juice

1 cup sesame paste (taheeni)

½ cup cold water

1½ cups finely chopped parsley

Additional salt to taste

1. Crush the garlic and pulverize it with the salt. Add a little of the lemon juice and work the mixture to a smooth paste. Blend in the taheeni and beat with a fork while adding the remaining lemon juice and the water.

2. Add the parsley and additional salt to taste. Serve cold with sesame crackers, toast or Armenian bread.

Yield: About two and one-half cups of sauce.

SESAME SEED BREAD

1 long loaf French or Italian bread

¼ cup (one-half stick) butter, at room temperature

2 tablespoons chopped parsley

Sesame seeds

1. Preheat the oven to 450 degrees.

2. Split the bread in half lengthwise. Blend the butter with the parsley and spread the mixture on the bread. Sprinkle each half liberally with sesame seeds and place the bread, cut side up, in the oven. It may be placed on a sheet of aluminum foil, if desired.

3. Bake until the bread is heated through and golden brown on top. If desired, the bread may be placed briefly under the broiler before serving.

Yield: Four to six servings.

BENNE WAFERS

½ cup sesame seeds
1 tablespoon butter
1 cup brown sugar, firmly
    packed
3 tablespoons flour
1 egg, beaten
1 teaspoon vanilla
¼ teaspoon salt

1. Preheat the oven to 350 degrees.

2. Put the sesame seeds in a small, heavy pan and roast in the oven until slightly brown. Remove from the oven and add the remaining ingredients.

3. Mix thoroughly and drop by teaspoonfuls onto well-buttered cooky sheets. Bake until firm, five to eight minutes. Remove carefully from the sheets while still warm.

Yield: Thirty wafers.

SESAME SEED BRITTLE

1½ cups sugar
½ cup honey
2 tablespoons water
1 teaspoon lemon juice
¼ teaspoon cinnamon
1 cup (one-third pound)
    sesame seeds

1. Cook the sugar, honey, water and lemon juice in a saucepan over low heat, stirring constantly, until the sugar is dissolved.

2. Continue cooking over low heat, without stirring, until the

mixture reaches 300 degrees on a candy thermometer (a brittle, hard thread will form when a few drops are tested in cold water), about twenty minutes.

3. Remove from the heat and stir in the cinnamon and sesame seeds. Pour the brittle onto a buttered cooky sheet in a thin layer. Loosen before the candy hardens. When cold, break the brittle into pieces.

Yield: About one and one-half pounds.

SESAME CHICKEN

1 three-and-one-half-pound chicken, cut into serving pieces	1 cup fresh bread crumbs
1 cup buttermilk	2 tablespoons finely chopped parsley
6 tablespoons butter	3 tablespoons sesame seeds
½ teaspoon dried tarragon	Salt and freshly ground pepper to taste
1 tablespoon lemon juice	

1. Place the chicken pieces in a mixing bowl and add the buttermilk. Refrigerate several hours, turning the pieces occasionally.

2. Drain the chicken and pat dry with paper towels. Melt the butter and add the tarragon and lemon juice. Combine the crumbs, parsley, sesame seeds, salt and pepper. Dip the chicken pieces first in butter, then roll them in the crumbs. Arrange the pieces on a baking dish and spoon the remaining butter over the chicken. Cover tightly with foil and refrigerate one hour.

3. Preheat the oven to 300 degrees.

4. Bake the chicken, basting occasionally with pan drippings, for one to one and one-half hours.

Yield: Four servings.

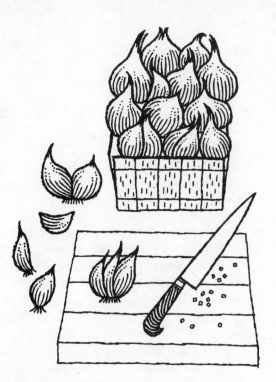

Shallots

SHALLOTS (sha-LOTS) may be counted among the cornerstones of fine French cuisine. They are a member of the onion family and they are an almost ideal blend of mild flavor and aroma. In effect they possess to a coveted degree some of the best traits of onion, garlic and scallions. They are worth seeking at a greengrocers or, failing that, growing in the home garden.

Shallots are rather small, they have a brown skin and may be somewhat elevated in cost in this country. One box lasts a long time, however. Shallots make a splendid contribution to salad dressings; they are delicious when chopped and sprinkled on steak; and, as any French chef can testify, their uses throughout epicurean cuisine are without number.

BILLI BI

2 pounds mussels
2 shallots, coarsely chopped
2 small onions, quartered
2 sprigs parsley
Salt and freshly ground black
   pepper to taste
Pinch of cayenne pepper

1 cup dry white wine
2 tablespoons butter
½ bay leaf
½ teaspoon thyme
2 cups heavy cream
1 egg yolk, lightly beaten

1. Scrub the mussels well to remove all exterior sand and dirt. Place them in a large kettle with the shallots, onions, parsley, salt, black pepper, cayenne, wine, butter, bay leaf and thyme. Cover and bring to a boil. Simmer five to ten minutes, or until the mussels have opened. Discard any mussels that do not open.

2. Strain the liquid through a double thickness of cheesecloth. Reserve the mussels for another use or remove them from the shells and use them as a garnish for the soup.

3. Bring the liquid in the saucepan to a boil and add the cream. Return to a boil and remove from the heat. Add the beaten egg yolk and return to the heat long enough for the soup to thicken slightly. Do not boil. Serve hot or cold.

Yield: Four servings.

Note: This soup may be enriched, if desired, by stirring in two tablespoons of hollandaise sauce before it is served.

COQ AU VIN

1 three-and-one-half-pound
   frying chicken or two two-
   pound broilers
Salt and freshly ground black
   pepper
½ cup diced salt pork
2 tablespoons butter
½ pound small onions
½ pound mushrooms

2 to three chopped shallots
   or one-half cup chopped
   scallions
1 clove garlic, minced
2 tablespoons flour
2 cups dry red wine
3 sprigs parsley
½ bay leaf
⅛ teaspoon thyme
2 tablespoons chopped
   parsley

1. Cut the fryers into quarters or the broilers into halves and season with salt and pepper.

2. Parboil the salt pork five minutes, drain and sauté in the butter until brown. Remove pork and reserve. Sauté the chicken in the fat left in the pan until brown on all sides.

3. Add the onions and mushrooms. Cover pan and cook slowly until the onions are partly tender and beginning to brown. Remove the chicken to a hot platter. Pour off all but two or three tablespoons of the fat. Add the shallots and garlic and cook one minute. Blend in the flour. Add the wine and cook, stirring, until boiling.

4. Return the chicken to the pan. If the wine does not cover the meat, add water. Tie parsley sprigs, bay leaf and thyme in cheesecloth and add to the chicken. Add reserved diced pork.

5. Simmer on top of the stove or cook, covered, in a 400-degree oven until the chicken is tender, thirty minutes or longer. Remove the herb bag and skim the fat from the surface, if desired. Arrange the chicken, onions and mushrooms on a platter, cover with sauce and sprinkle with chopped parsley.

Yield: Four servings.

MUSSELS À LA MARINIÈRE

1 cup dry white wine
3 shallots, coarsely chopped
4 sprigs parsley
½ bay leaf
½ teaspoon thyme
Freshly ground black pepper
   to taste
3 tablespoons butter
3 pounds mussels, scrubbed
   and debearded
¼ cup chopped parsley

1. Combine the wine, shallots, parsley sprigs, bay leaf, thyme, black pepper and butter in a kettle. Bring to a boil and simmer about three minutes.

2. Add the mussels to the kettle, cover and cook quickly over high heat. Occasionally shake the kettle up and down, holding the lid tightly in place. This will redistribute the mussels so they

will cook evenly. Cook five to ten minutes, or until the mussels are opened. Discard any mussels that do not open.

3. Using a large spoon, dip the mussels into soup plates. Spoon the cooking liquid over the mussels and sprinkle with the chopped parsley. Serve immediately with hot, buttered French bread rubbed with garlic, if desired.

Yield: About four servings.

The following is one of the classic dishes of French cuisine. It is authentic in every respect, and shallots are an essential ingredient for absolute success. Chopped green onion may be substituted for the shallots but without the same glory in flavor.

SOLE DUGLÈRE

6 fillets of sole
Salt
Freshly ground black pepper
4 tomatoes, peeled, seeded and chopped
7 tablespoons butter
3 shallots, finely chopped

3 tablespoons finely chopped parsley
2 tablespoons finely chopped chives
1/3 cup dry white wine
1/2 cup fish stock
2/3 cup fish velouté
1 cup heavy cream

1. Preheat the oven to 400 degrees.

2. Split the sole fillets lengthwise and remove the tiny bone unit down the center. Sprinkle the fish on all sides with salt and pepper. Roll the fillet halves like a jelly roll and secure them with toothpicks.

3. Cook the tomatoes in two tablespoons of butter about two minutes.

4. Rub the bottom of a deep, ovenproof skillet with three tablespoons of butter and sprinkle with salt, pepper and shallots. Spoon half the tomato mixture over the skillet. Arrange the rolled fillets in the skillet and spoon the remaining tomato mixture over them. Sprinkle with parsley and chives and pour over them the wine and fish stock. Cover closely with a lid or aluminum foil and bring to the boil on top of the stove. Place the skillet in the oven and bake exactly twenty minutes.

5. Remove the skillet from the oven. Immediately turn off oven heat and leave the oven door open. Transfer the sole to a heatproof platter, cover with foil and place in the oven to keep warm while sauce is prepared.

6. Place the skillet in which fish cooked over high heat to reduce the liquid one third. Add the velouté and heavy cream. Stir rapidly with a wire whisk and cook five minutes. Turn off the heat beneath the skillet and quickly stir in two tablespoons of cold butter. Pour the sauce over the fish and serve immediately.

Yield: Six servings.

WILD RICE DRESSING

1 six-ounce package long grain and wild rice mix
½ cup dry vermouth
3 tablespoons finely chopped shallots
¼ pound mushrooms, coarsely chopped
2 tablespoons butter
Livers from 2 Rock Cornish game hens or chickens, chopped (optional)
1 or two eggs, well beaten
Salt and freshly ground pepper to taste

1. Preheat the oven to 350 degrees.

2. Cook the rice mix according to package directions. While still hot, stir in the dry vermouth. Cool to room temperature.

3. Sauté the shallots and mushrooms in hot butter for four to five minutes and add the livers. Stir into cooled rice.

4. Add the eggs (two will give a more "bound" dressing) to the rice and add salt and pepper to taste. Turn into a lightly greased baking dish and bake thirty minutes.

Yield: Four servings.

Sorrel

*Like garlic, SORREL seems to belong to the ranks of
food which are adored or abhorred with kindred passion.
It is an acid green although it, oddly enough, symbolizes
affection. The French in particular are fond of sorrel
soup, called potage crème d'oseille or potage Germiny.
Sauces of sorrel go well with fish, particularly those of an
oily nature, and some folks like a little sorrel chopped
into green salads. Sorrel has been characterized as a
sour-leaf version of spinach.*

SORREL SOUP

1 pound fresh, unbruised
   sorrel leaves
½ cup chopped onion
¼ cup butter
1 cup light or heavy cream

2 beaten egg yolks
3 cups chicken broth
Salt
Freshly ground black pepper

1. Trim the sorrel and rinse well. Dry the leaves and chop or slice them into thin shreds.

2. Cook the onion in butter until tender. Add the sorrel and simmer five minutes, stirring until sorrel is wilted.

3. Combine the cream and egg yolks and beat until well blended.

4. Bring the chicken broth to a boil. Reduce the heat and gradually add the cream, stirring rapidly with a whisk. Do not boil.

5. Stir in the chopped sorrel and season the soup with salt and pepper to taste. Heat thoroughly and serve hot.

Yeld: Six servings.

EELS IN GREEN SAUCE

½ pound or more fresh spinach, well trimmed

⅓ pound or more sorrel, well trimmed

3 tablespoons oil

3 tablespoons butter

3 pounds eels, cleaned and cut into one-and-one-half-inch lengths

Salt and freshly ground pepper to taste

¾ cup dry white wine

3 tablespoons finely chopped shallots

3 cups fresh or canned chicken broth or fish stock

Juice of one lemon

2 teaspoons chopped fresh thyme

2 egg yolks

1 tablespoon finely chopped fresh basil

Lemon slices

1. Rinse the spinach and sorrel and drain well. Using a large sharp knife, slice the greens into very thin shreds. This is called a chiffonnade.

2. Heat the oil and butter in a large skillet and add the eels. Sprinkle with salt and pepper. Cook, stirring carefully, about three minutes. Drain the eels in a colander.

3. Add the wine and shallots to the skillet and simmer two minutes to reduce slightly. Add eels, chicken broth, lemon juice and thyme; simmer five minutes. Add the chiffonade of greens and simmer ten minutes longer. Remove the skillet from the heat.

4. Beat the yolks with the basil, gradually adding a little hot broth from the skillet. Add about one-half cup broth in all. Stir into the eels.

5. Return the skillet to heat and bring just to the boiling point, stirring and shaking the skillet. Do not boil or the yolks might curdle. Add salt and pepper to taste. Remove from the heat and chill. Serve cold. Garnish with lemon slices.

Yield: Twelve servings.

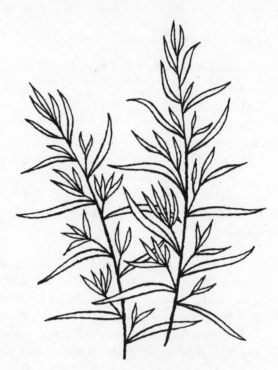

Tarragon

Nothing in the repertoire of herbs and spices has a more appealing and seductive flavor than TARRAGON. It is mysterious, gently pervasive, and is deeply satisfying to the palate.

Tarragon is an essential in Béarnaise sauces, it adds a beguiling touch to tartare sauce and it complements poultry, veal and eggs. It is commonly blended with vinegar, which is, in turn, used as a basis for salad dressings. It is one of the classic fines herbes *of French cuisine, combining eloquently with chopped parsley, chives and chervil. Tarragon symbolizes unselfish sharing.*

TARRAGON VEAL CROQUETTES

3 tablespoons butter
⅓ cup flour
1 cup milk
1¾ cups minced cooked veal
1 tablespoon chopped tar-
ragon
1 tablespoon chopped chives
1 tablespoon chopped parsley

2 eggs
2 tablespoons sherry
Salt and freshly ground black
pepper to taste
1 tablespoon water
Sifted bread crumbs
Fat for deep frying

1. Melt the butter, blend in the flour, add the milk and cook, stirring with a wire whisk, until the mixture boils and thickens.

2. Add the veal, tarragon, chives, parsley, one egg, sherry, salt and pepper. Cook, stirring, until the mixture thickens. Chill.

3. Shape into one-quarter-cup-size croquettes. Beat the remaining egg lightly with the water. Coat the croquettes with the crumbs, beaten egg and again with the crumbs. Dry on a rack thirty minutes.

4. Fry in fat heated to 390 degrees, just until golden brown. Drain on absorbent toweling.

Yield: Ten croquettes.

POULET À L'ESTRAGON

(CHICKEN WITH TARRAGON)

1 three- to three-and-one-half-
pound chicken, cut into
serving pieces
Salt and freshly ground black
pepper
5 tablespoons butter
2 tablespoons finely chopped
tarragon

3 tablespoons finely chopped
shallot
½ cup dry white wine
1½ cups heavy cream
3 tablespoons flour
1 tablespoon Calvados or
applejack (optional)

1. Sprinkle the chicken pieces with salt and pepper. Melt three tablespoons of the butter over high heat and place the

chicken pieces, skin side down, in it. Cook until golden brown and turn the chicken. Sprinkle with half the tarragon and the shallot. Cover closely and cook over low heat fifteen minutes.

2. Remove the cover and sprinkle with the wine. Cover and cook fifteen minutes longer. Transfer the chicken to a warm bowl and keep covered while making the sauce.

3. Add one cup of the cream to the skillet and stir to blend well. Blend the flour with the remaining butter (to make a beurre manie) and add it, a little at a time, to the simmering sauce. Add just enough to reach the desired consistency. Cook five minutes, then add the Calvados and stir. Add the remaining cream.

4. Return the chicken parts to the skillet and spoon the sauce over the chicken. Sprinkle with the remaining tarragon and serve immediately on a hot platter.

Yield: Four servings.

BAKED FISH WITH ALMOND STUFFING

½ cup (one stick) plus two tablespoons butter

4 tablespoons chopped onion

3 cups soft bread crumbs

½ cup chopped celery

½ cup chopped green pepper

2 tablespoons chopped parsley

3 eggs, lightly beaten

Salt

Freshly ground black pepper to taste

2 teaspoons chopped fresh or one teaspoon dried tarragon

½ cup chopped toasted almonds

1 five- to seven-pound striped bass, sea bass or red snapper, cleaned, washed and dried well

1. Preheat the oven to 400 degrees.

2. Melt two tablespoons of the butter and cook the onion until tender but not browned. Add the bread crumbs, celery, green pepper, parsley, eggs, 1 teaspoon salt, pepper, tarragon and almonds. Mix well and use to stuff the fish. Sew up the cavity.

3. Melt the remaining half cup of butter. Line a large baking dish with aluminum foil and pour a little of the butter over the foil. Lay the fish on the foil and sprinkle with additional salt and pepper.

4. Bake the fish about an hour and fifteen minutes, basting frequently with the remaining melted butter. The fish is done when it flakes easily when tested with a fork.

Yield: Six generous servings.

STUFFED SHRIMP WITH TARRAGON

16 large raw shrimp
Salt and freshly ground black
    pepper to taste
6 tablespoons melted butter
1 clove garlic, finely minced,
    or more if desired
2 tablespoons finely chopped
    shallot or onion

½ cup finely chopped mush-
    rooms
½ cup dry bread crumbs
1 tablespoon chopped pars-
    ley
½ teaspoon freshly chopped
    tarragon or one-fourth tea-
    spoon dried
1 cup dry white wine

1. Preheat oven to 350 degrees.

2. Remove the shell from the shrimp but leave on the last tail segment. With a sharp knife split the shrimp lengthwise along the upper vein, but do not cut all the way through. Rinse the shrimp and dry them between absorbent paper toweling. Place each opened-out shrimp between waxed paper and pound lightly with a rolling pin. Do not pound hard or the shrimp will split. Score the shrimp lightly with a knife to prevent them from curling as they cook. Sprinkle with salt and pepper.

3. Melt one tablespoon of the butter and cook the garlic, shallot and mushrooms briefly, about two minutes. Add the remaining butter, bread crumbs, parsley, tarragon and salt and pepper to taste. Divide the mixture over half the shrimp and top each with another shrimp, sandwich-fashion. Place the shrimp in a shallow baking dish and pour the wine around them. Bake until shrimp are pink, basting occasionally. This should take ten to fifteen minutes. Serve hot with lemon wedges.

Yield: Four servings.

RAGOUT OF POTATOES

½ pound sliced bacon, cut into half-inch strips
Water to cover
2 large onions, coarsely chopped
1 clove garlic, finely minced
3 pounds potatoes, cut into one-inch cubes (about two quarts)

1 cup chicken stock
Salt and freshly ground black pepper to taste
1 tablespoon fresh tarragon leaves or one-half teaspoon dried
2 teaspoons wine vinegar
1 tablespoon olive oil
Chopped parsley

1. Place the bacon strips in a saucepan and add water to cover. Cover the pan and bring water to a boil. Drain bacon and dry on a paper towel.
2. Place bacon in a heavy pan and sauté three to five minutes. Remove all but three tablespoons of the fat. Add the onions and garlic and continue cooking until the onions become translucent.
3. Add the potatoes, stock, salt, pepper and tarragon. Cover and simmer slowly about 15 to 20 minutes, or until potatoes are tender and most of the liquid is absorbed. Excess liquid may be removed by evaporation or by mashing a few of the potato pieces.
4. Add the vinegar and oil and toss lightly. Sprinkle with the chopped parsley and serve hot.

Yield: Six servings.

GREEN MAYONNAISE

6 raw spinach leaves, washed well, patted dry and coarsely chopped
1½ tablespoons fresh tarragon leaves
1 tablespoon chopped chives or the green part of scallion
1½ teaspoons chopped dill, fresh or dried

1½ teaspoons fresh marjoram
1 tablespoon lemon juice
1 egg
½ teaspoon dry mustard
½ teaspoon salt
½ teaspoon sugar
1 cup olive oil
1½ teaspoons tarragon vinegar

1. Combine the spinach, herbs, lemon juice, egg and seasonings in the container of an electric blender. Blend at high speed ten seconds.

2. Immediately reduce the speed to low and add half the olive oil in a slow stream. Stop the motor and add the vinegar. Blend at high speed and immediately add the remaining oil in a steady stream. The mayonnaise should make immediately.

Yield: About one and one-half cups.

SCRAMBLED EGGS WITH TARRAGON

¼ pound butter	1 tablespoon freshly
12 eggs, lightly beaten	chopped or 2 teaspoons
½ cup heavy cream	dried tarragon
	Salt to taste

1. Heat the butter in a chafing dish or large skillet and add the eggs. Cook over moderate heat, stirring the eggs constantly with a rubber spatula. Cover all the bottom of the skillet with the spatula and push the eggs toward the center as they set. Do not let the eggs harden.

2. While the eggs are semi-liquid add the cream, tarragon and salt and cook, blending with the spatula. Serve immediately.

Yield: Six servings.

ROCK CORNISH GAME HENS WITH TARRAGON BUTTER

2 Rock Cornish game hens, split in half as for broiling	¼ pound butter
1 clove garlic, sliced in half	1 tablespoon tarragon
Salt and freshly ground pepper to taste	1 tablespoon fresh parsley, finely minced

1. Preheat the oven to 350 degrees.

2. Trim off the excess skin at the neck and the fat at the tail of each half of hen. Rub the skin side with the cut garlic clove; salt and pepper lightly. Place the hens, skin side up, in a lightly buttered baking dish, one and one-half to two inches deep.

3. Melt the butter in a small saucepan and add the tarragon and parsley. Mix well. Baste the hens well with the tarragon butter and roast for one hour, basting every fifteen minutes. Serve with wild rice dressing (page 297).

Yield: Four servings.

SHRIMP SHRODER

1 pound raw shrimp
3 to four tablespoons butter
2 tablespoons minced shallots or green onions
1 to two cloves garlic, finely minced

1 teaspoon tarragon
1 teaspoon fresh parsley, finely minced
½ cup dry vermouth

1. Shell and devein the shrimp and set aside.

2. Melt the butter in a skillet; add the shallots and garlic and sauté briefly.

3. Add the shrimp and cook on both sides just until they begin to turn pink. Add the tarragon and parsley and toss. Pour in the vermouth, bring rapidly to a boil and simmer until the shrimp are done, from three to five minutes, depending on the size. Serve with rice.

Yield: Two servings.

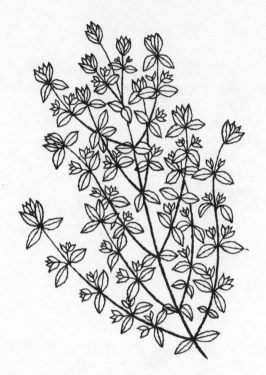

Thyme

THYME (pronounced TIME) is of the essence in French cuisine. More often than not it is paired with that other indispensable ingredient, the bay leaf. There is almost no stew, soup or ragout that does not call for a pinch of one, a leaf or two of the other.

The plant known as thyme is handsome and adorns many a rock garden and garden walk, emitting an unforgettable aroma when trod upon. Thyme is another favorite of the honeybees, particularly those which feast on the thyme growing wild on the slopes of Greece's fabled Mount Hymettus. English thyme is gray-green; woolly thyme is lavender and lemon thyme has a pink aspect.

Generally, thyme is used sparingly as a "background" flavor, but it is also delicious when stressed in such a dish as creamed onions.

Thyme symbolizes courage.

NEW ENGLAND CLAM CHOWDER

2 quarts clams	1 teaspoon thyme, tied in a
¼ pound salt pork	cheesecloth bag
2 cups finely cubed potatoes	½ teaspoon salt, or to taste
1 large onion, finely	¼ teaspoon freshly ground
chopped	white pepper
1 tablespoon flour	2 cups milk
Reserved clam juice plus	2 cups heavy cream
enough water to make two	2 tablespoons butter
cups	

1. Have the clams opened and reserve the juice.

2. Cut the salt pork into fine dice and chop it. Cook over low heat in a large kettle until beginning to brown.

3. Add the potatoes and cook three or four minutes, stirring occasionally with a wooden spoon. Add the chopped onion and continue stirring until the potatoes and onion are soft but not brown. Sprinkle with the flour.

4. Add the reserved clam juice and water, thyme, salt and pepper and bring to a boil.

5. Chop the clams fine and add them to the simmering mixture. Let cook twenty to thirty minutes, until the potatoes are tender. Add the milk and cream and bring to a boil.

6. Remove the thyme tied in cheesecloth and correct the seasonings. Just before serving, stir in the butter. When the butter melts, serve piping hot with buttered toast.

Yield: Six servings.

MARINATED BEEF BORDELAISE

2 cups red Bordeaux wine	2 tablespoons oil
2 cloves garlic, crushed	1 teaspoon vinegar
2 tablespoons chopped	½ teaspoon salt
onion	⅛ teaspoon freshly ground
1 bay leaf	black pepper
1 teaspoon thyme	3 pounds boneless chuck
2 sprigs parsley	beef

1. In a deep bowl combine all ingredients and let stand six to eight hours, occasionally turning the beef in the marinade.

2. Remove the meat, reserving the marinade. Pat the meat dry with a paper towel. In a heavy kettle, brown well in hot oil on all sides. Drain off the oil.

3. Strain the marinade and add one cup to the meat. Cook, partly covered, over low heat until the meat is tender, about two hours, adding more marinade as needed.

Yield: Six servings.

PORK LOIN ROAST WITH THYME

1 six-pound pork loin roast
3 teaspoons salt
1 teaspoon freshly ground black pepper
1 teaspoon thyme
½ teaspoon nutmeg
2 carrots, cut into half-inch slices
2 medium onions, peeled and thinly sliced
1 clove garlic, crushed
2 whole cloves
2 ribs celery
1 bay leaf
1¼ cups dry white wine
1¼ cups bouillon or consommé
Juice of half a lemon
½ cup water

1. Preheat the oven to 475 degrees.

2. Wipe the meat with a damp cloth and rub it with a mixture of the salt, pepper, thyme and nutmeg.

3. Arrange the carrots, onions, garlic, cloves, celery and bay leaf over the bottom of a roasting pan and cover with the roast. Pour one-half cup each of the wine and bouillon over the roast and place in the oven. Bake, uncovered, twenty minutes, or until the roast is golden brown. Reduce the heat to 350 degrees and continue roasting three to four hours, basting occasionally.

4. Fifteen minutes before the roast is done, transfer it to a hot platter and squeeze the juice of half a lemon over it. Return to the oven while making the gravy.

5. Pour off the fat from the roasting pan and add remaining wine, bouillon and water. Boil rapidly, stirring and scraping the

sides and bottom of the pan. Cook until the gravy is thickened and only about one cup remains. Serve the meat hot and the gravy in a separate dish.

Yield: Six to eight servings.

SOLE FILLETS EN PAPILLOTE

3 fillets of sole
6 thin slices of cooked ham
½ cup (one stick) butter
Salt and freshly ground black
    pepper to taste

1 teaspoon lemon thyme
    leaves
3 tablespoons chopped pars-
    ley
Lemon juice to taste

1. Preheat the oven to 400 degrees. Cut six pieces of parchment or aluminum foil into ovals about thirteen inches at the widest point.

2. Cut the sole fillets in half. Place a slice of ham on half of each piece of parchment or foil. Top the ham with a slice of sole. Dot the fish liberally with one-quarter cup of the butter. Sprinkle with salt, pepper, thyme and parsley. Fold the other half of the parchment over and twist the edges to seal the ends envelope-fashion. The edges must be thoroughly sealed to enclose the juices as the food cooks.

3. Place the packets in a shallow pan and bake fifteen minutes.

4. Meanwhile, melt the remaining one-quarter cup of butter and season to taste with lemon juice. Serve the packets unopened with the melted lemon-butter on the side.

Yield: Six servings.

CREAMED ONIONS

2 pounds small white onions
¼ cup (one-half stick) butter
¼ cup flour
½ teaspoon salt

¼ teaspoon freshly ground
    pepper
1 cup milk
1 cup heavy cream
1 teaspoon thyme

1. Steam the unpeeled onions in a covered colander over boiling water for approximately thirty minutes, or until tender. Remove skins.

2. Melt the butter, remove from the heat and blend in the flour, salt and pepper. Add the milk and cream slowly, stirring. Return to the heat and bring to a boil, stirring constantly. Add the onions and simmer two minutes.

3. Stir in the thyme. Serve immediately.

Yield: Six to eight servings.

LAMB SHANKS WITH EGGPLANT AND THYME

1 cup finely chopped onion
1 clove garlic, finely minced
2 tablespoons butter
6 lamb shanks
Flour for dredging
Salt and freshly ground pepper to taste
1 teaspoon thyme
½ cup oil
1 cup crushed, peeled tomatoes
½ cup dry white wine
1 bay leaf
1 small eggplant, peeled and cut into one-inch cubes

1. Preheat the oven to 325 degrees.

2. Cook the onion and garlic in butter until soft but not brown. Set aside.

3. Wipe off the shanks with a damp cloth. Combine the flour, salt, pepper and thyme and coat the shanks with the mixture.

4. Heat the oil in a large skillet and cook the shanks on all sides until golden brown. As the shanks are browned, transfer them to a large casserole. Add the onion and garlic mixture, the tomatoes, wine and bay leaf. Bring to a boil on top of the stove and cover. Bake two hours.

5. Drop the eggplant cubes into a little boiling salted water and cook briefly. Drain. Add them to the lamb and continue baking, basting the lamb occasionally, about thirty minutes or until lamb is fork tender.

Yield: Six servings.

GARDINER'S BAY FISH SOUP

3½ pounds fresh fish bones
2 quarts water
1 onion, sliced
4 cloves garlic, sliced
2 ribs celery without leaves
6 sprigs fresh thyme or one teaspoon dried thyme
2 bay leaves, broken in half
15 peppercorns
1 cup dry white wine
1 dozen cherrystone clams
3 tablespoons olive oil
2 onions, coarsely chopped

1 small sprig rosemary
2 tomatoes, cored and quartered
1 quart potatoes, peeled and quartered (about six whole potatoes)
¼ cup heavy cream
2 tablespoons Pernod, Ricard or other anise-flavored liqueur
2 tablespoons finely chopped parsley

1. Place the fish bones, water, sliced onion, one clove garlic, celery, half the thyme, one bay leaf, peppercorns, wine and clams in a kettle.

2. Bring to a boil and cook twenty minutes. Strain through a colander, pushing to extract as much liquid as possible from the solids. Reserve the liquid.

3. Heat the oil and add the remaining garlic, thyme and bay leaf and the chopped onions. Add the rosemary, tomatoes, potatoes and reserved stock. Bring to a boil and cook forty-five minutes. Force through a sieve or food mill equipped with a fine blade to purée some of the solids. Beat well with a wire whisk and bring to a boil. Add the cream and simmer five minutes. Add the liqueur, stir in the chopped parsley and serve hot.

Yield: Six servings.

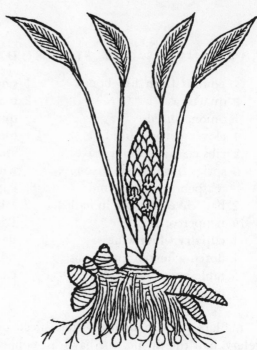

Turmeric

TURMERIC (TURM-uhrick) is principally used in curries, pickles and chowchows. Turmeric, in fact, is the spice which, more often than not, gives the yellow color to commercially packaged curry powders.

Turmeric is derived from the dried root of a brilliant, orange-hued tropical plant which is related to the ginger family. When powdered, turmeric is brilliant yellow and may be used in almost any curried dish.

BRAISED CAULIFLOWER

(A curry dish)

1 medium onion, sliced
2 teaspoons fresh ginger, diced, or one-half teaspoon powdered ginger
2 tablespoons vegetable oil
2 small cauliflowers, cut into flowerets

1 tablespoon turmeric
2 teaspoons cumin
1 teaspoon salt
½ teaspoon freshly ground black pepper
1 tablespoon mustard seed
½ cup water

314

1. Sauté the onion and ginger in the oil.

2. Stir in the remaining ingredients, cover and cook until the cauliflower is tender, about ten minutes, adding a little water if necessary to prevent burning. Serve with other curried dishes and dal (page 180).

Yield: Six servings.

BILL CLIFFORD'S KEEMA WITH PEAS

(A curry dish)

1½ pounds ground lamb or beef
2 medium onions, chopped
1½ teaspoons salt
2 teaspoons turmeric
1 tablespoon coriander
½ teaspoon crushed red pepper, or to taste
1 cup canned Italian peeled tomatoes or four medium fresh tomatoes, peeled and chopped
1 package frozen green peas

1. Cook in a skillet all the ingredients except the tomatoes and peas for ten minutes, stirring to break up the meat.

2. Add the tomatoes and simmer, covered, twenty minutes.

3. Add the peas and simmer until tender. Serve with other curried dishes and dal (page 180).

Yield: Six servings.

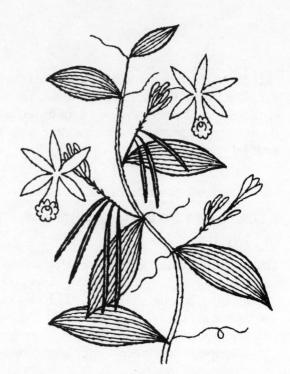

Vanilla

It seems almost poetic justice that VANILLA with its splendid flavor is the dried bean of an orchid. The plant from which it is taken has a long stem and attaches itself to trees by a scheme of aerial rootlets which also penetrate the soil.

Vanilla, like cacao, was first cultivated by the Indians of Mexico who, oddly enough, never made the happy liaison of products to produce vanilla-flavored chocolate.

A list of all the uses for vanilla would fill several volumes but it is, of course, best known as a flavor of ice cream. Vanilla is available in two forms, either as a dried bean, which professional chefs prefer, or as a liquid extract. When buying the latter care should be taken to purchase "pure" vanilla extract; it is far superior to the imitation product.

SWEDISH APPLECAKE WITH VANILLA SAUCE

½ cup (one stick) butter   2⅔ cups applesauce
4 cups zwieback crumbs

1. Preheat the oven to 375 degrees. Butter a nine-inch baking dish.
2. Melt the butter in a skillet, add the crumbs and stir until brown.
3. Line the baking dish with a layer of the crumbs, then alternate layers of applesauce and remaining crumbs, ending with crumbs on top.
4. Bake twenty-five to thirty-five minutes. Cool before unmolding and serve with vanilla sauce.

Yield: Ten servings.

VANILLA SAUCE

6 egg yolks   4 teaspoons vanilla extract
4 tablespoons sugar   ½ cup heavy cream, whipped
2 cups cream, heated

1. Beat the egg yolks and sugar in the top of a double boiler. Add the heated cream and cook until thick, stirring constantly.
2. Remove from the heat, add vanilla and cool, beating occasionally. When cold, fold in the whipped cream carefully.

Yield: Ten servings.

VANILLA CRUMB CAKE

2 cups plus three table-
    spoons sifted flour
2 teaspoons baking powder
½ teaspoon salt
½ cup shortening
2½ teaspoons vanilla
1 cup granulated sugar
2 eggs
1 cup chopped dates or seed-
    less raisins
1 cup milk
⅔ cup coarsely chopped
    pecans
¾ cup brown sugar
1 teaspoon cinnamon
2 tablespoons butter
¼ cup sifted confectioners'
    sugar
2 teaspoons cream

1. Preheat the oven to 350 degrees.

2. Sift together two cups of the flour, the baking powder and salt. Set aside.

3. Blend the shortening with two teaspoons of the vanilla. Gradually mix in the granulated sugar. Beat in one egg at a time. Stir in the dates or raisins. Add the flour mixture alternately with the milk.

4. Turn into a well-greased and lightly floured 9 x 9 x 2-inch pan and sprinkle the pecans over the top. Combine the brown sugar, cinnamon, butter and the remaining three tablespoons flour and sprinkle this mixture over the nuts.

5. Bake until a cake tester inserted in the center comes out clean, about one hour and ten minutes. Mix the confectioners' sugar, cream and remaining one-half teaspoon vanilla and drizzle over the cake while it is still warm.

Yield: Nine to twelve servings.

PAULA PECK'S PRINCESS CAKE

1 cup (two sticks) butter	Pinch of salt
2⅔ cups sifted flour	¼ teaspoon cream of tartar
1 teaspoon vanilla	1⅔ cups sugar
8 egg whites	

1. Preheat the oven to 350 degrees. Grease and lightly flour a ten-inch tube pan.

2. Cream the butter and one and one-third cups of the flour until light and fluffy. Add the vanilla.

3. Beat egg whites with salt and cream of tartar until they hold soft peaks. Add the sugar, a tablespoon at a time, beating well after each addition. Beat whites five minutes, or until very firm.

4. Fold one-quarter of the beaten egg whites into the butter-flour mixture. Pour the mixture over the remaining egg whites. Fold gently while sprinkling the remaining flour in. Do not overmix.

5. Pour into prepared pan. Bake about one hour, or until the cake is golden brown and shrinks from the sides of the pan.

6. Cool in the pan ten minutes before turning out to cool on a rack.

Yield: Twelve servings.

LADYFINGERS

3 eggs, at room temperature, separated
⅛ teaspoon salt

½ cup sugar
1 teaspoon vanilla extract
²⁄ cup sifted cake flour

1. Preheat the oven to 350 degrees.
2. Grease and lightly flour a ladyfinger baking tin or cover baking sheets with unglazed paper.
3. Beat the egg whites and salt together until foamy. Add one-quarter cup of the sugar gradually and continue beating until the meringue is stiff. Set aside.
4. Beat the egg yolks with the vanilla extract, adding the remaining one-quarter cup of sugar gradually, until the mixture forms stiff peaks. Fold in the stiffly beaten egg whites.
5. Sift about one-quarter of the flour at a time over the egg mixture. Fold in lightly.
6. Using a pastry bag and a round tube, force the batter into the prepared ladyfinger tin or force it out in strips three and one-half to four inches long on the prepared baking sheets. Leave half an inch between strips.
7. Bake the ladyfingers until they are a light golden brown, about twelve to fifteen minutes. Cool on a rack.

Yield: Eighteen ladyfingers.

WHITE SUGAR COOKIES

1 cup (two sticks) butter, at room temperature
1½ cups sugar
2 eggs, beaten
2 tablespoons milk

2 teaspoons vanilla
5 cups sifted flour, approximately
2 teaspoons baking powder

1. Preheat the oven to 375 degrees.

2. Cream the butter and sugar. Add the eggs, milk and vanilla and mix well.

3. Sift together about three cups of the flour and the baking powder. Stir into the creamed mixture. Add enough additional flour to make a stiff dough. Shape the dough into four balls and chill.

4. Roll each ball of dough on a floured surface to one-quarter inch thickness and cut into desired shape. If desired, decorate with raisins or nuts or sprinkle with cinnamon or colored sugar.

5. Place on ungreased cooky sheets one-half inch apart and bake until no imprint remains when a cooky is pressed gently, about twelve minutes. Decorate as desired. Store in a tightly sealed container.

Yield: About five dozen cookies.

BLACK AND WHITE SOUFFLÉ

4 tablespoons (one-half stick) butter
4 tablespoons flour
1⅓ cups hot milk
½ teaspoon salt
3 ounces unsweetened chocolate
2 tablespoons cold coffee

6 egg yolks
½ cup plus one tablespoon sugar
2 teaspoons vanilla
10 egg whites
12 ladyfingers (page 319)
Kirsch or cognac

1. Preheat the oven to 375 degrees.

2. Melt the butter in a saucepan and stir in the flour. When well blended, add the milk, stirring briskly with a wire whisk. When thickened and smooth add the salt and simmer over low heat three minutes, stirring constantly. Remove from the heat. Spoon half the mixture into another saucepan.

3. Gradually heat the chocolate with the coffee. When the chocolate is melted, add the coffee-chocolate mixture, three of the egg yolks, beaten, and one-quarter cup plus one tablespoon sugar to one of the saucepans. Mix well with the whisk.

4. To the mixture in second saucepan fold in the remaining sugar, remaining beaten egg yolks and the vanilla. Beat the egg whites until stiff and fold half of them into each soufflé mixture.

5. Turn the chocolate soufflé mixture into a two-quart buttered and sugared soufflé dish. Dip the ladyfingers in kirsch and arrange them over the chocolate soufflé.

6. Pour the vanilla soufflé mixture over the ladyfingers and bake the soufflé thirty-five to forty minutes. Serve immediately with zabaglione.

Yield: Six to eight servings.

VANILLA BREAD-AND-BUTTER CUSTARD

3 eggs, beaten
⅓ cup sugar
¼ teaspoon salt
1½ teaspoons vanilla
¼ cup cold milk

2 cups milk, scalded
2 tablespoons butter
2 slices white bread, one-quarter inch thick

1. Preheat the oven to 325 degrees.

2. Combine eggs, sugar, salt, vanilla and cold milk. Stir in the hot milk. Pour into a buttered one-quart casserole.

3. Butter one side of bread and place over top of custard, buttered side up, just before placing in the oven. Place in a pan of hot water. Bake until a knife inserted in the center comes out clean, about one hour.

Yield: Six servings.

CHARLOTTE RUSSE WITH KIRSCH

8 egg yolks
1 cup sugar
2 cups milk
1 one-inch length of vanilla bean
2 envelopes unflavored gelatin

¼ cup cold water
¼ cup kirsch
2 cups heavy cream
12 ladyfingers, split (page 319)

1. Combine the egg yolks and sugar and work the mixture with a wooden spoon until smooth. Bring the milk to a boil with the vanilla bean. Add it gradually to the yolk mixture, stirring rapidly with a wire whisk. Cook over boiling water until thick.

2. Soften the gelatin in the cold water and add it to the custard, stirring until the gelatin dissolves. Remove the vanilla bean. Cool the custard but do not let it set. Add the kirsch.

3. Whip the cream until it stands in moist peaks and fold it into the custard.

4. Line a one and one-half to two-quart mold with ladyfingers arranged in a daisy petal pattern. Stand ladyfingers close together around the sides of the mold.

5. Pour the custard mixture into the mold, cover with wax paper and chill until set, about two hours. Any extra custard may be molded in individual custard cups. Unmold and serve.

Yield: Eight to ten servings.

CHARLOTTE AUX POMMES

6 to eight pounds crisp eat-
  ing apples
1 cup apricot preserves,
  forced through a sieve
1 cup plus two tablespoons
  sugar
2 teaspoons vanilla extract

3 tablespoons butter
½ cup dark rum
10 to twelve slices homemade-
  type white bread
1 cup clarified butter (page
  1)

1. Peel, core and slice the apples thin, making about four quarts. Place in a pan, cover and cook over very low heat, stirring occasionally, until tender, about twenty minutes.

2. Add one-half cup of the apricot preserves, one cup of the sugar, the vanilla, butter and one-quarter cup rum; mix well. Boil the mixture, stirring, for about ten minutes or until the water content has almost entirely evaporated and a very thick paste remains. There should be at least six cups of apple purée.

3. Preheat the oven to 425 degrees.

4. Remove the crusts from the bread and cut shapes exactly to cover the bottom and sides of a cylindrical six-cup mold that is at least three and one-half to four inches high and about five and one-half inches in bottom diameter.

5. Sauté the pieces of bread in four tablespoons of the clarified butter and place them, overlapping each other, around the inner circumference of the mold. Trim the protruding ends.

6. Pack the apple purée into the mold, allowing it to form a dome about three-quarters of an inch high. Cover with four or five butter-dipped bread strips. Pour any remaining clarified butter over the ends of the bread around the edges.

7. Set in a pan and bake about thirty minutes. When the bread is golden brown, the charlotte is done.

8. Remove from the oven and cool fifteen minutes. Unmold carefully. If there is danger of collapse, cool further before un-molding.

9. Boil the remaining preserves, rum and sugar until thick and sticky. Spread it over the charlotte. Serve hot, warm or cold.

Yield: Six to eight servings.

CRÈME BRÛLÉ

3 cups heavy cream
Pinch of salt
½ vanilla bean or two teaspoons vanilla extract

⅓ cup granulated sugar
6 egg yolks
⅓ cup brown sugar

1. Preheat the oven to 300 degrees.

2. Heat the cream, salt, vanilla bean or extract and the granulated sugar over boiling water or low heat.

3. Beat the egg yolks until light in color and gradually blend in a little of the hot cream mixture. Gradually stir in the remaining cream mixture.

4. Strain into a 10 x 6 x 2-inch buttered baking dish. Place in a pan of hot water and bake one hour and twenty minutes. Increase oven temperature to 325 degrees and bake twenty-five minutes longer, or until a knife inserted near the center comes out clean. Do not overbake.

5. Cool and chill thoroughly. Just before serving, sprinkle the surface with the brown sugar. Place the dish in a pan of cracked ice and broil two to three minutes, or until the sugar is melted, being careful not to burn the sugar. Serve at once.

Yield: Six to eight servings.

MONT BLANC AUX MARRONS

1½ pounds chestnuts
Water
3 cups milk
1 two-inch piece vanilla
   bean
¾ cup sugar

2 tablespoons butter
¼ teaspoon salt
1½ cups heavy cream,
   whipped
Vanilla
Sugar

1. Cut a cross in the flat side of each chestnut. Cover with water and boil fifteen minutes. Drain, cover with cold water, shell and peel off brown skin. The skin is easier to remove while the chestnuts are wet and warm.

2. Meanwhile, scald the milk with the vanilla bean in the top of a double boiler over direct heat. As each chestnut is peeled, add it to the milk. Cook over boiling water until the chestnuts are very tender, about thirty minutes. Drain. (The milk may be used later for a pudding.)

3. While the chestnuts are cooking, boil the sugar and one-third cup water to 236 degrees (a soft ball will form when dropped into cold water).

4. Purée the chestnuts in a food mill or sieve. Add the sugar syrup, butter and salt and blend well.

5. Force the chestnut mixture through a ricer, letting it fall into a nine-inch ring mold. Place any purée that falls outside in the mold. Turn out on a serving plate and chill.

6. Fill the center with whipped cream, flavored with vanilla and sweetened to taste.

Yield: Twelve servings.

CREAM RICE MOLD

½ cup long-grain rice	1 envelope (one tablespoon)
2 cups milk, scalded	unflavored gelatin
2 eggs	¼ cup cold water
½ cup sugar	1½ teaspoons vanilla
¼ teaspoon salt	¾ cup mixed glacé fruit
¾ cup cold milk	1 cup heavy cream, whipped

1. Mix the rice and the hot milk in the top of a double boiler. Cover and cook over boiling water until tender, or about forty-five minutes.

2. Combine the eggs, sugar and salt in a saucepan. Blend in the cold milk. Cook, stirring, over very low heat until the custard coats a metal spoon.

3. Soften the gelatin in the cold water and add it to the custard in the saucepan. Strain the custard and mix it with the cooked rice. Add the vanilla. Chill until the mixture begins to set. Fold in the glacé fruit and tne whipped cream. Turn mixture into a five-cup mold and chill until ready to serve.

4. Turn out onto a chilled platter and garnish with currant jelly and additional glacé fruit, if desired.

Yield: Six to eight servings.

PEARS HÉLÈNE

6 Bartlett pears	Vanilla ice cream
2 cups water	Creamed fudge sauce (page
1¼ cups sugar	327)
1 two-inch piece vanilla bean or one teaspoon vanilla extract	

1. Peel the pears, cut them lengthwise into halves and remove the cores.

2. Combine the water, sugar and vanilla in a saucepan. Bring to a boil, stirring. Add a few pear halves at a time to the sugar

syrup and cook gently until tender. Chill the cooked pears in the syrup.

3. When ready to serve, arrange two drained pear halves in each dessert dish. Top each with a ball of ice cream and hot fudge sauce.

Yield: Six servings.

CUSTARD SAUCE

4 egg yolks	2 cups milk, scalded
¼ cup sugar	1 teaspoon vanilla
⅛ teaspoon salt	

1. Beat the egg yolks slightly in the top of a double boiler. Add the sugar and salt and stir in the scalded milk slowly.

2. Cook the sauce over water that is kept just below the boiling point, stirring constantly, until it thickens.

3. Add the vanilla and serve over cake, ice cream or stewed fruit.

Yield: About two and one-half cups.

CHOCOLATE BUTTER CREAM

1 six-ounce package semi-sweet chocolate pieces	4 egg yolks
	1 teaspoon vanilla
¼ cup boiling water	½ cup (one stick) butter

1. Empty the package of chocolate bits into the container of an electric blender. Add the boiling water, cover and blend on high speed twenty seconds.

2. Turn off the motor and add the egg yolks and vanilla. Cover and turn the motor on high speed.

3. With the motor on, uncover the blender and drop in the soft butter. Blend until the frosting is smooth, about fifteen minutes. If the frosting is too soft, chill in the refrigerator until of spreading consistency.

Yield: Enough frosting to fill and frost an eight-inch cake or twelve cupcakes.

CREAMED FUDGE SAUCE

1 cup sugar
¼ cup light corn syrup
⅓ cup cocoa
½ teaspoon salt
½ cup water

1 teaspoon vanilla
2 tablespoons butter
½ cup heavy cream,
   whipped

1. Mix the sugar, corn syrup, cocoa, salt and water in a saucepan and cook to 228 degrees on a candy thermometer.
2. Add the vanilla and butter. Mix but do not beat. Fold in the whipped cream. Serve over cake or ice cream.

Yield: About two cups.

VANILLA DIVINITY

2⅓ cups sugar
½ cup light corn syrup
½ cup water
¼ teaspoon salt
 2 egg whites

Red, green or yellow food
   coloring (optional)
1 teaspoon vanilla
1 cup pecans or walnuts,
   coarsely chopped

1. Cook the sugar, corn syrup, water and salt to 264 degrees (it will form a hard, almost brittle ball when dropped into cold water), stirring only until the sugar is dissolved.
2. When the syrup is almost ready, beat the egg whites in an electric mixer or with a rotary hand beater until stiff. Add the syrup in a fine stream, beating constantly. Replace the beater with a wooden spoon when the mixture becomes heavy. If desired, color the mixture pink, green or yellow.
3. Add the vanilla and continue beating until the mixture just holds its shape when dropped from a spoon.
4. Add the nuts, mix quickly and drop as speedily as possible by rounded teaspoonfuls on wax paper or a lightly greased surface. Or turn the divinity into a greased 8 x 8-inch pan. Coat with melted semi-sweet chocolate and sprinkle with chopped

nuts. Cool, turn out of the pan, invert the candy and cut it into squares.

Yield: Twenty-four pieces or one and one-quarter pounds of candy.

WHITE TAFFY

2 cups sugar	⅛ teaspoon salt
½ cup light corn syrup	1 teaspoon vanilla
⅔ cup water	

1. Grease one 9 x 9-inch pan or two 8 x 8-inch pans if two people are going to pull the taffy. Also grease a large surface for cutting the candy.

2. Cook all ingredients except the vanilla to 268 degrees (it will form a firm, nearly brittle ball when dropped into cold water), stirring only until the sugar is dissolved. Pour into the greased pans.

3. When candy is cool enough to handle, pour the vanilla into the center and fold the corners over the vanilla so it will not be lost. Pull, using the finger tips, until the candy is rather firm and white.

4. Stretch into a long rope about three-quarters inch in diameter. Lay the rope on the greased surface and cut it at once into pieces of desired size. Separate the pieces to prevent sticking together. Serve on a buttered plate or, if the candy is to be kept, wrap each piece in wax paper, foil or transparent Saran and store in a sealed container.

Yield: About sixty one-inch pieces or one pound two ounces candy.

Note: The taffy may be colored and flavored, before pulling, with a suitable flavoring oil. For example, color the taffy pink and flavor it with wintergreen; color it pale green and flavor it with spearmint; color it yellow and flavor it with lemon, or leave the taffy white and flavor it with peppermint.

CREAM TAFFY

2 cups sugar	¼ teaspoon salt
¾ cup water	1 cup heavy cream
¼ cup light corn syrup	1 teaspoon vanilla

1. In a three- or four-quart saucepan cook the sugar, water, corn syrup and salt to 250 degrees (it will form a hard ball when dropped into cold water), stirring only until the sugar is dissolved.

2. Add the cream and cook slowly, stirring as needed to prevent sticking, to 260 degrees (almost brittle). Pour into a greased pan.

3. When cool enough to handle, pour the vanilla into the center and gather the corners toward the center so the vanilla will not be lost. Remove from the pan and pull with the fingers, dipped in cornstarch if necessary to prevent sticking, until rather firm and a light cream color.

4. Stretch into a long rope about three-quarters inch in diameter. Lay the rope on a greased surface and cut it at once into one-inch pieces.

5. Wrap in foil, transparent Saran or wax paper.

Yield: About 120 one-inch pieces or one pound three ounces candy.

DAVID DUGAN'S SPRITZ CHRISTMAS COOKIES

¼ pound butter	1 teaspoon vanilla
¼ pound margarine	2 cups cake flour
2 tablespoons solid white vegetable shortening	½ teaspoon salt
	¼ teaspoon baking powder
1 cup sugar	1¾ cups unbleached flour
2 eggs	Red and green colored sugars

1. Preheat the oven to 375 degrees.

2. Cream the butter, margarine and vegetable shortening. Gradually add the sugar, beating constantly. Add the eggs, one at a time, and the vanilla.

3. Sift together all the remaining ingredients except the colored sugars and add slowly to the batter, beating on low speed. Use a cooky press to press the mixture onto ungreased Teflon cooky sheets. Decorate with colored sugars and bake eleven minutes.

Yield: About seventy-two cookies.

Watercress

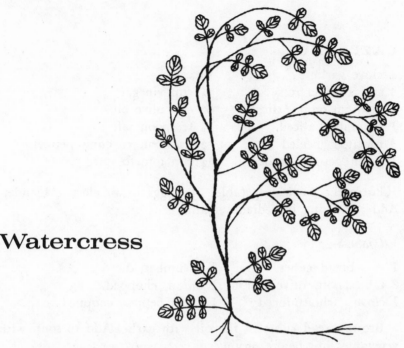

WATERCRESS, the delicate peppery plant with the handsome dark or pale green leaves, symbolizes stability and power. It is easily cultivated and today it is grown commercially on a wide scale, but the watercress growing wild in clear brooks and streams is more appealing to the herbalist and gourmet than a host of daffodils.

Perhaps the most elegant of sandwiches are those of a finger shape with a watercress and mayonnaise filling. Watercress salad gives a mildly pungent punctuation to a meal and watercress soup is a joy. So are platters garnished with sprigs of the natural greenery.

GAZPACHO

1 clove garlic	4 eggs
4 sprigs watercress	¼ cup vinegar
1 medium onion, sliced	¼ cup olive oil
1 cucumber, sliced	⅛ teaspoon salt
3 tomatoes, peeled	⅛ teaspoon cayenne pepper
1 green pepper, seeded	¾ cup tomato juice

Purée the garlic, vegetables and eggs in an electric blender. Add remaining ingredients. Chill.

GARNISH:

1 cup bread cubes	1 cucumber, diced
2 tablespoons olive oil	1 onion, chopped
1 clove garlic, minced	1 green pepper, chopped

Brown bread cubes in the oil with garlic. Add to soup with vegetables just before serving.

Yield: Eight servings.

SHRIMP SALAD WITH GREENS

1 pound fresh spinach	1 teaspoon Dijon or Düsseldorf mustard
1 bunch watercress	
14 medium shrimp, cooked, shelled and deveined	3 tablespoons lemon juice
	1 clove garlic, minced
¼ cup peanut oil	1 tablespoon chopped dill
¼ cup olive oil	Salt and freshly ground black pepper to taste

1. Rinse the spinach in several changes of cold water. Drain. Cut the leaves in half. Wash the watercress, drain it and trim off the stems.

2. Slice the shrimp into bite-size pieces.

3. Combine the oils, mustard, lemon juice, garlic, dill, salt and pepper. Whip with a fork until well blended.

4. Combine the greens and shrimp. Toss with the dressing. Season to taste.

Yield: Six servings.

WALNUT AND WATERCRESS SANDWICHES

½ cup finely chopped watercress
½ cup broken walnut meats
½ cup cream cheese
Salt to taste

2 hard-cooked eggs, sieved
Butter
12 slices white bread, trimmed

1. Combine the watercress, walnuts, cream cheese, salt and eggs in a mixing bowl. Blend well and correct seasonings.

2. Butter the bread and spread six of the slices with the filling. Cover with remaining bread slices.

Yield: Six servings.

Woodruff

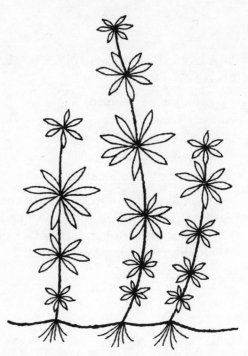

WOODRUFF *symbolizes modest worth and that is a sermon in itself. It is a plant of almost overpowering sweetness and therefore limited uses.*

Woodruff grows wild in many European countries, where it is used as a flavoring for candies, wines and punches or "bowles." The flavor of woodruff reaches a peak of sorts around the first of May, when it is drunk in May wine. Some people say that woodruff is preferably used in an old-fashioned sachet to keep away the moths.

LUCHOW'S MAY WINE BOWL

½ cup dried woodruff
¼ cup superfine granulated
sugar
½ cup cognac
2 bottles Rhine or Moselle
wine

1 bottle champagne or club
soda
½ cup whole fresh straw-
berries

1. Tie the woodruff in a small piece of cheesecloth. Place it in a bowl and add the sugar, cognac and one-half bottle of the wine. Cover closely and let stand overnight.

2. Strain the woodruff-wine mixture into a punch bowl containing ice cubes or a large chunk of ice. Add the remaining still wine, champagne and strawberries. Serve in stemmed glasses.

Yield: Eight to ten cups.

Herbs and Spices with Limited, Quaint, or Questionable Virtues

ANGELICA symbolizes inspiration. It is used in making cordials and liqueurs but it is principally used in a candied form. In that form it is cut into various shapes and is used to decorate desserts.

BALM symbolizes pleasantry and is generally called lemon balm for a fairly obvious reason. It may be used in fruit cups and salads. It can add interest to fish dishes and cream soups.

BERGAMOT symbolizes "your whims are quite unbearable." Bergamot makes a rather whimsical cup of tea.

BIRCH symbolizes meekness. Birch bark may be made into a wine of dubious merit.

BORAGE symbolizes both bluntness and courage. It tastes like cucumber and is greatly admired by the makers of Pimm's Cup.

A blade or two of BUFFALO GRASS, when dried, gives a splendid character to vodka if it is allowed to steep in the liquid. Vodka flavored with buffalo grass is called zubrowka in Poland and Czechoslovakia. For want of a blade of buffalo grass, imported zubrowka may be purchased in fine wine and spirit shops.

BURNET symbolizes affection. It, too, tastes like cucumber and is not amiss in salads and as a flavoring for vinegars.

CAMELLIA symbolizes unpretending excellence. Dried camellia petals have been used in tea.

CAMOMILE, which symbolizes energy in adversity, is greatly admired in France as a basis for tisanes or medicinal teas.

The CARNATION symbolizes fascination. The petals of the carnation have been candied and preserved; they have also been used in vinegars and as a colorful garnish in salads.

CORN SALAD or field salad is one of the most delicate of salad greens. It is deservedly popular in France, where it is known as *mâche* or *doucette*. During the fall and winter it is available in limited quantities at certain greengrocers. To make a salad, wash the leaves well, drain them and mix with sliced beets, julienne strips of celery and a well-seasoned French dressing.

COSTMARY symbolizes impatience. A tisane of costmary is said to be very good for head catarrh.

FIELD SALAD is corn salad. Which see.

HOREHOUND is a bitter herb whose leaves and juice are used to make a rather unpleasant, perverse-tasting candy which enjoyed a peculiar fame some years ago. It is said that horehound candy may be still be purchased.

HYSSOP symbolizes cleanliness. Bees like it and sometimes flavor their honey with it. It is rumored that a hyssop flip can be made with hyssop water, sugar candy and the yolk of an egg.

LAVENDER symbolizes distrust. It, too, is used in tisanes. We have it on authority of Mrs. C. F. Leyel, the British herbalist, that the effect of lavender is very pronounced and beneficial.

LOVAGE has been made into cordials and can be candied like angelica.

MARIGOLD symbolizes grief. The leaves used sparingly add a fascinating if bizarre flavor to salads and soups. Some people with a great sense of daring or humor or both deep-fry marigold leaves and serve them with cocktails.

NASTURTIUMS symbolize patriotism. The bright leaves of the nasturtium plant add a gay conceit to commonplace green salads.

PANSIES, the bard reminds us, are for thoughts. Why else would the French call them *pensées*? Pansy leaves (perish the thought) have in less enlightened days been used in syrups.

SWEET CICELY is chervil. Which see.

TANSY symbolizes "I declare against you." It has been used as a flavoring for custards and in cakes.

Index